Julia A. Ericksen

Dance with Me

Ballroom Dancing and the Promise of Instant Intimacy

New York University Press • *New York and London*

NEW YORK UNIVERSITY PRESS
New York and London
www.nyupress.org

References to Internet websites (URLs) were accurate at the time of writing.
Neither the author nor New York University Press is responsible for URLs
that may have expired or changed since the manuscript was prepared.

Library of Congress Cataloging-in-Publication Data
Ericksen, Julia A., 1941–
Dance with me : ballroom dancing and the promise of instant intimacy /
Julia Ericksen.
p.   cm.
Includes bibliographical references and index.
ISBN 978-0-8147-2266-4 (hardback) — ISBN 978-0-8147-2285-5 (ebook) —
ISBN 978-0-8147-2298-5 (ebook)
1. Ballroom dancing—Social aspects.   I. Title.
GV1746.E75 2011
793.3'3—dc22   2011015754

New York University Press books are printed on acid-free paper,
and their binding materials are chosen for strength and durability.
We strive to use environmentally responsible suppliers and materials
to the greatest extent possible in publishing our books.

Manufactured in the United States of America

10 9 8 7 6 5 4 3 2 1

Live in fragments no longer. Only connect . . .

—E. M. Forster, *Howards End*

For Scott and all the dance teachers who have enriched my life

Contents

Color illustrations appear as a group following page 128.

Preface

The Passion

I am a college professor who loves her career. My marriage has lasted forty years. Our children like us, our grandchildren live close. We can afford life's small luxuries.

So why has a new love turned my once-gray hair blond and my nails long and red and replaced my professional suits with flouncing skirts? Why do I waste time talking about my desires and searching the Web for my passion?

In academia, to worry about clothes and appearance is to lack seriousness. The sensible person I used to be knows that this new behavior is unsuited to my age and status. I do not care.

I stand holding hands with a handsome man half my age. We are at the Heritage Classic DanceSport Championships in Asheville, North Carolina, about to perform the cha-cha. Scott Lazarov, my teacher, whispers reminders: "Straight legs," "Direction and rotation." He is a gifted teacher, and when he is pleased with me, I glow.

Preparing for competition involves endless repetition of steps I thought I knew, and improvement is hard and slow. It also involves endless worries about appearance, hence the hair and nails. At the Heritage, Scott picks out a dress, bright red with purple bands and red and purple stones. Transparent fabric covers my stomach. A dress I would have once dismissed as tacky now looks glamorous. So do my makeup, my false eyelashes, my elaborate hair, and my high-heeled Latin shoes.

Returning home, I wake at night longing for Asheville. My husband understands. In our years together, we have learned that for love to last, we need additional loves.

We began weekly dancing lessons four years ago, and it was some time before Scott acknowledged my existence. At parties, many wanted to dance with him; he has a seemingly effortless charm. One time watching me dance the swing, Scott admired my skirt. Later, he asked me to dance and suggested that I take lessons with him. Seduction was easy; by then I would have fallen for any top teacher who suggested I could dance well.

Ballroom dancing is about love and also about sex. When Scott and I work on the foxtrot, knees bend slightly, heads and chests are back, and torsos grind together. The correct leg position dictates that my right leg is between his legs and his left leg is between mine. None of this shows when we dance, because smooth dancing appears romantic, not sexy. The sensation of being held and floating along adds to the excitement and makes me feel light-headed and young.

I joined the women's movement in the 1960s, abandoning flirting and female artifice. I have helped countless women students achieve rich and independent lives. Over a recent lunch, a former student told me that dancing has weakened my messages. But age-inappropriate behavior is women's last rebellion.

I have always excelled at things that can be learned from books. Ballroom dancing involves physical and experiential learning. Sometimes I cannot master a technique after hours of trying, yet still I persist.

The Heritage is full of women like me with successful careers and demanding lives. At work, most compete against men; many have broken through, or at least bumped against, the infamous glass ceiling. In dancing, they shed their professional armor, entering a place where men lead, women follow, and the only things that matter are how well you dance and how glamorous you look.

I once asked Scott why he danced, an activity American men often avoid. This manly man said he dances for the moments when everything is perfect and the audience is yours. In performing, his face radiates absolute joy, and his connection to his partner is palpable.

We all seek this feeling. I am in love with the dancing world and with the person I become when I join for a while.

To establish my credentials as an insider in the dance world, I published the above piece in the *Philadelphia Inquirer* on September 5, 2006, at the start of my research. I often showed this piece to dancers I wished to interview. The headline read, "An Age-Inappropriate Last Rebellion" and continued with the byline of "*Julia Ericksen is a sociology professor at Temple University who dances at DanceSport Academy in Ardmore.*" At the bottom of the piece my email address was listed with an invitation to contact me.

I received about seventy-five uniformly positive responses, from dancers, from former students, from others who saw aging as a time to let loose, and from those with passions other than mine.

Acknowledgments

When I am asked how I came to write a book on ballroom dancing, I typically joke that I did it because it gave me an excuse to hang around dance studios. Yet it is hard to imagine that I could have written it if I did not love to dance, a love I inherited from my parents, Harry and Kathleen Smith, who met on a blind dancing date. As a child, my father taught me to follow by dancing me around the living room. My parents did not live to see me write this book, but they did enjoy seeing my husband and me learn to dance, after many years away from it.

Many people facilitated the writing of this book. First I must thank the dancers who gave of their time to be interviewed. The generosity of the professional dancers was amazing. For them, time is money, and I interviewed them in their studios, where they took long breaks from teaching to talk to me at length about all aspects of their dancing lives.

I must thank my teacher, Scott Lazarov, for introducing me to professional dancers, when he and I went to compete in pro/am. He helped established my credentials and paved my way to later interviews after dancers went home. These dancers, in turn, introduced me to their students and to other teachers in their studios. Scott was particularly helpful with American dancers, and it would have been difficult to gain introductions to them without him.

Paul Richardson introduced me to many of the top international-style dancers. Often it is difficult to get in touch with them, but Paul not only gave me email addresses; he told the dancers what I was doing and got them to agree to interviews. Again, this would have been difficult without Paul's help. Both Paul and Scott became unofficial advisers to my research, answering my many questions, and I learned a lot about the organization of the dance world through discussions with them. Both were generous with their time and input, and Paul was particularly helpful in explaining the intricate politics of the dance world. John Larsen was also helpful in answering my questions, and he read my glossary of terms just to make sure I said everything correctly.

I must thank Jonathan Marion for his compelling photographs of every aspect of the dance world. Jonathan typically photographs professional competition, for that is his academic interest, and he took wonderful professional pictures for this book. He also took pictures of pro/am, pictures of studio parties, and pictures of lessons. His photographs illustrate my words, making the glamour and the emotions of the dance visual to the reader. His introductory chapter in this book adds a fascinating dimension to our understanding of the sociology of emotions. Jonathan read an early version of the manuscript, and his suggestions were helpful.

Scott Lazarov and Barbara Capaldi were generous in letting me use their studios to photograph lessons and parties. I would like to thank all the students and teachers who allowed us to photograph them in lessons and at parties. I must also thank everyone who graciously let me use their photographs. Without the visual images, the book's arguments would be weaker.

Many of my colleagues were generous with their time and interest in discussing my work. Some have even seen me dance! In particular, I would like to thank Bill Overton, Sue Wells, Richard Immerman, Kevin Delaney, Judith Levine, and Dustin Kidd. Temple University provided me with the funds for travel and to pay student workers. Alyssa Richman was involved from the beginning undertaking a literature review on dance and performance, which helped me to get started. Veronica Burnazacki is a native Russian speaker, and she helped me in numerous ways. She went to the interviews with Russian speakers and helped translate when they ran into difficulty. Most had excellent English, but we occasionally ran into problems with idioms. Veronica also transcribed many of these interviews and was helpful in explaining what speakers were saying when I could not quite understand the tapes. Ocean Dull transcribed interviews. A former dancer with the Pennsylvania Ballet, Ocean had insightful comments about dancers' motives. Three other students who ably transcribed interviews were Shea Ogden, Mairead Conley, and Clarissa Marks. Finally, I must thank Elizabeth Cozzolino. Beth took responsibility for creating a bibliography, for making sure all the pictures and their captions were in order, for proofreading the manuscript, and for editorial assistance. Her help was invaluable.

My editor, Ilene Kalish, at New York University Press was helpful in every way. She believed in the book from the beginning, stayed in touch when I needed her, turned material around fast, and gave me great suggestions to improve the manuscript. I would also like to thank three anonymous reviewers, whose comments helped improve the book.

Finally, I wish to show my appreciation to my family. My children, Polly, Andrew, and Monica, have families of their own now but never fail to show enthusiasm for my endeavors. All have watched me dance numerous times and are lavish in their praise, even when praise is not due. My grandchildren, Miles, Drew, Blake, and Olivia, think I am a hip grandma, which is high praise in my world. Drew is a talented dancer in her own right and has been making tentative forays into the world of ballroom. Watching her come to terms with the physicality of partner dancing gave me insights into the learning experiences of young dancers. Finally, I must thank my husband of many years, Gene Ericksen. He, too, has taken dance lessons, in part to please me. He has also driven countless miles and attended numerous dance parties while I checked out the social dance scene. He constantly showed me newspaper articles that I might find interesting while working on this book. Ours is a relationship that involves the kind of intimacy only found when a relationship has lasted a long time and faced many different challenges. Gene is the most interesting person I know, so writing this book has been made more pleasurable by his presence.

Readers will see that this book is a labor of love. The dance world has enhanced my life and given me permission to transgress our culture's rules about aging.

Introduction to Photographing Emotion

Jonathan S. Marion

WALKING IN THE door to DanceSport Academy in Ardmore, Pennsylvania, for the first time on July 28, 2010, the first person I see is dancer Jean Paulovich (figures 3.3 and 7.2), and although he does not recall my name, we instantly recognize each other based on a photo I took of him at his first professional competition, at the 2004 Yankee Classic DanceSport Championships in Boston, Massachusetts.[1] That we each knew who the other was more than six years later—and both recalled the exact pose and costume in that single photograph—illustrates the power of image in the world of competitive ballroom. More than just a means of facilitating entry and access *into* ballroom,[2] the inextricable intertwining of looking, seeing, and knowing[3] enables images to convey understandings not possible from words alone. It is in this light that I hope you enjoy the images in this book and, more important, that they not only help illustrate the textual content but also provide insights.

Paralleling Isadora Duncan's comment, "If I could tell you what it meant, there would be no point in dancing it,"[4] much the same can be said of photography: if I could tell you, there would be no need to show it. But photographs are tricky things. Because we each bring our own backgrounds, experiences, and understandings to the images we see, it is easy to mistake *self*-evident content and meaning as universal, enduring, and fixed.[5] Indeed, "photographs are ambiguous. They may be worth a thousand words, but it can be any thousand words."[6] It is therefore important for scholars to think about and understand the strengths (and weaknesses) of both text and image[7] and to harness and juxtapose these tools accordingly. "Used correctly photographs and words can work together to produce the desired ethnographic meanings,"[8] and the following comments detail the considerations that went into the three interrelated processes of crafting, selecting, and captioning the images in this text.

Crafting

Increasing understanding of the neurological links between perception and understanding[9] explain how and why images have the potential to move viewers. This demands ever-greater attention to how social scientists take and use images in their work. Just as the anthropologists John Collier Jr. and Malcolm Collier suggest that "artistry is only a means, for the end is cultural authenticity" in ethnographic film,[10] so too with photography. Which is not to say that there is ever an objective, true, or real "thing" to be captured in an image but rather that responsible visual research should always be informed by and reflect the visual cultures in question.[11] So how then do I go about trying to take images that are not simply *of* ballroom dancing but *are* ballroom dancing?

To start with, I try to craft images that are not only "good pictures" but that tell a story, using composition, movement, and emotion to do so. Compositionally, I try to depict what someone watching from my vantage point would actually "see." As such, my default approach involves (1) shooting level images—since the human brain "corrects" for minor variations in angle—and (2) focusing on one couple at a time (since this is the basic "unit" of ballroom dancing).[12] Indeed, to the extent that it is persons who dance—and not their arms, legs, or heads—I generally try to follow Karl Heider's filmic guideline of framing whole bodies.[13] This is not to say that I never take close-up images but to point out that I do so deliberately and for specific reasons, including the following:

- If a couple, judge, or spectator is so close to me that I cannot see their whole bodies, all at once, with my naked eye
- If I am focusing on a specific action that is not about the whole body, such as a competitor applying eyeliner or lipstick in a mirror
- If I am trying to call attention to a specific element—such as an expression—that might not be visible unless cropped in on more tightly[14]

Likewise, I share Freeman's perspective that "environment can add a greater sense of the context and the space in which the activities depicted are taking place,"[15] and so I try to shoot in a way that captures the immediate surroundings as well, such as the ballroom floor, audience, or lighting.[16]

These compositional considerations also apply in postproduction. I try to do minimal editing, and, as with my original image composition, I try to let myself be guided by what someone else would see if he or she had been in the same place at the same time. For example, whereas different light sources (e.g., tungsten, fluorescent, flash) all have different color temperatures, the human brain adjusts what is seen to eliminate the color casts captured by a camera's sensor. For that reason, I will adjust color balance in postproduction. Likewise, while interesting angles make for exciting photographs—a tool I use in much of my more artistic, less ethnographic photography—my default approach in ethnographic settings is to shoot leveled images (whether vertical or horizontal), and straightening is one of the few postproduction manipulations I regularly perform. I may also crop tighter in postproduction, but only when deliberately directing focus and when I can use words (be it in a talk, as a caption, or in body text) to provide appropriate context.

Where I use composition to provide focus and context, I try to capture the overall nature of ballroom dancing—interpersonal performance predicated on bodily action—by highlighting movement. This means many things, however, as dancers of different levels move in very different ways. For most starting dancers, for instance, lines and shapes are often brief and hesitant, so I need to click the shutter quickly, before the action disappears. This same approach does not work with elite competitors, however, who "hit" their lines and shapes and then continue to stretch until reaching their personal maximums.[17] Here I need to stay focused on the couple, waiting and allowing them time to produce the pinnacle of their own movement in order to accurately represent the tone of their performance. Likewise, while I often use flash (a) to maximize the punch and color of my images and (b) to highlight the couple from the background (as our brain naturally processes for our eyes), I run the risk of having an image look posed. To counteract this, I seek to capture movement by waiting for maximal stretch or catching a dress or hair flying through the air.

Finally, in crafting images that tell the ballroom story, I rely on the emotion that is being performed by focusing on competitors' eyes and expressions. Here, when I say "focusing on," I do not mean in a technical sense but rather that this is what I am looking at through my viewfinder before deciding whether to snap the shot in front of me. Since dancing is a partnered activity, I try (when possible) to take images where both partners' faces can be seen. Likewise, I try to make sure that eyes are open and expressions appropriate (which can vary from dance to dance, as seen in the contrasting color images of Katusha Demidova and Arunas Bizokas). Although this has been a slow process (indeed, early on I was cutting off feet and hands as my attention focused on eyes and expressions), with practice (and familiarity with my equipment) I have learned how to "feel" how tight I can get without regularly checking the bottom of the frame—and thus losing focus on the emotions being portrayed on the floor.

Selecting

The final photo selections for this book followed two parallel tracks. For many images, I sorted through my digital archives; others were shot on site (both at competitions I was attending and at the studios shown in this book). In each case, the two key questions were these:

1. Does this image add to what is being discussed?
2. Is it acceptable to those whom it depicts?

Starting with Julia Ericksen's original wish list, we therefore (1) identified topics amicable to visual depiction (e.g., not dancers' ideas and feeling, which were already—and best—conveyed in their own words), (2) discarded images that only illustrated rather than explained (or duplicated the content of others), and (3) composited images where such juxtapositions evoked greater understandings.[18]

Equally important, however, was the recognition that "*no photograph is more important than the wishes of its subject.*"[19] As such we tried to start by selecting competition images that we thought the people depicted would like and by getting permission to shoot all of the studio images taken for this book. Then, and most importantly, we got explicit permissions for each image used in this book. While the press was only concerned with my permissions (as the copyright-holding photographer), I am a visual anthropologist deeply aware of and committed to the ethical implications of working with visual imagery.[20] Ericksen fully recognized and appreciated this perspective, and between us we received permission—in person, online, and by phone—for each of the photographs readers find here.

Captioning

While images speak to each of us, they do not speak for themselves. Rather, "their meaning and significance are defined by context."[21] While this facilitates photo elicitations on the one hand (an underutilized and often invaluable ethnographic tool whereby research participants provide context to the researcher),[22] it also mandates thoughtful and appropriate framing (i.e., contextualization) when images are used in and presented as part of scholarly discourse. "The ethnographicness of any image or representation," as Pink has pointed out, "is contingent on how it is situated, interpreted and used to invoke meanings and knowledge that are of ethnographic interest."[23] Far too few scholars provide informative captioning, however, let alone link images to written text, thereby generating a dialogue between these different media and modes of representation. This is unfortunate, as deliberate attention to how visual and written data intercontextualize each other facilitates both broader and deeper understandings.

This book has taken the linking of image and text very seriously from the outset. Unlike most such texts—where images are gathered post hoc from whatever sources are available—Ericksen chose to collaborate with only one photographer (in this case me). Although this certainly is not the only viable approach, it did allow us to build a common understanding of how images were going to fit into this work. Reading an early version of the manuscript before I started selecting archival images and shooting new materials for this book started the dialogue between image and text, a process that continued as we worked together to select the final images (as noted earlier). Finally, in preparing the captions, attention went to (1) what references were already in place (in the text), (2) what context was lacking, and (3) what elements in the image might need highlighting for those not "in the know" regarding ballroom culture and community. Additionally, and as part of the photo-permission process noted earlier, captions were adjusted to reflect the few instances when any concerns arose. Ultimately, then, careful attention to the relationship between text and image is the vehicle whereby the images presented herein reach their full potential to illuminate the issues at hand.

ACKNOWLEDGMENTS

Thanks to Julia Ericksen for inviting me to be part of such an interesting project and for her truly collaborative approach to producing the images in this book. Thanks also to the ballroom-competition organizers and photographers who have facilitated my ongoing research and photography, as well as to Guido Carlo Pigliasco and David Marion for critiques and input on earlier versions of these comments.

Introduction

Entering the World of Ballroom

IT IS THE last night of the 2008 United States Dance Championships (USDC), and the most popular event is under way: the final of the Open to the World Professional Latin Championship. Six finalists dance the five dances that constitute every Latin competition: cha-cha, samba, rumba, paso doble, and jive.[1] As the first dance ends, the crowd favorites, Riccardo Cocchi and Yulia Zagoruchenko, begin whizzing around the floor doing promenade runs to the fast-paced samba music with its heavy drum beat and complicated syncopation. They flirt with each other; they flirt with the audience; they smile and wink as they perform intricate movements in quick succession without missing a step. Their partnership is less than a year old, but both are experienced at engaging the crowd.[2] As Yulia moves her long, slender legs, the movement of her dress accentuates their elegance and speed. The audience sits at tables around the edge of the floor or on stadium seating stacked up behind the front tables, or they stand wherever there is space. They are whistling, cheering, and calling out dancers' names and competition numbers as the master of ceremonies encourages them with, "Who's your favorite couple out there, ladies and gentlemen?" I am in a floor-side seat cheering and yelling with the rest of the crowd. As Ruud Vermeij[3] notes in his advice book for Latin dancers, whereas theatrical dancers perform a role and thus "become the dance," competition dancers perform as themselves, and their fans come to see them more than the dance.[4] The audience has been anxious to see Riccardo and Yulia dance together, since they placed second a few months earlier at the Blackpool Dance Festival in England. Blackpool is the most prestigious and difficult competition in the world, and up to this point, Americans have rarely done this well.[5] Color plate 1 shows the couple competing at USDC a year later, when they had moved up on the international stage by coming in first at Blackpool in the jive.

The samba ends, and the men move their partners into new spots on the floor. In the rumba, as with several Latin dances, couples do not progress around the floor, so competitors pick spots depending on the direction they will take and where they expect others to go. They try to maximize the chance that each judge will have a clear view of them for at least some of the time and that the audience will notice them too. Inexperienced competitors sometimes crowd the center of the floor because they want the judges to see them, but these experienced finalists spread out. As the music starts, the dancers alternate clinging to one another and turning away. Rumba is a slow, erotic dance; the mood is hot and heavy, and the Latin rhythms are languid. The women bend and hyperextend their legs as they twist and turn around their partners. They slide their feet along the floor toes first, transferring weight from leg to leg and settling their hips after each move to produce rumba's emblematic rolling hip action.

Dimitry Timokhin and Natalia Petrova, another new couple, are dancing for Russia, and the audience gives them a warm welcome. Dimitry and his previous partner, Karina Smirnoff, had made the finals at Blackpool. But when Karina became a regular on *Dancing with the Stars*, the popular ABC reality show, she no longer had time to compete. Dimitry's new partner, Natalia, is one of the fastest women on the floor, and after the fourth dance, the dramatic paso doble, excitement builds with the jive. Jive is the most energetic of the dances, and its position at the end tests dancers' stamina; these finalists have already danced several rounds. This is the most exciting part of the show, as the dancers kick and spin at breakneck speed. Women's dresses bounce and swirl, their rhinestones flickering in the lights; men slide across the floor; and the audience gets louder. This crowd knows how difficult it is to reach the skill level displayed before them.

In Latin dancing, the action portrays a world of swaggering men and "their" women. The dancers depict a man's world where women are beautiful objects with the power to inflame a man's passion but not to reject his demands. Women follow the men's lead and often supplicate their bodies before them. Sometimes they turn away, rejecting their partners' overtures, only to be turned back face to face with fire and passion. The men strike dominant poses in tight-fitting shirts and pants set off by high Cuban heels. They appear to pull and push the women around, spinning and turning them, demanding their attention. Hips gyrate, legs flick in and out. The women glitter. They wear high-heeled strappy sandals, with bare legs or fishnet stockings, and skimpy clothing adorned with many crystals and sparkling necklaces, bracelets, and hair ornaments. Both men and women are deeply tanned.

I think back to my first competition, the Millennium DanceSport Championship, several years earlier.[6] I had gone to compete as an amateur dancer with a professional partner, and at night we watched the professionals. The professional competition sent my head spinning, and I did not know where to look. Concentrating on any one couple meant ignoring others. My head flipped back and forth, and I was unable to take it all in. By USDC, I am an experienced enough dancer and competitor to have learned to focus on the dancers I want to see, and I can quickly distinguish the best couples. I understand good technique and can see who is fast but not artistic and who makes up for being slower by dancing with elegance and grace. I note which couples relate to the audience and how well couples connect with each other. The connection is key in ballroom; the dancers are always a couple, and they must show this to those who are watching. This is what I want to show in this book—how to read ballroom, where to look, and how to see the connections.

Each dance is scored separately by each member of a panel of judges, and as expected, Riccardo and Yulia win the professional competition easily, losing only two first-place marks out of a possible ninety-five. The Russians come in second, and an exciting new Lithuanian couple, Justinas Duknauska and Ekaterina Lapaeva, come in third.[7] The sixth-place couple, Delyan Terziev and Boriana Delcheva, had hoped to improve their results from the previous year, when they achieved third place. Since they also fell from third to fifth in the closed competition,[8] Keith Todd, writing in *Dance Beat* magazine a few days later, suggests that they need an infusion of energy and that they rethink what they are doing.[9] Even more surprising, Dimitry Kurakin and Violetta Kurakina, a relatively unknown couple who shocked everyone by winning the rising-star event in Blackpool, do not even place into the finals, although Todd is of the opinion that they probably should have.

The other important competition on the last night is the Open to the World International Standard, a style of dancing that is called "ballroom" elsewhere in the world and sometimes in the United States.[10] Here, too, there are new partnerships. Jonathan Wilkins and Katusha Demidova, who have won this event ten years in a row, ended their partnership several months ago. This year they are each competing with a new partner. Jonathan is now dancing for his native England with former Blackpool professional champion Hazel Newberry, and Katusha still dances for the United States with Blackpool amateur champion Arunas Bizokas. When Hazel has to withdraw after the first round, suffering from an ongoing shoulder injury, the open final becomes the same all-U.S. final as the closed final two days earlier. Arunas and Katusha have been scoring slightly ahead of Jonathan and Hazel in international competition, and the audience murmurs its disappointment not to see the couples compete against each other. Katusha is a crowd favorite, blond, elegant, and always beautifully dressed. I find her relationship with her new partner to be a little more aloof than her former partnership appeared to be. Arunas does not emote enough for my taste, although his technique is of the highest caliber. The judges may have felt this too, because the other top U.S. couple, Victor Fung and Anna Mickhed, challenge them more closely than previously, especially in the tango and the quickstep.

The motif of ballroom dancing is "dancing as one," and couples must maintain a closed hold throughout the dance. A closed hold means that they must stay in the classic ballroom hold, with the woman's left hand on her partner's upper arm and his right hand around her back. They hold each other's free hand up and away from their bodies. Maintaining this hold is perhaps the most difficult skill in all of competition dancing, yet these couples speed around the floor with their bodies swinging and swaying together, making their steps look effortless. As with Latin, it is all about gender, but here the theme is romantic rather than erotic, and the lush music reflects this. Ballroom dancing is less exciting for the audience than Latin is; its lesser popularity is manifested by lower attendance, and the audience is less inclined to call out competitors' names. The first rounds of the professional ballroom competition start early in the evening, and many in the audience have not yet arrived. The couples' dancing as one makes it harder for audience members to have confidence in their own judgments about which couple is best, and since eye contact between audience and dancers is less frequent than in Latin, there is less opportunity for the audience to feel connected to individual dancers. If there is no connection, there is no emotional excitement, and that is what is most craved here—to feel the sex and the romance. Some couples, such as Igor Litvinov and Julia Ivleva, have been dancing together for over a decade. They bring their students to competitions and have no shortage of fans who call out their number. Even so, the noise level for ballroom dancing remains low compared to Latin. To paraphrase Vermeij, unlike Latin, ballroom becomes more about the dance than the dancers. For me, the sight of all six finalists carefully following the line of dance around the floor is more satisfying, if taken as a whole, though I do register a drop in audience enthusiasm.

The professional dance competitions are the most eagerly awaited events, but they constitute a small proportion of the total. The bulk consist of pro/am competitions—professional teachers dancing with their adult students. Pro/am competition has been unique to America until recently. Elsewhere, dancers usually start as children dancing as amateur couples, rising through the junior to the adult ranks. They turn professional only after achieving success as amateurs. In the United States, few dancers start as children, although this is changing with the influx of immigrants from the former Soviet Union. However, dancers here may more easily turn professional, because many adults learn to dance as a hobby, which provides teaching jobs for the professionals. Some students become passionate enough to want to compete with their teachers, and this supports the competitive careers of many professionals. Only a few professional dancers are so highly acclaimed that they can support themselves by coaching and performing. Most take students to competitions and dance pro/am with them. Pro/am students often dance in several of the four different styles that constitute competition ballroom in America. The four styles include the two international styles described earlier, which are danced all over the world, and two American styles, smooth and rhythm, which are similar, but not identical to, ballroom and Latin. In the past, most Americans learned American style only, but the influx of foreign professionals has increased interest in international style. At the USDC, a day is given to each of the four styles, with a fifth day for events that cannot fit into the other four, such as preteen and junior competitions, and a variety of showdance and cabaret events.[11] Each evening is confined largely to professional competition, when those who danced during the day turn out to watch their idols strut their stuff.

The USDC is not the biggest ballroom competition in America, but it is arguably the most prestigious because this is where the national titles are bestowed on both professional couples and pro/am dancers. The governing body for professional dancers in America is the National Dance Council of America (NDCA),[12] which is, in turn, a member of the international governing body the World Dance Council (WDC).[13] The most prestigious titles in the United States for amateur couples are awarded by a different governing body, USA Dance,[14] which has its own competitions and is a member of a different international organization, the International Dance-Sport Federation (IDSF).[15]

Both Riccardo and Yulia came to the United States as adults, having previously danced for their countries of birth—Italy and Russia, respectively.

This gypsy existence is common for international-style dancers. Often they dance for one partner's country of origin, but the example of Riccardo and Yulia is the norm with couples who dance for the United States. The names of the finalists in international style at USDC indicate that most of those dancing for the United States are immigrants. As is fitting for a nation where almost everyone's ancestors came from elsewhere, the American audience takes Riccardo and Yulia into its heart and takes national pride in their accomplishments.

The USDC is held at the Royal Pacific Hotel at Universal Studios in Orlando, Florida, but the dancers have little time to take in the theme park. The women spend their days in glittering dresses, sporting sleek hair that either does not move or swings perfectly back into place, rhinestone jewelry, lots of thick makeup, artificial tans, and high heels. The competition spawns a cottage industry, with designers and sellers of dresses, shoes, jewelry, and practice wear all hoping to attract the dancers' attention. Everything is laid out to attract consumers (as can be seen in the pictures of shoes and jewelry in color plate 2). Some designers sponsor professional dancers or even top students, loaning them dresses to wear until an audience member decides to buy the dress literally off a dancer's back. In addition, one can take coaching, have a massage, or have one's makeup and hair done. Hair may be turned into the elaborate upswept designs favored by many professionals, enhanced by the addition of extra hair pieces. Photographers sell photographs of each dancer's performances, and dancers may have their events videotaped to learn from their mistakes. Competitors may also buy books, music, instructional videos, and every conceivable accessory.

In addition to competing, I am taking field notes on the competition for this book. I climb to the top of the bank of seats and watch the pro/am Latin competition below. I am interested in the relational aspects of ballroom, since this is what distinguishes it from other dancing. Latin dancing, as noted earlier, is all about the display of sexual interest and intimacy between partners. Ballroom is more subtle in its emotional display, but again connection is key. I especially note that when young professional men dance with older women, a few of them seem unable to emote. I quote from my notes spoken into a recorder as I watched:

> One man is dancing with an older woman wearing a black and brown outfit. He's a beautiful dancer, but he's not looking at her while they're dancing. He's looking all around the room instead. I don't think he ever lays

eyes on her, in fact. Even when she looks at him, he does not return her look. He's showing how great he is by dancing professional-level chore-ography. She's really struggling to stand on her own and is having a hard time keeping up. She looks really uncertain as time goes on. I'll switch to another couple and look at them, a Latino man dancing with an Asian student. The age difference is similar, but he's much more relational with her. They're looking at one another now. They're connected. He's hovering over her. It's a completely different experience to watch them. He's holding her, and he puts his hand on her face and looks into her eyes.

The experience of the teacher ignoring the student surprises me, because, at my dance studio, teachers do not treat older women this way. I cannot help but think that what I saw that day is a manifestation of our stereotyp-ical ideas about gender and aging—that older women are not attractive and that intimacy between an older woman and a young man is somehow offensive. It is not that this teacher cannot look at the student; it is that he will not connect, he will not be intimate with her. Fortunately, it is a behav-ior seen in a minority of professionals.

When the competition switches to beginners, I notice how many top professional competitors are on the floor. Unlike that first teacher, these dancers take noticeable care of their students. The competition I am watch-ing takes place in the afternoon, before the Latin final described at the be-ginning of this chapter. Delyan Terziev, who will be a finalist in the evening competition, dances with several students during the day. In the Bronze Scholarship,[16] he makes eye contact with his student, and he looks like he is interested in her and in dancing with her. The jive is fun rather than sexy, and she appears relaxed as she basks in his smiles. Delyan's wife, Boriana Delcheva, sits on the sidelines with his two other students. She watches intently as he dances and will give the students detailed feedback. This is common when professional couples compete together and husbands take students to dance pro/am. Figure I.1 shows professional dancer Carolina Orlovsky-Telona watching her husband, Felipe Telona, dancing with his longtime student Ruby Yap. Although a few teachers are not particularly respectful, the majority are like Delyan, attentive to their students' needs for care and preparation.

The USDC is held during the first week of September, a week that marks the beginning of classes at Temple University, where I teach sociology. I am on study leave but still feel negligent of my duties as I try to make sense of an exotic culture bearing little resemblance to the academic life

Fig. I.1. Wifely support. Carolina Orlovsky-Telona watches Ruby Yap with Felipe Telona Jr. at the 2010 Desert Classic DanceSport Championships, Palm Desert, CA. © 2010 Jonathan S. Marion.

that constitutes my everyday world. This has been a long journey, one that started as a child watching my parents dance around the living room. In my early teens, I took group classes at my local village hall in the north of England. I stopped ballroom dancing in my late teens when it became unfashionable, but I always regretted leaving it behind.

My husband and I have birthdays six weeks apart, and some years ago, he suggested that we celebrate them by taking dance lessons. He knew I would like the idea but was surprised when, a few hours after his casual suggestion, we were signed up for lessons. We started with a joint private lesson and quickly got hooked. We progressed to separate lessons, because it is easier to learn when your teacher focuses entirely on you. We increased the frequency of lessons over time. Competing took a little longer. I could not imagine wearing competition dresses or makeup, and the idea of holing up in a hotel, at a place I did not want to visit, seemed strange. My husband was the first to try, and he came home with such extravagant tales that I soon followed and fell hopelessly in love with the whole experience.

Many of the students who compete are professional women with lives like mine, and yet all are passionate about dancing and competing in a world that differs completely from their everyday lives. This book is my attempt to understand the fascination it holds for participants.[17] Many of the women who dance have benefited from second-wave feminism on their paths to success. Yet they dance in a world that seems traditionally gendered, where appearance is all important, and where men lead and women follow. This is a world where men are men and women are girls, no matter their age. Why, I wondered, do successful women choose this world as the place to spend their precious leisure time? Why do they want to spend time and money visiting a world in which they would likely not want to live? What motivates teachers? How do they learn to satisfy students' desires?

At the same time, professional dancers earn a living by it, usually by teaching or coaching and sometimes by putting on shows. Students can spend tiny fortunes on lessons and competitions. What are they buying? What are the teachers selling?

Ballroom dancing seems a perfect example of what sociologist Viviana Zelizer has called "the purchase of intimacy."[18] This phrase describes the commercialization of emotions in everyday life. In ballroom, professional competitors learn to display an emotional relationship for dance audiences to enjoy and consume. They also learn to provide students with an intimate experience. I argue that it is this intimate experience that seduces students, particularly women students, into the world of dance. Of course, both students and professionals have long-term relationships that they must manage in addition to the instant intimacy of the dance floor. Furthermore, students and their teachers develop complex relationships over time, relationships that can deepen over shared experiences and confidences, even while governed by the demands of the marketplace. This book explores the development and attractions of these emotions.

In the beginning, I intended to confine the book to competition dancing, both professional and pro/am. The art of emotional display is most highly developed in professional competition, and in pro/am, adults are able to pay for the instant gratification of dancing with professionals and to enjoy the spoils of competition without devoting their lives to it. However, in preparation for my research, I started exploring the dance lessons and activities available in the Philadelphia area, where I live, and as I began to discover the offerings, I found a more nuanced picture than I originally imagined.

When my husband and I decided to learn, I contacted the studio most convenient to our work, a studio in the center of the city, where rents are high and lessons are correspondingly expensive. Students take private lessons by appointment, after which they leave and another student replaces them. Many students have "standing appointments," locking up particular times for their lessons. The studio has weekly social dances, where students practice their steps. Instructors attend these parties and dance with each student in turn. At this particular studio, outsiders are unwelcome at parties, although that is not the case at all dance studios. At our current, more enlightened studio, in Ardmore, a suburb of Philadelphia, instructors see parties as a way of attracting new students. Figure I.2 shows studio owner Scott Lazarov dancing with four different students during a party in July 2010. In rapid succession, he danced with these among other students, finishing by dancing a polka with another teacher, Tim Jones, to celebrate Tim's birthday.

I discovered many classes and parties on the outskirts of Philadelphia, either in low-rent areas or in places used for other purposes, such as a local YMCA. These programs are less expensive to run, and studio owners offer group lessons, packing in as many students as possible in order to cover costs. For example, the Atrium Ballroom on the edge of Camden, New Jersey, an impoverished suburb, is nestled among liquor stores, strip joints, and fast-food places. It is on a major highway that can be reached quickly from over a large area; those within a forty-mile radius can drive to the studio within an hour or less. On Sunday afternoon, there is a "Ballroom Mix Party," starting with a group lesson focusing on a particular dance, for example, a month of international tango. This is followed by several hours of social dancing, during which dinner is served to those who want it—and many do. The whole program costs twelve dollars. The generous parking lot is jammed, and by five p.m., folks are lined up for supper. Supper is a convivial affair, as can be seen in figure I.3. The standard of the social dancing is high. Dancers of all ages crowd the floor, and regulars move from partner to partner with ease. I counted over one hundred attendees on a typical Sunday, compared with perhaps thirty at the downtown studio parties described earlier.

It did not take me long to realize that these social dancers should be included in my research—at least as a brief comparison—if I want to understand the passion for dancing among a variety of American adults. Many participants are older, single adults who know one another from years of

Fig. I.2. The hard work of a dance teacher. Scott Lazarov dances with a variety of partners at a July 2010 practice party at DanceSport Academy in Ardmore, PA. © 2010 Jonathan S. Marion.

Fig. I.3. Dining at the Atrium, July 2010. © 2010 Jonathan S. Marion.

attendance and who appear to want physical and emotional connection without commitment. Social dance students learn by dancing with each other and by rotating partners. Social dance differs from competition dance because it is aimed at the performers, not the audience.[19] There is more emphasis on steps than on technique, because social dancers want to be able to dance with strangers. They are not being judged on form, and students do not learn choreography, although they often learn sets of steps. I decided to interview dancers of all kinds, although I confined myself to those who dance mixed Latin and ballroom, rather than those who focus on individual partner dances, such as salsa, East Coast swing, hustle, West Coast swing, or Argentine tango. Each of these single dances has passionate devotees who dance many nights a week in the venues available in most large cities.[20] They concentrate on perfecting a particular dance rather than learning the variety of dances that the ballroom studios teach. Widening my scope to include each of these dances would have made the research unmanageable.

Professional dancers follow a prestige ranking. At the top are those who compete in international competition, followed by those who compete in American style. The top dancers earn their livings doing shows and giving demonstrations, but these are few in number. Some supplement these activities by coaching amateur and professional couples. Most dancers who compete, however, teach students who want to compete with their teachers in pro/am competitions. The most successful teach only pro/am students, but most also teach private students who do not compete, at least not often, and they may give group classes in some aspect of the dance (for example, "Latin Styling") for students and even other professionals who want to improve. After these dancers retire from professional competition, they usually continue to teach pro/am. Ranked below these professionals are those who teach social dancers.

The top students are those who go to many competitions, dancing with the same professional teacher and paying for many hours of lessons. A larger group of dancers compete but not as often as they would like to, and these are also interested in social dancing. Another group of students takes private lessons but only performs at showcases organized by the studio. Under them are the social dancers who spend time in group lessons and attend many social dances. They may watch competitions but do not compete.

Ballroom dance is an increasingly popular activity. As we shall see, teaching ballroom is one of the few ways that dancers can make a living through dance. Every large city has many studios, and students may choose to go dancing every night of the week. The popularity of ballroom dancing had been growing even before *Dancing with the Stars* began to appear on television, but that show has increased its popularity. The tenth-season premiere in March 2010 finished in a virtual tie with *American Idol* for the week's top spot, with 24.2 million viewers.[21] The large number of immigrants who love dancing, from both Asia and eastern Europe, has also helped to increase the number of studios.

I conducted sixty formal interviews with all these types of dancers and found that the categories are more permeable than described here.[22] Some professionals, particularly women, find that they have to teach social dancing in order to pay for their own lessons and to keep competing. Some professionals start out competing in amateur competitions, although this is more common in other parts of the world where pro/am does not exist. This is changing with the influx of immigrants from eastern Europe, and competitions often include amateur dancers, particularly children and adolescents. In addition, many studios, except for the top ones, supplement their income by teaching special-occasion dances, most commonly for weddings. And dancers change category. Some students compete for a while and then decide they prefer social dancing, or vice versa. Others do well in pro/am competition and turn professional, hoping to make a career out of their passion.

For purposes of simplicity in discussing dancers, I have divided them into competition professionals, social dance professionals, competition students, and social dance students. Each of these groups is divided by gen-der, making eight groups of dancers in all. Some do not fit such tidy pack-aging, but the typology works for the most part. In chapter 1, I lay out my arguments about ballroom and the commodification of intimacy, including an outline of my research questions and methodology.

1

The Purchase of Instant Intimacy

ALTHOUGH PHOEBE, A diminutive woman in her sixties, had studied ballroom dance for over twenty years, dance had never lost its glow. She explained, "I don't have a social life. I only have a dance life. . . . I sacrifice everything for it; friendships, family, they come second." Phoebe had always loved to dance, and as a teenager, she had persuaded her father to pay for ballet lessons, after having, as she put it, "taught it to myself really." She resumed these lessons in adulthood, and at one point, the instructor began to teach the class something he called "ballroom performance." This involved teaching the students a choreographed number. They learned no technique, just steps, which bothered Phoebe because she wanted to dance correctly. Phoebe had also been taking private ballet lessons with the same teacher, she said, "for no particular reason, except to get better and because I loved it." She decided to change the lessons to half ballroom and half ballet "to learn how to do it right." Her teacher upped the ante:

> He asked if I knew what a dance competition was, and I said, "No." He told me, and he said, "There's a division called 'Newcomers.' You dance with a teacher, and it's for someone who's only danced three months. You have to do only three steps in each dance." He wanted to know if I might be interested in that, and I said, "Yes, it sounds like fun." He then said, "Well, good, because it's in three weeks, and I've already signed you up." . . . I was . . . just sold. . . . Ballet class you get to perform in front of the mirror and whoever is in the class, but this is performing.

Phoebe's passion for ballroom competition continued. She described herself as being "as serious as any professional." She was currently on her fourth teacher and planned to compete about six times over the coming year at some of the bigger competitions. Dance provided meaning and happiness in Phoebe's life. She lived in a small apartment with only her cat for company and worked in a demanding but tedious job. On a lesson day, she said, "I'm always in a good mood, because this is my joy. It's what I've waited all day to do. I wake up in the morning, and my first thought is, 'Is this a dance day, or is this not a dance day?'"

Phoebe practiced a double consciousness about the intimacy involved in the student-teacher relationship. She wanted to be the favorite student of every teacher, and she had had crushes on each of them. However, she added, "I know that it's a crush. It's not ever been real." A previous teacher had had about "seven students, but a core group of four," and, she said, "we all fought for his attention." Phoebe added, "I think it was so immature, when I look back on it. We were all adults in our forties. . . . 'Who's the favorite?'" When this teacher retired, Phoebe thought that she would never "want to dance with anybody else." However, she quickly discovered, "It's not him at all. It's the dance that I love." The hope for a perfect dance relationship was important in framing Phoebe's desire for closeness, but, in turn, the desire for intimacy helped create her love of dance.

Phoebe's commitment to dancing, and her desire for the connection that dancing provided, positions ballroom dancing as an example of what sociologist Viviana Zelizer has called "the purchase of intimacy," that is, an understanding of intimacy as inevitably mixed with economic activity in the modern world.[1] Intimacy, just like any commodity—a pair of shoes, a bag of potato chips—can be bought and sold. However, because we view intimacy and commerce as incompatible, people carefully negotiate the connections between the two. While we can see the economic basis of commercialized intimacy, such as sex work, we do not always recognize that close personal relationships, such as courtship and marriage, also depend on a complex set of economic entanglements. The dance world is somewhere between these two—more obviously commercialized than marriage but more genuinely close and personal than sex work.

Dance and Intimacy

Ballet dancers who know the choreography can partner any number of dancers in a role,[2] but ballroom dance partners learn together. This appears to require an intimate connection, something we think of as developing slowly by means of personal revelations and increasing mutual dependency. Yet, in ballroom, the emotional connection of the couple develops quickly. From the first lesson, the teacher's warmth and apparent pleasure in the lesson create a feeling in the student of being special. Furthermore, dance professionals learn to display an emotional connection with their professional partners as well as their students, whether or not they feel it. In addition, dance involves a physical connection not normally available outside a sexual relationship.[3] Dancers hold one another. They sweat together. Becoming comfortable with this can be difficult but pleasurable. Dance intimacy, then, involves a quick intimacy, a public display, and a physical connection. I call this "instant intimacy."

Instant intimacy is not only about the speed with which the relationship develops; it is also about physical closeness. Inside the dance studio, on the competition floor, and on the social dance floor, partners touch, hold hands, hug, and kiss with seeming abandon. Partners do bodily favors for each other, like massaging a sore back or pinning a pair of pants that have come unstitched. These same dancers, particularly if there is an age disparity between teacher and student, behave more formally in public spaces, only relaxing their guard in the safety of the dance space.

Zelizer examined the way couples negotiate the economic implications of long-term familial relations. She looked at court records of cases involving fights over the appropriate economic rewards for intimate caring to see the ways that couples combine economic transactions and intimate relationships and the stories they tell to explain the intermingling of the two. I am interested in intimacy and its portrayal in relationships that are ephemeral, not lasting. I argue that the attractions of instant intimacy are a feature of a world with high divorce rates and late average age at marriage. In such a world, many people organize their lives around short-term relationships, forgoing the demands of more encompassing connections. Furthermore, even long-married persons often wish for a safe variety in their intimate life, one that is emotionally satisfying but limited.

Phoebe explicitly purchased emotional connection. Her income was between fifty thousand and seventy-five thousand dollars per year, and she spent most of it on dance. Because she did not earn enough to cover both her day-to-day living expenses and dancing, her savings were dwindling. Although she was an extreme case, she was by no means unique in her willingness to put dance first. Zelizer notes in her book on money and its social meanings that money is not entirely fungible; that is, individuals segregate according to use.[4] Phoebe recognized her dancing as an extravagance but was frugal in every other aspect of her life.

Phoebe's teacher and competition partner was a highly ranked professional. Although he worked as an independent teacher and did not have to share his fees with a studio owner, Phoebe's lessons were costly.[5] When asked how much she spent on dancing, Phoebe became nervous, saying,

"Oh, dear, I don't want to go there. . . . I don't want to figure it out. . . . I'd rather be ignorant." In order to pay for competitions, she cut corners wherever she could. Where most student competitors eat hotel food, often with their teachers as part of the competition package, Phoebe took food with her and ate in her room.[6] She stayed at the competition only on the days she was competing, which saved on tickets to the evening shows and on hotel bills but meant that she rarely got to watch the professional competition. She danced in one style only—American smooth—so she could usually confine the dancing to one day and use one dress at a time. She was spending about two thousand dollars per competition, which is less than most students pay. She attempted further economies, such as selling her old dresses—a difficult feat because many students have dresses to sell, and fashions change quickly. She had resolved not to buy new dresses but found this decision difficult to sustain. When she started dancing with her current teacher, the pressure to spend increased:

> Each one's different. This one's incredibly controlling. . . . I always have somebody do my hair, because I can't do it, but I did my own makeup, and the first few times he didn't say anything except, "You need more makeup." I went, "I have so much makeup on." "That's not even makeup." I put more on, and the last time, he said, "I don't like your makeup. . . . It doesn't look professional. I want you to have it done." I went, "It costs more, come on." He went, "No, I really insist." So I had someone do it, and he was like, "See what a difference it makes? How many people came up to you and said how terrific, how beautiful you looked." . . . I make mine a little more natural looking. When you're older, I think you look better if it's more natural looking. . . . I love black, and I had a black dress made. . . . This teacher, when he finally saw it on me . . . wasn't very enthusiastic. . . . I saw a dress . . . that I really loved, and it's red. . . . We tried it on, and he said, "It's much too big. It can't be fixed. My partner can make it for you." We copied that dress, only we made it a lot better. . . . The back has three little scoops, and she said, "We could make the back open completely if you want." I went, "Oh, I kind of like my back still." She came back three days later and said, "No, he says it should be closed." . . . I was just imagining him saying, "Oh, no! She's too old."

Here we see the way in which money was the medium used to secure a relationship but also the way in which the relationship influenced Phoebe's decisions about money. Phoebe wanted her teacher to care about her but worried that he viewed her as old. She interpreted his autocratic behavior as evidence of his interest, and she let herself be talked into wearing more makeup than she found flattering.

Phoebe was explicit about her ambivalence over the commercialized nature of the intimacy she obtained from dancing. On the one hand, she described what she greatly valued:

> all the different kinds of relationships you can have with your teacher. You can be friends. You can flirt. . . . I used to tell [one], "Oh, my God, you're so gorgeous," but it was more to relax him. . . . He would say, "I know they're all looking at my butt." He could talk about it. You're exploring the pro/am relationship, and I feel it can be a beautiful thing. It can be very supportive and very caring, and maybe it crosses the line.

Yet Phoebe worried about the commercial implications of her feelings:

> "It's just a job," I remind myself. "They're getting paid for this. . . ." For me, it's a passion, and I don't want to exaggerate what they feel for me. Maybe they don't. Maybe they—"Well, I like her, but it's still just a job." I always have to tell myself, "Maybe it's not a friendship. . . . It's just a job, and hopefully for them, it's a pleasant job." They usually say, "I love teaching. I love what I do."

Here we see the dilemma for teachers and students. Most teachers declare that teaching is more than just a way to make money and that they care about students and their performances. While it is clear that many do, students can never be certain, because they live in a culture with an apparent disconnect between caring and commerce.

Phoebe attempted to reassure herself that her teachers genuinely cared by putting considerable effort into creating friendships with them that extended beyond the dance floor. She despaired of her current teacher, who had proved resistant to her overtures. If she asked him to have lunch with her at a competition, he would "take a rain check." She fondly remembered the teacher over whom she had fought. She told me, "He preferred to be with us. He really didn't want to be with his colleagues. He would say we protected him. . . . We'd just talk about everything in the world; music, show business, politics." That is, Phoebe knew his feelings were genuine.

Phoebe noted,

> I would have trouble having that kind of conversation with some of the others. . . . Some are not very knowledgeable, or very educated, or they come from different cultures nowadays. . . . It has always been important to me to have a personal relationship with the person though. . . . I want to break that barrier, and I'm not happy until it's broken. . . . The best way to do it is to show them how interested you are in their career, and I usually am. . . . I also like to find out about their life, their past. . . . You start sometimes even talking about your personal life. They may even ask little by little. You don't talk during lessons, because that would be a waste of money. . . . At competitions, some include you afterwards, some don't. It doesn't hurt my feelings.

The former teacher had been born and raised in the United States, whereas the new teacher was an ambitious immigrant from one of the poorest countries in eastern Europe, so breaking down the barriers had proven difficult. However, Phoebe kept trying.

Intimacy, Gender, and Commerce

Ballroom dance always draws attention to two types of human bodies: male and female.[7] For many students and audiences, the gendered nature of this dancing is part of its attraction. Phoebe's husband had died shortly after she started. Male companionship was important to her; her main source came from dance lessons, always carefully calibrated in dollars. She described the dance relationship as one of equals. Although she understood that the man's role is to lead and the woman's is to follow, she argued that "the woman does fifty percent." She even noted that "there are certain times when you're leading the motion." She saw smooth dancing as "simply a love story of a man and a woman, whether they're fighting or flirting or playing or seducing." However, she liked the idea of "ceding something to them" because she saw it as "very feminine." In this way, dancing helped maintain her gender identity.

While the performance of ballroom appears traditionally gendered, in reality gender plays out in complex ways. Masculinity in American society has been conceptualized as an endeavor that requires the approval of other men.[8] Men who dance professionally, however, transgress this understanding, because, while other men may be an important audience during a performance, male teachers spend most of their days relating to and pleasing women. The intimacy rules that male teachers follow involve a mix of traditionally gendered and transgressive behaviors.

In contrast, professional women dancers must tread a fine line between telling male students what to do and showing them how to take charge. Some men find it difficult to be taught by a woman, which is one possible reason that there are many fewer male students than female. In addition, the flirting that is a part of studio life has a different and potentially more dangerous meaning when the student is male and the teacher female, rather than the other way around.

The idea that money can buy intimacy helps explain why Phoebe looked to the commercial dance world for a dose of romance.[9] Phoebe desired personal, but nonsexual, physical relationships with handsome young men, and she was willing to pay for them. At the same time, she was quite brutal in her description of the limits of these relationships, noting the emotional labor she undertook to achieve a closer connection.[10]

Romantic love is regarded in our culture as indispensible for true happiness.[11] For those who have not found it, love can also be bought by those who can afford it. Commercial relationships permeate all aspects of modern life, putting love and romance up for barter like any valuable commodity. Phoebe understood that she had to pay for the romance of dance. However, she did not view it as just another product; dance was special and worth much sacrifice. This is common when intimacy and money intertwine.

Phoebe was utilitarian in her approach to membership in the dance community, carefully calibrating how to cut corners without destroying the quality of the experience. She noted that her teacher found it "uncomfortable" to talk about money and that it was better when he could "make a joke of it," underscoring a desire to deny that intimacy is commercialized. We prefer to think that there is one true love in our life, a relationship impervious to the vicissitudes of the marketplace. Indeed, Phoebe justified her teacher's unwillingness to spend time with her by explaining that "he just wants to be with his partner, who is the love of his life."

Phoebe underscored this ambivalence over the commercialization of emotion in her description of her family's initial reactions after she became enamored with competitive dancing. Until they met her teacher, they were suspicious of his motives and worried that she was "being taken advantage of by this young man who wants her money." After her husband died,

Phoebe's children questioned her motives more strongly. They were embarrassed by her ardor for dance, telling friends, "My mother's lonely. She has nothing else to do. It's a nice little hobby that she's doing, but isn't she getting totally carried away? . . . Isn't it taking over her life? Why is she so obsessed?" Phoebe's daughter, a high school student at the time, was particularly uncomfortable. When her daughter's friends asked Phoebe how her dancing was going, the daughter would "freeze." This had changed in recent years. Her children had watched her dance and seen how happy it made her, but they did not like her to "go on and on and on about it."

Some critiques of love under capitalism assert that love cannot flourish when it becomes subservient to commerce.[12] Instead some people have argued that true love must be free of commerce, a view which has been called "one of the most important mythologies of our time."[13] I take the position that there exist many opportunities for people to purchase a romantic or intimate experience without the need for love. For example, when people go social dancing, they experience physical closeness and friendliness, but they typically leave alone.[14] They do not necessarily see the intimacy they purchase as commercial, but it is an experience that is bought and consumed.

Phoebe is but one example of many dancers I interviewed who saw love and romance as commodities, which enhanced their quality of life, and who had few qualms about their purchase. She and other students I interviewed saw the glamour of ballroom as additional evidence of its power to enhance romance. Phoebe called dancing "making love to these people."

In a study of the connections between love and late capitalism, Eva Illouz interviewed fifty couples about their romantic experiences.[15] Particular commodities became essential components of the romance, while, at the same time, the culture of romance invested some commodities with an iconography of love. Her couples echoed the types of romantic relationships that are prized in our culture: getting out of everyday space, doing something glamorous and exotic, and most especially, marking the time as different and celebratory.

The world of ballroom offers an ideal example of this type of romantic experience. While the relationship between commerce and romance is explicit, it has to be managed carefully. Even though romantic love is not involved, teachers understand that dancing provides an intimate and glamorous experience. Students expect to receive this, whether they are beginning social dancers or top pro/am competitors. The studio atmosphere contrasts with everyday life. Worries are to be left at the door. Students frequently report being tired and distracted by work at the beginning of a lesson, only to find these feelings disappear after a few minutes. Pleasure is the order of the day, even when students are being exhorted to try harder. The combination of hard work and emotional reward makes every experience an occasion, and competitions feel "like running away to join the circus."

The pursuit of romance on the dance floor is largely, but not exclusively, a female endeavor, especially in pro/am dance studios which emphasize technique, long-term commitments, and competition. It is less true in social dance venues. Here one finds middle-age and older, lower-middle-class men who live alone and use the dance floor as a way to obtain a small measure of noncommittal intimacy.

On the whole, men prefer to purchase other leisure activities. For example, baseball fans may attend fantasy camps and obtain coaching from retired players; 170 men each paid around forty-five hundred dollars to attend the 2008 Phillies camp in Clearwater, Florida,[16] while eighty men each paid ten thousand dollars for a week's practice with Duke basketball coach Mike Krzyzewski.[17] The intimacy that these men purchase—male camaraderie and an insider status in the masculine world of sports—is different from that achieved by dancing with a partner and synchronizing bodies and movement.

Men are the major purchasers of the wide variety of explicitly sexual services sold all over America. Sociologist Elizabeth Bernstein argues in her book on the transformation of prostitution that professional men with demanding jobs are increasingly seeking a "girlfriend experience" with high-end sex workers; they want all the trappings of a successful sexual relationship without the commitment.[18] The "girlfriend" is different from the dance teacher; girlfriends do a man's bidding, but teachers have their own ideas about what should happen. One could argue that women students want a "boyfriend experience," a relationship involving romance and commitment with physical affection but no sex. Women may well desire sex as much as men do, but even in a world of "hooking up," there are costs involved in developing a strong commitment to sexual pleasure.[19] Although some women are willing to pay the price for this—Bernstein's middle-class sex workers, for example—it is safer, particularly for older women, to pursue the stereotypical feminine alternative of romance to be found in private ballroom lessons.

In our culture, romantic love and affection are viewed as the prerogative of women, while men are seen as more concerned with the practical. Yet the practical is a way of loving, even if it is not always seen as such.[20] Our norms about appropriate gender roles portray men as independent and dominant and women as dependent and incapable of practical action. In ballroom, these qualities are not so clearly gendered. Dance teachers embody a mixture of male and female qualities, and the mixture plays out differently by gender.

Furthermore, as women have moved into the world of work and up the ladder of success, this description of the gendered nature of caring seems outdated. Yet career-oriented independent women who decide to enter the world of ballroom often revert to gendered stereotypes. Indeed, in an effort to recruit men, the Oxford University dance team sold T-shirts; the back of the women's read, "The only place where men are still in charge: On the dance floor."[21]

In an examination of advice books for women, Arlie Hochschild reported that the majority of them were "cool modern"; they counseled women that emotional life is commercialized and advised readers to defend themselves from emotional hurt.[22] Although many women accept sexual desire as normal and, indeed, want to engage in sexual experimentation, love and romance continue to be important to them, and they sometimes despair of finding them.[23] The world of ballroom provides a way to protect against hurt, because women understand what it is they are purchasing.

A Brief History of Dance

The Victorians had a different view of romantic love. Like many people today, they idealized it as a noncommercial relationship, but they also emphasized its spiritual importance. In 1892, when Clelia Mosher interviewed married middle-class women about the purpose of sex, the majority of her respondents approved of sex for nonprocreative purposes, but only if it led to a greater spiritual connection between the couple and, through that, to a closer connection with God.[24] During that time, however, a wave of secularization was emerging, and romance began to replace religious faith as the goal of marriage. The marketplace responded by producing commodities to enhance the desirability of the wearer and leisure activities, which could lead to romance.[25] One such activity was the commercial dance hall.

Dancing had been popular for centuries in Europe and America, despite Protestant declarations against it.[26] For most of the eighteenth and nineteenth centuries, closely chaperoned formal balls were held in private houses.[27] Readers of Jane Austen will remember the ceremony of asking for and accepting dances, the public commentary on who was dancing with whom, and the frequent partner changes during the dance, which allowed for little more than snatches of private conversation while on the floor.[28] Those lower on the economic ladder took their pleasures at country dances, where partners changed during the dance and vigorous steps precluded much in the way of intimate conversation or close touching. The waltz was introduced at the beginning of the nineteenth century and was considered scandalous because of the close position of the dancers and the opportunity it provided for a longer private conversation between partners.[29]

The social changes accompanying the rapid urbanization of the late nineteenth century led to shifts in social mores and in what was deemed acceptable in social relations between men and women.[30] By the end of the nineteenth century, there was greater acceptance of the waltz, but it was the introduction of ragtime music and the development of syncopated movements that created the dance craze of the early twentieth century. Ragtime developed among Black Americans, quickly becoming a craze in America and Europe. Many of the dances it inspired are no longer popular, but its endorsement of freedom and desire for rhythm continue.

By 1910, the growing dance craze persuaded restaurants that dance floors would increase business, which led to the building of numerous dance halls.[31] This trend continued after the end of the First World War.[32] Social dancing was so popular between the wars that taxi-dance halls, memorialized in the song "Ten Cents a Dance,"[33] flourished in America as places where single men, often immigrants, could obtain the company of women.[34] When sociologist Paul Cressey wrote about the dance hall in the early 1930s, he viewed it as a place for sexual and romantic relationships, not for dance itself.

One factor promoting the commodification of romance was women's increased economic independence. In the late nineteenth century, young working women changed their leisure activities from family to peer-group events with opportunities to meet young men and fall in love.[35] This gave rise to a heterosocial world of leisure centered on the movie theater and the dance floor. Spending one's time this way quickly proved attractive to middle-class girls, and they followed their working-class sisters out of the home and into the dance hall.

Commercial dance halls were, from their beginnings, associated with sex and romance. Dorothy Richardson, a teacher from upstate New York, moved to New York City around the turn of the twentieth century in order to support herself.[36] She was horrified to find that the women she worked with in various factories spent much of their earnings going to these "pleasure clubs."[37] The assumption that dance halls led to liaisons and even sex was a cause of concern, particularly since well-bred middle-class girls were anxious to experience the thrills and dangers of the public dance hall. Thomas Faulkner, the former proprietor of the Los Angeles Dance Academy, converted "from a dancing master and a servant of the 'evil one' to an earnest Christian and a servant of the Lord Jesus Christ." He answered the question about potential harm in dancing by describing the inherent dangers of letting beautiful young daughters of wealthy parents learn the waltz.[38] Faulkner's may have been an extreme position, but the late nineteenth century was replete with advice on proper ballroom conduct, and debate raged as to whether ladies and gentlemen might waltz together, even at private dances.[39]

By the early twentieth century, recognizing that New York City was "dance mad," writers began to call for reform to allow young people to enjoy the dance hall's pleasures while avoiding its pitfalls:

> No girl comes to the dancehall night after night and remains as she was when she began coming there. You cannot dance night after night, held in the closest of sensual embraces, with every effort made in the style of dancing to appeal to the worst that is in you, and remain unshaken by it. No matter how wary or wise a girl might be—and she has enough things in her daily life in factory and store to teach her—she is not always able to keep up the good fight. It is always a matter of pursuit and capture. The man is ever on the hunt, and the girl is ever needing to flee.[40]

When Beth Lindner Israels wrote these words in 1909, she did not agree with Faulkner that the inevitable end was prostitution, but she did think that girls who regularly went to ballrooms were "apt to lose the bloom of their youth."[41] The danger in the new dances, like the waltz and the two-step, lay in their emphasis on the couple rather than on the social group, so girls had little protection from men's sexual demands. Of course, for girls seeking romance, this was a major reason for dancing's attraction.

After the Great War, Victorian ideals had mostly disappeared. Love as the basis for a happy marriage had replaced duty and friendship. By the 1920s, magazines were full of advice about how to keep the romance alive in marriage—this was seen as the key to a successful adult life.[42] The popularity of the dance hall as a place to find romance continued to rise, and by the 1930s, when my parents met while dancing, it was a desirable place to socialize and meet new people.

In order to learn the new dances, young people needed lessons. The role of the dance teacher was long established, but the beginning of the twentieth century brought a rapid growth in opportunities to teach, partly fueled by the newly affluent middle classes. Dance instructor Arthur Murray began providing mail-order lessons in 1912. By 1925, he and his wife had founded their first studio, and in 1947, their chain was joined by a chain of studios from the Fred Astaire Organization. These two companies still franchise studios in the United States and, in the case of Arthur Murray, in thirteen other countries.[43]

Ballroom dancing continued in popularity throughout the first half of the twentieth century. New dances were added during this time, with the introduction of swing dancing and with a stream of Latin dances coming from Cuba, via New York. During the 1960s, however, dances such as the twist replaced partner dancing, and clubs replaced ballrooms. Many dance studios fell on hard times during this period, and it was not until the introduction of disco dancing and the hustle in the mid-1970s that a small revival began.

Since the seventies, couple dancing has grown slowly in popularity, and some dances have experienced a boom. For example, the lindy hop, a type of swing dancing popular in Harlem in the 1930s and 1940s, began a revival in the late 1980s, starting in Southern California and spreading to the rest of the country.[44] Mixed ballroom and Latin dancing has been experiencing a renewed interest due, in part, to the popularity of the television show *Dancing with the Stars*. College teams had started in Britain in the late 1960s and were popular by the 1980s.[45] American colleges soon followed suit, and many now have competition ballroom teams as well as social dance lessons. With the 2005 release of *Mad Hot Ballroom*, a movie about teaching children to dance in the New York's public schools, lessons in ballroom and Latin dance have swept across middle schools in America.[46] The resurgence of interest in ballroom has been noted in the press.[47]

The influx of immigrants from places with a strong interest in ballroom, especially from eastern Europe and Asia, contributed to this increase in demand.[48] By the beginning of the twenty-first century, the two studio chains, as well as many independent studios, were flourishing. Many eastern European ballroom dancers either immigrated with their families or were recruited to America to staff the growing number of dance studios. As a measure of this increase in popularity, membership in the United States

Amateur Ballroom Dance Association (USABDA) grew from two thousand in 1988 to more than fifteen thousand by 2005.[49]

Since the early years of ballroom, it has not been just a social activity. Beginning in 1910, when cabaret owners began to introduce ballroom acts, audiences have been willing to pay to watch dancing. The most popular couple in the early years, Irene and Vernon Castle, began dancing in 1912, and they helped professionalize exhibition dancing.[50]

The social class ramifications of ballroom have been written about elsewhere.[51] From the beginning, teachers of dance were at pains to keep dancing respectable. They wanted to distance the popular dances from their origins in Latin America and the new urban neighborhoods of Black America. These origins were tainted with explicit sexuality, which could have jeopardized the developing ballroom profession among middle-class white Americans. Irene Castle noted in her autobiography that she and Vernon were careful not to dance passionately and that their status as a married couple increased their wholesome reputation.[52] Even so, in 1914, one year after the Castles returned to the United States and brought the tango with them from Paris, the Vatican denounced it as immoral, along with the equally popular turkey trot.[53] This kind of criticism kept the Castles and other teachers ever vigilant.

If the Murrays, with their mail-order business and their franchise schools, had standardized social dancing, it was the British who set down the rules for professionals. Philip Richardson chronicled the explicit measures that English dance teachers took to agree on and to document the allowed steps and to remove the lower-class and non-European origins of some dances. Competitions started in England about 1919, and the Blackpool competition began in the 1920s. Concerned about the sexually explicit nature of the non-European dances, about two hundred teachers attended an informal meeting, which Richardson chaired. The participants began to legislate as to the permitted movements. They decried "dubious steps" originating "in low negro haunts" and agreed that there were to be no "dips, lift-ups, lifting of the feet, and other movements unsuitable in the ballroom."[54] They were particularly offended by the tango, which Richardson described as perfected "in the lower haunts"[55] of Argentina. They also declared that moving with the feet turned out as in ballet was to be replaced by parallel feet. This "English style" spread throughout the world and is known in America as "international style" to distinguish it from the homegrown American version.[56] Standardization continued over the next two decades. For example, Richardson called the rumba a "native dance of Cuba, purely Negroid in origin" and described the battles over which steps were to be allowed.[57] When American GIs brought over the jitterbug, the English teachers developed a "not unattractive" version, the jive.[58] Today, these dances are performed in more or less the same way as defined then, although constraints on the portrayal of sexual desire have loosened considerably, and technique has become more demanding.

Out of these beginnings arose the ballroom and Latin sections of the Imperial Society of Teachers of Dance (ISTD). The ISTD had started in 1904 but did not add ballroom to the curriculum until 1924. The ballroom curriculum was encoded in writing by Alex Moore in 1936, with Latin added in 1946.[59] To this day, the ISTD offers a curriculum and levels of certification in which teachers can become credentialed.[60]

This successful decision to routinize the steps of ballroom and Latin dances has not been without controversy, particularly where Latin is concerned. Many people believe that it caused Latin dance to lose its authenticity. For example, one of the most popular Latin dances is the samba. As danced in Latin competition, it involves a pulsating motion, along with many twisting, rotating, and extended body actions. The parade around the floor is an important characteristic of ballroom samba.[61] Samba originated in the Bahia region of Brazil but has its roots among the Yoruba of West Africa.[62] Samba as practiced in Brazil is often danced solo, and dancers frequently stay in one place. Aficionados of Brazilian samba are quite scornful of the ballroom version, which they view as inauthentic.[63]

Much has been made of the racial implications of the decisions made by the British developers of the ISTD.[64] Richardson's writing shows a fear of lowering the class standing of ballroom dancing if any suggestion of crudity was allowed. However, the underlying concerns were economic. Dance teachers wanted to make a living. They were typically working class themselves, and it was to their financial benefit to market ballroom dancing as an elegant activity. There was a fine line between the intimacy of partner dancing and a more explicit sexuality, a line which dance teachers were careful not to cross.

A second purpose of the strict curriculum was to anoint those who were qualified to teach. Richardson believed that the public would be reassured that ballroom teaching was a professional activity if everyone taught the same curriculum. This concern for credentialing, though only partially successful, has helped maintain the standing and income of teachers. Certification is more complicated in the United States, where a unique American style is taught in addition to international style. The American styles, called "smooth" and "rhythm," were pioneered by the chain studios, with each chain developing its own curriculum and certification. Independent studios in the United States use a third curriculum, DVIDA, so U.S. professionals may have any of a number of certifications, including ISTD. Regardless of the type of certification (if any), all teachers follow a similar curriculum.

The Life of a Dance Teacher

In the chapters that follow, I argue that in addition to curriculum, intimacy is a crucial part of the dance experience. But what of teachers? What benefits do they get? Just as Phoebe represents students in this chapter, George is a stand-in for teachers. He is an attractive and personable forty-three-year-old, with a charming southern accent, who has been teaching since he was nineteen. He was in his first year of college when a friend suggested that he might earn additional income teaching ballroom. He started out at a Fred Astaire studio, and as is typical of chains, he quickly began teaching, often finding himself just a few lessons ahead of the students. A former high school sweetheart, Susie, was also teaching at the studio, and George was quickly sold on dancing as a career:

> I dropped out of college and started to do dancing, because in college I was just having fun, sowing my oats and so forth. The manager who approached me about becoming an instructor . . . said, "George, you know there are some people who like the security of knowing that they show up for the job, they're there for so many hours a day, and they make such and such a week. I like knowing that through my own efforts I can make as little as a few hundred dollars, or I could make as much as a few thousand dollars a week, but it's all up to me." He said, "How do you like dancing? Do you like traveling?"

This lifestyle appealed to George, but he saw other advantages also: "I saw that after four years of college, I would have the credentials to get my foot in the door and maybe begin to learn something about this trade or that trade. In the dancing," he added, "I could learn the skill as I was going . . . and make money doing it."

To teach dance with so little experience was intimidating at first, but George is gregarious: "chatting with people and being with people of all ages was nothing that made me nervous." George is a master of instant intimacy. When I first met him at a competition, he was teasing and joking with me in no time as if we knew each other well. Later, when I visited his studio to interview him, he greeted me like an old friend. When he first started teaching, George said, he "felt inadequate in a lot of the different dances," but then he added, "I considered myself a professional pretty soon, because I knew more than most people." He was "doing it for four to six hours a day training," so he quickly jumped ahead of students who were taking one or two lessons per week.

Susie, who became George's wife, was a major source of encouragement and an antidote to the reaction of his parents. George was the youngest of five in a working-class family and the only child to attend college. His father was upset with George's decision to leave college before graduating. His father, George said, "had the idea that I wanted to be the best dancer in the world, and he's looking at things realistically. I'm already nineteen, and I haven't had all this training. He didn't see the business side." However, by age twenty-five, George and his wife owned a Fred Astaire franchise, and George described his father as now proud of him. George and Susie had struggled to make this happen, even sleeping in a small studio office at one point. Dancing provided George with a life of recognition and glamour that he had never imagined would be his. To become a business owner at age twenty-five with only a high school education was a heady experience.

By the time they bought the studio, George had entered the world of DanceSport competition.[65] This happened soon after he first learned to dance:

> Susie was the best girl there. I was the newest guy. She decided that we should dance together, so that she could help me to learn quickly. . . . There was a competition . . . three months from the day I started training, and she said, "We're going to it." I was so nervous, but I worked really hard, I mean, 'til four in the morning at times. . . . We got second place, but then, the nine competitions after that we got first place.

At Fred Astaire competitions, the level of dancing was lower than at national ones, where professional dancers have many years of experience. George explained that Fred Astaire had a "novice category" for teachers with less than a year of instruction. George felt proud that they had won at a national Fred Astaire competition early in their partnership. He quickly became hooked on American smooth and began competing in top national events. George explained that he loved smooth the best, "the oneness of it." He realized that "there's oneness in Latin and rhythm as well" but added, "When you're sailing around the room and you're one body, when it feels like a ride, it's just a neat feeling."

In focusing on the nondancing motives for dancing, it is easy to forget the love of dance. Dancing's physical pleasures are a great motivator in and of themselves. In fact, George felt that sometimes the money got in the way. He told me, "I love music. Dancing is relating with, being with people from all different walks of life. I like people, and what better way to do it than this." He did not like it, he said, when he had to ask for money: "it can get expensive, so you meet a lot of friends, you lose a lot of friends."

Dance Teachers and Intimacy

In addition to competing professionally, George began dancing pro/am. When I interviewed him, he was attending about six competitions a year, usually taking more than one student. George appreciated the students. He noted that without students' lessons, professionals "wouldn't be able to do what they did. Competitions wouldn't exist, because where would they get the money?"

When a student went with him to a competition where he was competing with his wife, George acknowledged that there was a down side: "You just danced all day, and now I'm dancing again with Susie in the evening." Yet, although teachers sometimes had to deal with difficult students, they recognized the economic importance of the students to their own careers. In addition to the financial rewards of taking students, they enjoyed the relationships they developed and the status they obtained from being known as a dancer whose students competed. Still, the emotional rewards of teachers are clearly different from those of students.

George had stopped competing about a decade before our interview. This happened for two reasons. First, as he said, he and his wife were "getting older, and the young ones are just getting better." However, they had also had difficulties with the Fred Astaire organization, which did not give their professional dancing the recognition that they believed they deserved. Eventually, George and Susie bought themselves out and became an independent studio.

George's appreciation for students, especially those who go to competitions and dance pro/am, contrasts with the perspective taken in a book that is highly critical of DanceSport.[66] Written by former professional competitor and dance professor Juliet McMains, the book's descriptions of pro/am are uniformly negative. McMains conflates actual people into what Max Weber called "ideal types," composites who stand in for the group they represent. This allows McMains a free range in creating portrayals of students and teachers, and she often portrays their relationships with teachers negatively. This portrayal is at odds with my experience, George's description, and the experiences of others whom I interviewed for this book.

When George took students to competitions, he enjoyed the contact he had with other professionals. Dancers work difficult hours—studios are typically open from midday until late evening—so it is hard to maintain nondancing relationships. Friendships with other dancers become important. Competition organizers recognize this, and they typically schedule professional parties, to which students are not invited, in the late hours. Since most students keep daytime hours, professionals are able to socialize among their peers without offending students. Teachers from different parts of the country quickly become close, utilizing the people skills they learn in becoming dance teachers.

George desired this contact with professional dancers, because they understood his life and validated his experiences. He lived in an area with many retirees, and a number of his students lived alone. Sometimes these students were demanding in their desire for emotional intimacy, and his professional friendships provided an outlet:

> Some students tend to think if they've paid your way to do something, they bought you and not your time. . . . As a professional, . . . it's not like, "Well, I'll just show up, and we'll dance. You're not gonna see me again." You must practice, and you are going as a team. So there should be some things to do together, but, at competitions, when I see [my friend], or I have other acquaintances there that I want to talk about things that are not of their business. Let our hair down, so to speak. . . . That's important to me because I'm doing this all the time. I don't have a whole lot of friends here.

This description reflects sociologist Erving Goffman's idea of frontstage and backstage.[67] Frontstage involves a public performance and necessitates embodying and maintaining standards of politeness and decorum. Even though teachers and students dance together, teachers are typically onstage when students are around, even when not on the dance floor. George joked with students, for example, but never at their expense. He always appeared content in their company. The art of instant intimacy as practiced by teachers involves enjoying students' company and including them in activities.[68] Backstage is usually occupied only by performers. Here the performer can step out of his or her public character. This does not mean, of course, that actors are not performing when they are backstage, but they are doing so as insiders.[69] Letting one's hair down is a perfect backstage activity, and George's use of this idiom suggests an intuitive understanding of the concept. Of course, the longer students and teachers dance together, the more students get to see the backstage personalities of teachers and the more instant intimacy turns into the long-term kind.[70]

There are several answers to the question of what teachers get out of the dance relationship. They are able to make a living teaching dance in a country that does not pay dancers well. They are also able to move in social circles otherwise unavailable to them. George, like most teachers who dance pro/am, had stayed in the best hotels across America and had taken students on dancing cruises. He considered this a pretty good life for a southern boy with one semester of college. He also recognized that teaching allowed him to compete. Pro/am students not only pay for their professionals to attend; they compose the audience for these same dancers when they compete. Furthermore, George, like many other teachers, saw his success in teaching dance as an affirmation of himself and his place in the world. He took pride in a top, but former, student, who now lived in a different part of the country.

Research Questions

In the stories of George and Phoebe, we can see the complicated ways in which professional and student dancers negotiate their relationships. However, other dance relationships—those between professional partners and those between social dance teachers and students, for example—are equally important. In each case, issues of intimacy must be negotiated. This process of negotiation gives rise to four research questions, which I attempt to answer in the remainder of the book: (1) How does the performance of intimacy in the world of ballroom differ from that recorded in other aspects of social life? For example, does the dance world's pressure for instant intimacy hamper or facilitate the development of genuine relationships? (2) How is the intimacy of the dance world experienced differently by professionals and students? (3) How do dancers develop dancing identities in a world where intimacy and its portrayal are to be turned on and off at will? And finally, (4) What are the gender and social class manifestations of developing an identity as a dancer, and how do these vary among immigrant dancers?

Although these questions entail discussions of dance as a performance, this is not a book about dance per se. Nor is it a book about dance as movement. It is about dance relationships. Dance teachers produce intimacy when they teach students, by making students feel welcome and at home in the studio. Dancing couples, whether professionals or pro/am, produce intimacy for audiences in an effort to show that a real relationship exists between partners. Finally, dancers, whether students or teachers, must integrate the instant intimacy of many dance relationships with other long-term intimate relationships. The world of ballroom dance can illuminate trends in the ways intimacy and romance are negotiated and portrayed in America.

Methodology

Academic women writing about ballroom sometimes feel the need to explain their attraction to an art form they consider to be sexist and even racist in its appropriation and modification of dance forms from other cultures. Most of the Latin dances and rhythm in ballroom are quite different from those danced in their countries of origin: Cuba, Argentina, Brazil, and the Black ghettos of the United States. Furthermore, there is a paucity of dancers of color, especially of African Americans, whether professionals or students. Most students are affluent, and although there has been an increase in the number of African American and Latino dancers in recent years, especially in social dance, the cost precludes more from participating. One exception is Asian dancers, especially Chinese Americans, who do participate in significant numbers. Teachers also tend to be white, and the influx of eastern Europeans guarantees that this trend will continue.[71] It is also possible that the world of ballroom holds little appeal to African Americans because of the formality of the steps, as opposed to the spontaneity of many popular dance forms.

In spite of these issues, I make no apology for the way I have been ensnared. Rather, I am grateful for having discovered a passion late in life, especially one which brings me such joy. However, dancers know that their world is sometimes viewed with suspicion, and McMains's book, with its largely negative portrayal, caused consternation in the ballroom world. Thus, I was apprehensive when I began to interview dancers. Although the public's understanding of ballroom has improved somewhat since *Dancing with the Stars* became popular, many ballroom dancers—particularly professionals—are unsure about exposing their dancing selves to nondancers. Other researchers have reported difficulty in getting dancers to agree to formal interviews rather than simply chatting off the record.[72]

I realized that I would improve my chances of success if I was identified as an insider who belonged to the world I was studying. This is the reason that I published the piece reproduced in the preface to this book. I added the piece to my website, the address of which is always listed at the bottom of any email I send. This enabled the dancers to whom I wrote to check out my insider credentials, and it proved crucial. Often those who agreed to be interviewed commented on their pleasure in reading the piece.

While my dance background helped me gain entrée to the dance world, my status as a student who competed may have caused some teachers to be cautious in their replies. For example, as noted earlier, teachers rarely complained about students. Was this because they knew I was a student and did not want to reveal their true feelings, or was it how they actually felt? Evidence is mixed. Sex workers may say whatever it takes to get business, even falsifying a sexual identity when necessary.[73] Yet middle-class sex workers often describe themselves as providing more than merely sex and describe the relationships that they develop with clients as meaningful and worthwhile.[74] Dance teachers hope for long-term relationships with students, not the transitory ones of many sex workers. So, although it is likely that I was not always told how teachers really felt, the fact that I almost never heard criticism of students, even in studios where I have spent much time, most likely indicates that teachers attempt nonjudgmental relationships, even if they do not always succeed. When I asked teachers what they did with a student they did not like, most reported that this was not common and then described the emotional labor they engaged in to change their feelings. Nonetheless, given that I was on the student side of the divide, it is likely that professionals were sometimes careful about what they told me.

Another potentially gray area is that of sexual identity. Did gay male teachers always reveal their sexual identity, given that some students prefer to dance with straight men? Again, I cannot be sure. Dancers insist that most gay men are out to the dance community, yet professionals speculate about the sexual identities of some married men who dance with wives.[75]

It is likely that some dancers were in the closet about their sexuality and did not tell me they were gay. Since I was not proposing to have dance lessons with the teachers I interviewed, there would have been no economic reason to lie. However, they might have seen no advantage in revealing potentially damaging information. Although the world of ballroom and Latin dance is fairly open about sexuality, gay dancers told me that there is still discrimination.

Sociologists have shown little interest in studying dance, even though gender, social class, and race all manifest themselves on the dance floor.[76] Furthermore, social dancing has remained popular in many parts of the world for over a century.[77] This academic avoidance is due, in part, to the difficulty of writing about "the art of motion" without a visual representation in front of the reader.[78] Even the photographs in a book such as this can only give a hint of the movement on the floor. The rise of culture as a central interest in sociological theory has opened the possibility of studying dance from a sociological perspective. My focus here is specifically on gender and class.

Sociologists often study that which they do not inhabit, but it would not be possible to write about ballroom as a nonparticipant. All who write about it are insiders.[79] This includes academic works,[80] books on the joys of dancing,[81] autobiographies and biographies of famous dancers,[82] and even novels.[83] None of these works uses extensive quotations from interviews with dancers, so, in my case, I would have had an additional problem of not knowing how to talk to dancers if I did not understand their issues.[84] I do not even think it would be possible to undertake research on ballroom as a student of a different type of dance, such as ballet, because of the unique status of the ballroom couple.

In addition to interviewing students and teachers at independent studios in various area of the country, I interviewed current and former teachers and owners at the two studio chains, Arthur Murray and Fred Astaire. I also interviewed social dance teachers and students. Finally, I interviewed some of the top American professionals competing at the time I was doing the research for this book.

Even though most of the top professionals in the United States look to Europe, especially England, as the place to compete, I have focused on the American experience. Dancing is different here because of the prevalence of pro/am dancing, which allows professionals to make a living teaching. Pro/am is spreading elsewhere, particularly in places such as Hong Kong, but students from these countries typically come to the United States to compete. As a result of the availability of teaching, most Americans turn professional when quite young to take advantage of this opportunity, whereas in other countries they stay amateur and often look elsewhere to support their dancing.

Book Layout

In the following chapters, I take the reader on a journey through the world of dance, with the intention of answering my four research questions.

In chapter 2, I start with the world of competition, where the work and the relationship are sold to judges and audiences. How do dancers express their connection on the dance floor, and what are the rewards of the hard work that makes these moments possible? In this chapter, I sometimes use professional competitors' real names. When I interviewed professionals, most gave me permission to quote them by name and were frank in their discussions. Since I wanted to protect dancers from potentially embarrassing revelations, I chose to treat professionals like students when discussing private aspects of their lives and to change names. However, in their public lives —in discussing their standings as competitors, for example—these dancers are so well known that there is no point in trying to maintain anonymity. No doubt those with a great familiarity with the dance world will make informed guesses as to the identities of some professionals throughout the text. Since some of these are dancers whose experiences are unique, I cannot prevent this, but I have been careful not to reveal embarrassing stories. Where only a first name is given, it is a signal that the name has been changed. When I use dancers' real names, I give both first and last name.

In chapter 3, I turn to the economics of ballroom. This chapter explores the explicit connection between commerce and intimacy. Some writers have argued that the dance world is inherently exploitative,[85] but, although exploitation happens, I take the position that most dance teachers and students are clear-eyed about their expectations. Students would like to be able to afford more lessons or to go to more competitions. Professionals might like more students who compete or more sponsors so they could teach less. Teachers and students have a clear understanding about the purchase of intimacy in their world.

In chapter 4, I examine the emotional connection between dancers. Using the concept of "emotional labor" developed by Arlie Hochschild, I show how dancers work at their emotions in order to create a partnership.[86]

In addition, they learn how to display emotions on the dance floor. In Hochschild's analysis of flight attendants and bill collectors, she developed the concepts of deep and surface acting; both are brought into play in ballroom, though in different ways for professional couples than for pro/am couples. And the process is different again for social dancers, and the implications of these differences for identity construction and maintenance are profound.

Chapter 5 is about the dancing body. Ballroom is a world where appearance is everything.[87] Often in interviewing a dancer I had previously seen competing, I was struck by how ordinary he or she looked away from the dance floor. In addition to clothing and makeup, dancers need to be in perfect physical shape. Many dancers engage in grueling physical exercise off the dance floor. Since romance is more believable for the viewer if the portrayer embodies desirability, I investigate this appearance work and its implication for the portrayal of intimacy.

Chapters 6 and 7 deal with identity formation. Chapter 6 focuses on how male dancers develop a dancer identity and learn to mesh it with their sense of masculinity. By "dancing identity," I mean coming to think of oneself as a dancer, with all that it entails, especially for men. In addition, men have to learn to deal with the class differences between teachers and students. This process differs for immigrants, who typically started dancing while children, and between students and professionals. Chapter 7 looks at the experiences of women learning to dance. They too must learn to think of themselves as dancers, an identity which appears to contain fewer contradictions for women than for men. However, as we will see, professional women dancers have a tougher time. The lack of male students makes it difficult to make a living. In addition, there are the same class, ethnic, and student-teacher ramifications for women as for men, although they play out differently. Although I do not intend to reify the gender divide, I have grouped the men into one chapter and the women into another, regardless of whether they are students or teachers. This is because the ballroom world is so carefully, if complexly, divided by gender.

Chapter 8 focuses on the aging dancer. What is life like for professionals after competition ends? Do old dancers retire gracefully, or do they just fade away? Are they able to sustain long-term relationships? There is an additional issue involved in the relative ages of students and teachers. Ours is not a world which looks kindly on older women learning to give hot and heavy looks to young men, and older students must learn to feel comfortable with this in order to dance and maintain their self-worth. This dynamic is complicated by the potential for misunderstanding the flirtatiousness and physicality of the dance studio, a place with unique rules about the display of sexuality. This was exemplified in a sign hanging on the door of a female director's office that read, "Sexual harassment won't be reported, but it will be graded."

Finally, chapter 9 contains a discussion of the implications of my findings for the research questions articulated in this chapter. Throughout this book, I let the dancers speak for themselves. I am hopeful that in the end the dancers' words speak of the realities of the dancer's life.

2

The Thrill of Performance and the Agony of Competition

IN *THE DANCING YEARS,* legendary dancer Bill Irvine tells a dramatic story.[1] He and his wife were up-and-coming dancers, having placed fifth at the 1961 British Championship at Blackpool. When they entered the competition the following year, the favorites were Peter Eggleton and Brenda Winslade,[2] a couple the Irvines had so far been unable to beat.

At Blackpool, the atmosphere is always intense:

> It's difficult to imagine the excitement that takes over the whole place. Ballroom dancing is an extremely enthralling occupation, taking up the entire life of those taking part and calling out extreme enthusiasm in those watching. . . . If you say to any ballroom dancer, "I reached the last six at Blackpool," he'll respect you more than if you name yourself the winner of almost anything else.[3]

The first round started with the waltz, and the audience was quiet throughout. They began cheering for Eggleton and Winslade in the second dance, the foxtrot—a dance for which Eggleton was noted. The third dance was the tango. When the Irvines performed a particularly fast movement, cheers arose from the crowd, so they repeated the movement, and the crowd went wild. Before the fourth and final dance, the quickstep, other competitors told Bill that he and Bobbie had become the crowd favorites.[4] He decided to change the order of their steps, so that they could start with a dramatic move:

> Immediately, the crowd was back at attention, screaming their heads off for us. It was fantastic. We went round the floor so fast—! I don't think we felt the wood under our shoes at all! It all seemed to go perfectly; nobody got in the way to spoil it. . . . Frank Albach was watching the dancing that night, . . . and when we came off the floor he said to me: "D'you

know, you covered that entire floor in about seven seconds flat!"[5] By this time, a lot of people were coming up to the competitors' enclosure to say, "You're going great, boy. . . . One famous competitor, who had by this time retired, said, "Bill, I think if you can keep up your pace, you can win. You're going so strong, though, that I don't think you can keep it up at Blackpool."[6]

After several elimination rounds, the results stunned everyone. Each couple had won two dances, so the winner had to be decided by the rarely used "skating system," which considers every judge's individual score, starting with the total number of firsts awarded to each couple. This took some time:

> Alex Warren came forward to the microphone. He gave a little resume of the skating system and ended, "The winning couple this evening have won thirty firsts, Bill and Bobbie Irvine." I had been sipping whiskey and smoking. To this day, I can't imagine what I did with my glass or the cigarette! All I know is I was on the floor—without Bobbie. I was carrying on like Cassius Clay, acknowledging the roar of applause from the audience. Bobbie ran on after me. As she raced up to me, I caught her in my arms and swung her around six foot off the ground. We couldn't speak, we were so happy. I cannot remember crying at school, but there were tears running down my cheeks at that moment. I had just never credited that this could happen to Bill Irvine of Kilsyth.[7]

Several themes resonate in this story. First, the audience's reaction enabled Bill and Bobbie to intensify their connection and change their choreography while dancing. Second, Bill strategically interacted with the crowd to gain their support, assuming that the judges would be influenced by the opinion of the knowledgeable crowd. As the dark-horse couple, skill was not sufficient; the Irvines needed to show a distinct personality, with which the audience could identify. Most of the audience danced, so they would have recognized that the Irvines were using them, but they were willing to suspend criticism and let themselves get excited. Audience-conscious performances, which the Irvines exemplified throughout their career, have become even more important over the years.[8] Third, this account is almost entirely about men. Brenda Winslade is never mentioned; it is as if Peter Eggleton is dancing alone.[9] Bill Irvine describes making all the decisions, with no input from Bobbie. All those commenting or offering judgments during the competition were men.[10] These men offered Bill advice on how to manage an audience of which they were part.

In addition to being about strategy and gender, this is also a story of social class. "Bill Irvine of Kilsyth" was the son of a coal miner from a small town outside Glasgow in Scotland. He had apprenticed as a butcher, before deciding that he might make a living as a dancer. He and Bobbie had been financially unstable on the way up, and their success was only beginning to pay financial rewards at the time of their Blackpool victory. When the winner was announced, Bill was so elated that he committed a major breach of ballroom etiquette by neglecting to escort Bobbie onto the floor. In describing his bad behavior, he compares himself to a famously badly behaved and egotistical black man, Muhammad Ali. Respectable working-class white men, such as Bill, might have been assumed to know better. It is ironic that Blackpool, a working-class town, frequently bestows social class advancement on its champions. Blackpool was built for day trippers from the nearby Lancashire mills, and its two beautiful ballrooms are testimony to the working-class nature of British dancing.[11]

Finally, the account illustrates how we all revise our history to explain our current selves. Sociologist John Gagnon calls this the "fictionalizing of the self."[12] Though true of most personal narratives, this phenomenon is perhaps most evident in describing events that seem, in retrospect, to have been life changing. Such stories are rehearsed by recounting them to oneself and are perfected in telling others. They become miracles, without which the speaker would not be where he or she is today. Winning Blackpool in a close competition against all expectations was certainly such a moment for the Irvines, but its importance undoubtedly grew over the years. The Irvines, one of the most renowned ballroom couples ever, were inevitably going to win Blackpool, if not in 1962 then soon after. In addition to being talented dancers, they knew how to project palpable excitement and romance to the audience.

The Excitement of Competition

Bill Irvine's narrative, with its vivid depiction of the excitement attending this world-famous competition, is a perfect introduction to ballroom performance. Elation, sustained by the fact of competition and experienced by audience and dancers alike, makes ballroom performance different from other kinds of dance. Many of the top competitors whom I interviewed told me similar stories. When I asked Katusha Demidova, who dances with Arunas Bizoukas for the United States, which competition result had made her the happiest up to that point in her career, she talked about their most recent Blackpool competition, where they had placed second:

> We did not know how we would place, and I have to say this Blackpool probably out of the whole career, out of all the time I was dancing, that was the most amazing feeling. I still sometimes sit down and just look at the tape. I can just refeel everything that was there. . . . I remember, by the time we figured out we were second, we were so stunned we couldn't even come out on the floor. I remember Arunas standing in front of me was like, "Oh, that cannot be true." And they were calling us, and somebody's like, "Get out!" It was amazing—I don't even know if it will ever repeat itself, the feeling we have there, probably not. It was a new partnership. It was a first competition, so it was no expectations whatsoever. When the numbers kept calling . . . I wasn't nervous the whole competition, and then I remember . . . I couldn't move. As wonderful as it was, because it came out great, that was tough. I'm talking to you; I'm reliving the whole thing. I have goose bumps.

This moment happened forty-six years after the Irvines' victory, yet the same expression of amazement and joy pervades Katusha's narrative.

At the time of this interview, no American had ever won the British ballroom competition at Blackpool.[13] Katusha's ambition was to be the first. She had grown up in the former Soviet Union, but she said, "I consider myself American," and added, "I would love to win the Worlds[14] and the British for this country." She wanted to dance, she said, "so that people in the years to come just remember us"—in other words to dance like Bill and Bobbie Irvine.[15] Since the interview, she and Arunas have won both competitions. Color plate 3 shows their ability to perform different emotions as called for. In the picture on the left, the couple performs the tango with fierce determination and aggressive body movements, whereas, on the right, the foxtrot is all smiles and fun.

Of course, most top dancers do not expect to win Blackpool or the World Championship. They do, however, hope to rise in the rankings; everyone I interviewed who competed at the professional level could tell me their precise ranking and their goals for improvement. Paul Richardson, for example, who modestly considered himself and his partner, Olga Rodionova, to be in "the top twelve" in the world standings, knew how well he had done with every partner with whom he had competed.[16] He also knew whom he had beaten and who had beaten him.[17] Keeping an exact account of one's standing is typical of professional dancers. When couples rank this high, it is difficult to differentiate among their technical skills, so their ability to project excitement and connection becomes more important. Maximiliaan Winkelhuis predicts that of two equally skilled couples on the floor, those who produce "the strongest total concept will win." In other words, "Likeability for a couple is perhaps as important for success as pure technical skill."[18] In order to achieve this, he urges couples to develop a clearly recognizable concept with which audiences can identify.

Using research from advertising, Winkelhuis argues that there are three components to dancers' communication with the audience. The *content*, that is, technique and choreography, counts for 7 percent; the *tone*, or personality, counts for 38 percent; and *body language*, which includes the physical body, body toning, wardrobe, and makeup, as well as floor craft, use of space, musicality, and facial expression, counts for 55 percent.[19] Body language is illustrated by a number of dancers in this book, including Natalka Cap and her teacher, Jose DeCamps, in figure 2.1.

Sport, Art, and Show

When dancers talk about their rankings, they sound more like athletes than artists. In fact, there is widespread debate in the world of ballroom and Latin dance about whether it is more of an art form or a sport.[20] If dancing is mainly a sport, then technique and athleticism should be valued over emotional connection. The International DanceSport Federation (IDSF), which organizes major amateur competitions, is the association recognized by the International Olympic Commission as the official sponsor of DanceSport. The IDSF presents ballroom as a sport, albeit a sport with artistic merit, like ice dancing.[21] The IDSF has been in conflict with its professional counterpart, the Word Dance Council (WDC).[22] The WDC emphasis is on art, not sport; its instructions tell adjudicators to judge two aspects: technical merit and artistic impression.[23] Since dancers usually compete as amateurs before becoming professionals, they move from one governing body to another. Thus, they begin their careers considering themselves athletes but must become artists when they turn professional. In addition, professional dancers typically perform shows in addition to competing. Several dancers I interviewed said they think of dance

Fig. 2.1. Body language. American rhythm champion Jose DeCamps dancing with his student Natalka Cap at the 2009 United States DanceSport Championships, Orlando, FL. © 2010 Jonathan S. Marion.

as an art when doing shows but as a sport during a competition, where the emphasis is on winning.

In Ruud Vermeij's book on Latin dance, he identifies a third goal of Latin dance: show. He argues that show is particularly strong in America but that it exists all over the world. Show is distinguished from art by its preoccupation with "elements of display, public exhibition, outward appearance and performance before an audience."[24] The aim of art is to create something new, whereas the focus of show is the display in front of an audience. Of course, it is not as simple as this, because all good dancers are impressive athletes who integrate elements of both art and show in their performances. It is hard to distinguish among art, show, and athleticism in figure 2.2, in which Paul Cloud showcases Borbala Bunnett's strength and flexibility, as well as her glamour and grace.

However, top dancers' descriptions of why they danced sometimes alluded to the conflict among these three goals. Some dancers described dance as an intrinsic part of who they are and said that without it they would find life difficult. For example, Rita Gekhman—a top ballroom competitor who in partnership with her former husband, Garry Gekhman, had won the United States Showdance Championship—described the meaning of dance in her life as follows:

> People laugh at me because I don't smoke; I never tried. I don't drink; I don't enjoy that. I don't take drugs, never tried. I never did anything like people do to feel high. The only time I really felt high is when I'm on the dance floor. When I would go out there, I was like, "Damn, that's what I want to do." . . . It makes you feel alive. The feeling that you get in dancing is incomparable to anything else I've ever experienced.

Watching the Gekhmans perform their winning silver robot showdance at the 2007 Ohio Star Ball—a scene from which is shown in color plate 4—to the music of Herbie Hancock's "Rockit," one is struck by the art and the showmanship rather than the athleticism, even though both dancers are in excellent physical shape.[25] Garry and Rita are dressed in silver from head to toe, with silver makeup covering their faces and arms. Their eyes are made up to look as if they are wearing tiny sunglasses, and their robotlike faces betray no emotion. Rita's long black hair is arranged in thick silver spikes all over. In spite of the appearance and the robotlike quality of movement, the Gekhmans dance strictly in the ballroom style in which they competed. In rapid succession, they perform tango, foxtrot, Viennese waltz, and

Fig. 2.2. Getting it all together. Borbala Bunnett, dancing smooth with Paul Cloud, combines strength, flexibility, glamour, and grace. 2009 San Diego DanceSport Championships, San Diego, CA. © 2009 Jonathan S. Marion.

quickstep, as robots might dance them, sometimes interspersing with break dance and sometimes dancing like broken robots. Their timing is so perfect that each seems to move the other without touching and with no eye contact. In plate 4, the couple can be seen dancing without their hands touching. Bodies alone move as one. As Tony Meredith noted on *America's Ballroom Challenge*, this dance illustrates the couple's amazing connection,[26] a feat made even more extraordinary by their ability to execute it without using facial expressions. They barely look at each other throughout the entire performance, and their use of ballroom frame is perfect. The audience is brought into a relationship between two robots who can only have mechanical hearts. Rita Gekhman looks like someone born to dance.

Some dancers I interviewed combined the ability to portray a close and intimate connection with a more personal view about the pleasures of dancing with a particular partner. Such dancers tended to believe that authentic feelings were paramount. Ben Ermis, who won the United States Professional Smooth Championship three times with his wife, Shalene Archer Ermis, added a personal note to his love of dance:

> I love to dance, because I get to be creative. I get to use my musical background. I might have gone further in my music, if I had not stumbled on dancing in the first place. I'm allowed to use my body as a musical instrument without actually making music. I love to dance, because a big part of it is what it became with Shalene. Had it not been for that—what dancing means to me as a result of my partnership with her—I'm not sure it would be exactly the same.

In this statement, Ben sees his dancing as art.

Ben and Shalene performed a showdance at the Ohio Star Ball in 2006, as part of the "best of the best" competition, in which the winners of each of the four divisions compete for the final prize. As winners of the American smooth, the Ermises danced a Viennese waltz. Rules are relaxed for these dances, and sometimes the dancers change styles in the middle or do a themed performance in costume, like the Gekhmans. As can be seen on video,[27] Ben and Shalene do none of this. Dancing to "You and Me," sung by boy band Lifehouse, they enter the stage slowly, hand in hand, heads together, and begin to social dance like a couple in love. Winkelhuis considers the invitation to dance one of the two most important steps in a dance performance. He argues that "you create in this step the human relationship with your partner before the real action starts." This, he explains, is because "ballroom dancing comes from social dancing," and "it is all about the connection of a man and a woman."[28] Ben and Shalene exemplify this point at the beginning of their dance. He is in a dinner jacket and white tie, and she wears a sparkling blue dress revealing her long muscular back and arms. As the couple dances, the mood continues. The lifts seem effortless as they spin round and round, repeatedly looking at each other tenderly. The words of the song express the feeling of being in a sea of people and only seeing each other; they enhance the emotionality of the dance. The audience feels that they have watched a private and authentic moment of love.

Like the Gekhmans, the Ermises emphasized the art and the show of the dance. However, other dancers emphasized sports and competition. Many American men find it easier to incorporate dancing into a sports persona than an artistic one. Eugene Katsevman, a Latin dancer who had moved to the United States from the Ukraine in his early teens, adopted this viewpoint:

> I think there is something very special about this particular type of activity that appeals to my personality: the whole even marriage of competition and artistic expression that works just right. I don't think I will be satisfied in a more classical dance environment, where it's all about performance, and competitions are very rare. I think a more clear sport would be okay for me, but I would miss on the creative.

This perspective is evident in the jive performed by Eugene and his partner, Maria Manusova, at the 2007 IDSF championship. Amateurs at the time, they had been thoroughly socialized into considering dance a sport. Dancing to "Svaluation" by Italian rocker Adriano Celentano, Eugene dominates the action with high kicks and jumps. At one point, he stands twisting his feet and swinging his hips from side to side. At another, he pushes Maria in front of him and slides several feet beside her. Both dancers swing their arms wildly, and Eugene pays little attention to Maria, except to direct her and turn her as needed. His energy appears to be higher that hers, and the dance is a display of true athletic virtuosity.[29] Jive is not as relational as other Latin dances, and Maria and Eugene perform like two individuals who just happen to share the floor. That this was typical of their jive can be seen in color plate 5, taken at the 2009 USDC. Other dancers manage to make the jive seem more relational, for example, one performed around the same time by then World and Blackpool champions Brian Watson and Carmen Vincelj. In their exuberant version, Brian and Carmen manage to engage the audience while sharing the experience with each other through looks, touches, and synchronized movement, which has the effect of letting the audience in on a series of private jokes and moments.[30]

Although the athletic nature of dance competitions was typically emphasized by young men, some younger women agreed. Katya, an amateur ballroom dancer who had been to all the major competitions with an amateur partner, said, "I like the movement; I like performing, and I like competing—I like the whole image you create, as a couple on the floor." She explained why she liked competing: "I'm a very competitive person—always have been in my life with everything else I've done."

The tensions among art, sport, and show have dance critics bemused and sometimes disapproving. In reviewing two ballroom shows, *New York Times* dance critic Alastair Macaulay bemoans how athleticism and show have replaced art.[31] The photograph accompanying his critique shows Natalie Woolf and Craig Smith, the World Professional Showcase Champions, performing a signature move that is hard to describe in words. Natalie leans back and slowly lifts Craig up until his head is on her stomach and his bottom and legs are in the air. Macaulay finds the athleticism in this performance "staggeringly aggressive" and argues that these shows and others like them have taken "most of the dance out of these dances." He also finds the performances degrading to women, although he concedes that the women "cheerfully consent." For Macaulay, art has been pushed into the background in modern ballroom dancing.[32] Using terms such as "rape," Macaulay appears to object to ballroom's performative "exploitation." Audiences for ballroom are invited into an erotic moment, not commonly found in other kinds of dance.[33]

Performing as a Way of Life

Unlike Rita Gekhman, some dancers who had been dancing since they were children no longer asked themselves why they liked to dance or even if they did like it. Colin had been dancing since he was five. He struggled with this question, finally answering, "I honestly don't know," adding, "I think I found something that was meant to be, because I don't remember ever making this conscious thing of, 'I love to dance.' . . . I've never questioned my life in dancing." Peter had also been dancing since he was young and said much the same thing: "You don't ever think about it. It's just what you do. It's like breathing. It's just something that I'm used to. What else would I do?" Peter justified dancing by explaining, "I've got a pretty good life, and I enjoy it; that's as simple as I keep it. I don't think too deeply about it."

Dancers sometimes have to work hard to find the joy of dance amid the constant teaching, traveling, and practicing. Katerina grew up in Moscow, the child of amateur ballroom dancers.[34] She and her partner-husband moved to America when an opportunity arose to teach and turn professional. They had been competing together for ten years at the time of my interview with them. Katerina described herself as a disciplined and hard-working dancer, and the couple has a reputation for strong technical skills. When they go to competitions in the United States, her husband takes with him pro/am students, who usually do well. My question about why Katerina loved to dance took her by surprise:

> I never think about this. It's been a long time. I asked [my husband's] students the same question. . . . They really looked at me. They gave me such answers, I nearly cried. I thought, "My God! People are really passionate about this." One lady would write to me that "I feel it's my life. I feel so happy when I dance." Many people, especially from lower level, do it from passion, from the enjoyment. I guess we already lost a little bit of that. . . . We have to always come to that, to bring it out. It doesn't come as natural, because it's been a long time. . . . One lady, when she stopped dancing, very famous, she said that "I just want to wish to the other people who still compete that they never forget why they started dancing. Remember what you feel when you just started dancing and why you stayed in this sport. It's going to make you happier." I guess, also, a better dancer, so I try to do it.

The joy of dancing, which should produce natural emotions in the dancer, becomes difficult to maintain when competition is fierce and hours of practice are long. This is a couple with a deep personal connection who never argued about dancing. Yet they strove for a genuine connection on the dance floor and needed to resort to emotional labor[35] to produce and demonstrate the feelings that their students appear to find spontaneously.[36]

The appearance of an emotional connection in dancing is what separates ballroom from sport. No one tells a top quarterback what expression to have on his face when throwing a pass, but the right facial expression in dance competition has long been crucial. Len Scrivener, dancing with his wife, Nellie Duggan, won Blackpool three times between 1949 and 1953.[37] Here is his opinion on the appropriate look for competition:

> I am not for a moment advocating any special facial expression, but I do strongly condemn that fixed grin which some competitors and demonstrators put on as a mask the moment they take the floor. . . . Consider for a moment the present Foxtrot tunes most popular among good dancers. Here are a few:—Unforgettable; Half as Much; If You Go; Too Young. Every one of these melodies, as well as the lyrics I am sure you will agree, expresses a mood diametrically opposed to a fixed grin.[38]

Scrivener saved his most savage criticism for couples who did not achieve the proper facial expression in the tango, in which he declared that "a broad grin . . . surely betrays the fact that the performer is a fraud."[39] In other words, the emotions being portrayed in the dance must look authentic and are essential to the performance.

Judging Competition

Judges are part of the dance audience. What are they looking for? Jonathan Marion answers this question in his book on the culture of competitions by referring to an online article on judging, written by former U.S. ballroom champion Dan Radler.[40] Radler lists fourteen different criteria that judges use, and Marion argues that judges examine each in scoring every competitor. The list is formidable: posture, timing, line, hold, poise, togetherness, musicality and expression, presentation, power, foot and leg action, shape, lead and follow, floor craft, and finally, intangibles. Marion shows photographs of what each looks like when done properly. No doubt judges look at all these things. However, given the number of couples on the floor at once (often as many as twenty) and the short time span of each dance (less than two minutes), judges cannot give equal weight to each of these criteria for every couple. Douglas had been a judge for many years, and he conceded that it was not possible for judges to examine everything. He told me that each judge has a specific priority, adding,

> My priority is about musicality. For most judges, it's about speed, structure, impact, and all that. That's necessary, but to me the context of dance

Fig. 2.3. Judges line the floor, making notes and looking at each couple in turn, during the 2009 United States DanceSport Competition. © 2009 Jonathan S. Marion.

is music, and that to me is the number-one thing. As a musician and as an individual who has been a musical dancer and as a choreographer, I see all kinds of flaws in this area, and that tends to influence me a lot.

Figure 2.3 shows the array of judges on the floor at the 2009 USDC. As can be seen, a lot is going on, and judges cannot take it in all at once.

Douglas also agreed with Ruud Vermeij that "the results a couple have had in previous competitions can color the results of today."[41] Douglas tried to avoid this:

When I judge a competition, I almost put myself in a trance. . . . I try to wipe the slate clean, and I just look out there, and I just let my eyes be drawn. Within about twenty seconds, I have my winner, my second, third, fourth person. I start writing down, look at it, see if what I've written down is true, . . . switch a place here. That's how I do it. I have an absolute horror of allowing myself to be influenced by the results of a previous competition. . . . I have to try to judge, and then what I've done I'm happy with.

Some professional dancers conceded the difficulty of the judge's task. Others, however, accused judges of favoring those dancers whom they had coached. Boris, who competed professionally and took students to dance pro/am, was skeptical, saying, "All judges, they're all teachers, so they make living from their teaching." As a result, he believed that they had to favor those they taught, in order to obtain and retain students. He added, "Everybody has ego: 'Oh I'm teaching this couple, so that's my boy.'" To Boris, this meant that judges would "automatically support and have preference for these couples and style," because it reflected well on them as a teacher if their students did well. Finally, he thought, it "depends from the country: they like people from the same country."

Colin did not agree:

> Is there an unfair element in judging? Of course, because people judge by emotions, feelings, business. I think, for the most part, it ends up being fair, because there are enough respectful people in the business that care about dancing. . . . There are competitions that I am sure all couples can point to and go, "Oh, this is bullshit." . . . It's like human nature. If something starts being unfair, there's enough people that start questioning that, and it always seems to come back.

When Colin coached younger dancers, he was careful to tell them to let go of these concerns:

> You've got to keep your feet rooted to the ground, when results start to happen. . . . 'Cause people sometimes have a bad result, and they get a negative thing about their dancing. . . . I say, "Do you think, if you were a cook, it would be different? Do you think this is just ballroom? It's called life." . . . Once they start thinking like that, they get resentful of the results, and then they get resentful of their teacher and the judge. I say, "You're going down the wrong avenue. Just work on your dancing. Never mind the judges. Your job is to turn their opinion, and you do that by just working on your dancing."

Douglas put the issue differently:

> I don't know the judging is always fair, but I think, for the most part, we get a pretty accurate result. I like to see judges disagreeing. Out of the disagreement, there comes a general consensus of opinion. If you have a

competition with a fair number of judges, you get pretty fair results. Sometimes, I have disagreed with the majority, but I still thought the person who won—who was not my winner—deserved to win.

Douglas added that judging was difficult, and some judges had regrets. They wanted to do a perfect job and feared that they had not made the right decision. Judging, he said, "takes a toll on you."

Students' Pleasures

Due to the high stakes and uncertainty, professional dancers find competition to be hard and stressful. However, their dancing must appear effortless, emotionally engaged, and impervious to judicial criticism. The intimacy displayed in competition becomes part of the emotional labor of dance performance, and most professionals become adept at producing the required emotions. When professionals dance with students, their work is different. Even the top students require more physical and emotional support while dancing than do professional partners, and beginning students require even more care. New students do not always know where they have to be on the floor; they are not always good at holding up their own frame and so rest their arms on the teacher as they tire. They do not know how to engage their core muscles and lengthen their bodies. Teachers must help with all of this and more. The work of a teacher with a beginning student can be seen in figure 2.4. Janet Carrus does a good job of holding her frame for a beginning-level student, but compared to any number of pictures of professionals in this book, including figure 2.2, her posture shows her to be a beginner whose teacher has to do a lot of the thinking for both of them.

For students, however, the story is different. Students dance for pleasure, and they pay to do this. There is no reason to continue if there is no pleasure to be had. Students may find pleasure in the dance itself, in touch and intimacy, in the relationship with a teacher, in the rush of competition, or most likely in some combination of these. When students and teachers compete, they spend extra time together, which increases the level of intimacy between them, something students typically desire. Studios often have rules about how much time teachers can spend with their students under normal circumstances. The practice originated in the chains to allow teachers to end a lesson when the allotted time was up. One reason that they continue to exist is so that teachers will not play favorites among students and make

Fig. 2.4. Bronze-level pro/am. Janet Carrus with Edgar Osorio at the 2010 Desert Classic DanceSport Championship. © 2010 Jonathan S. Marion.

other students jealous. However, at competitions, the rules are relaxed, and students engage in a multitude of social activities with teachers. Students and teachers may travel together, eat together, and even visit local tourist attractions, if time permits. All these activities increase the student's sense of being special to the teacher.

Some students, however, considered themselves too serious for any of this. Hortense, a smooth dancer who competed regularly, danced because she wanted to win. When I asked her how serious she was, she answered that she was a ten "on a scale of one to ten, with ten being extremely serious." She spent much of her day thinking about competing; she had left a teacher because, she said, "his dedication was not at the same level as my dedication"; and she had organized her lessons to focus on what she wanted to learn:

> The first thing I like to do, and I have made it part of what we do every time, is I warm up, and he can pick whatever song he wants to warm up with—whether it's Latin, smooth, or whatever—so that I can get my legs moving, my knees, my ankles engaged. . . . Then we'll decide which of our four dances we need the most work on and start there and go from the beginning and counting. . . . Sometimes we'll stop everything and just work for an hour on footwork or frame or stretching our head, . . . which is, of course, not everybody's favorite, but sometimes you have to get back to basics. We may do basics for an hour, and then we may work on all four routines for an hour. And I'll say, "Well, that doesn't feel comfortable for me. We have to change that." So we have lots of dialogue back and forth.

When not having lessons, Hortense told me, "I practice dancing in my head. I videotape everything that is worthy of videotaping, and then I study it at night so I can see what mistakes I'm making." Even at the grocery store, she practiced holding her frame while walking around. She considered herself to have "grace, personality, and elegance" but thought she needed to work on "technique, footwork, and frame"—a good performer who could make up for technical weakness through her ability to project the character of the dance and her pleasure in doing it.

Why was competing so important? Hortense answered,

> Because I'm an extremely competitive person, which I've discovered in the last six years. . . . I am also a performer, and I believe that I've been, very late in life, given a God-given talent. I like to inspire other people,

especially young people. I morph into another person when I'm dancing to music that I enjoy with confidence and with a partner that I feel connected to.

At the studio, Hortense did not socialize, because she was "there to work." Nor did she perform in student showcases, because she considered herself a better dancer than the other students. Given how seriously she took herself, it is not surprising that Hortense was not interested in forming dance friendships. In fact, she disapproved of teachers' "encouraging women who are financially stable to get to competition when they don't belong there." When she first became interested in competing, Hortense had decided, "I was not going to do it until I was really good, no matter how long it took." "Really good," of course, did not mean that Hortense danced like a professional. A few of the top students who dance pro/am are better than some of the professionals, but the difference in the two levels is immediately apparent to the audience.

Leanne was one of the most successful student competitors. Unlike Hortense, she was engaged in the social life of her studio and made friends with her opponents. In fact, she told me that she did not really have friends outside of family and the ballroom. She loved taking lessons and was hard put to say which parts she liked best. Leanne found performing to be the easiest part of dancing. As she put it, "I'm a bit of a showboat." She also described herself this way: "more self-competitive than I am with other couples." Leanne's relationship with her professional partner-teacher had "evolved over time" as she improved:

> I still feel the student-teacher relationship, but not like I used to. I credit that to him as a good teacher in helping me develop to where I feel like he's taught me how to become more of an independent dancer, more of a partner, and not just totally dependent on him. . . . I want to be responsible as a dancer to do what I need to do, but then 'course there's those times that I need him to be just a teacher: "Take care of me please." . . . At this stage in our dance partnership, what I want to achieve more is . . . to give him the opportunity to dance more by not having to take care of me. . . . We do some side-by-side things, where I can't really see what he's doing behind me, and I'll be like, "Well, what d'you look like? Did you look good, or were you watching me the whole time?" He's like, "No, I trusted you." So that always makes me feel good, if I feel like he's able to dance, because I'm doing what I'm supposed to.

In this comment, Leanne perfectly describes the difference between a student and a professional. When her teacher danced with his professional partner, he always felt like he was able to dance his own part to the best of his ability, something Leanne was not sure he could always do with her.

Unlike Hortense, who held herself apart and disapproved of the pro/am world in some ways, Leanne felt totally at home:

> One of the things that attracted me, not just about competition but about this whole dance community, was the fact that I've always been a fairly optimistic person, and I've always had a lot of enthusiasm and a lot of energy, and I love to be around people that are positive, enthusiastic, happy people. For the most part, I believe that dancers have that, and you go into this environment and you're surrounded by people that are doing what they love to do, so they're happy and they're positive. It's a little bit of escape, for sure, for most of us from the day-in, day-out life that we might live.

For Leanne, the combination of intimacy, friendship, approval, and glamour on the dance floor made the experience worth the price. A now-single woman with grown children, her success as a dancer had great meaning to her. As she put it,

> Basically I go out on the floor every single time to this day feeling like I'm the luckiest person in the world to have the opportunity to do this. . . . No matter what the results are at the end of the day, at the end of the competition, I'm here because it makes me happy and because it adds joy to my life. . . . It truly is a total escape from everything. I have such a joy and such a passion for it, when I'm out there for a few minutes, nothing else matters but that. It's just pure heaven.

Not all students compete, even in competition studios, because the expense is prohibitive. These students want to exhibit the technique and performance skills they have learned, so studios organize showcases with family and friends as the audience. In some ways, performing at a showcase is harder than at a competition. As one student noted, unlike competition, the showcase performance is solo, "and everybody's eye is on you." Many find performances more difficult in front of their nearest and dearest, because the failure goes home with them.[42]

Although showcases mainly serve to provide a performance outlet, they also motivate students to improve. Ellen had not been having lessons very long when her studio had a showcase, and she did not want to perform at first. Then she decided, "I'll try the showcase, and if I don't enjoy the experience, then I'll just concentrate more on the social dancing with my husband, and I'll do fewer lessons." She smiled as she added, "I came back, and I said, 'The good and the bad news is that I absolutely loved it.'" Ellen wrote later to tell me that she was now competing.

Student Disappointments

Showcases did not always go well. Wendy, who had been dancing for a number of years when I interviewed her, described an Argentine tango she performed with her teacher at a studio showcase. She had an entertaining spin on her mixed satisfaction:

> It really felt good. At the end of the evening, he was back in his street clothes, and he came over to the table to say hello. He wasn't even saying this as a teacher. He said, "That felt really good. I was just dancing with you on the floor, and I don't care what it looks like on the video." Then I saw the video, and I went, "Oh, my God. I'm so glad it felt good, but it doesn't look good. Let's hang on to what it felt like."

Disappointment in the performance was not uncommon with showcase dancers. Competitions are better at making students feel satisfied, because they can recover from one unsatisfactory performance in subsequent heats. Isabel, who competed successfully at the national finals, experienced a disappointing showcase:

> What really destroyed my confidence was the showcase. All the time we were practicing a routine, it was supposed to be a foxtrot. But it really turned out to be more like a jazz. We were doing things apart, and it was my balance. . . . The room was large, and all the people there, and I'm sitting there waiting for my turn. I'm thinking, "God, I don't know what this routine is. I can't think what I'm supposed to do." It started out all right, but then I got lost in it somewhere, and I tried to pick it up. It really flustered me, and I was absolutely petrified. That left me with a very insecure feeling, anytime now that I get to do something.

Isabel was not alone in her performance anxiety. Claudia was a competition student, but she found it stressful when her teacher changed choreography on her right before her first showcase performance, and she panicked:

> I reacted in a very typical way. I got very upset, and I challenged him on it. That was the wrong thing to do, and he came back at me like a panther. . . . That was upsetting, because the chauvinism was alive and well. I was really demoralized from that experience. . . . I hate to admit this, but I burst into tears and was speechless. Right after that we didn't say another word to one another, and we went out on the floor and performed a perfect performance. Oddly enough, I guess what happens is that kind of stress or humiliation kicks in and you just say, "I'm going to perform perfectly." But I'm not proud of that moment, to tell you the truth.

Whereas an experienced professional dancer might have been able to walk away from the blowup, Claudia felt that it damaged her relationship with her teacher. The relationship was part of the reason she danced, so she switched teachers shortly afterward.

Yet Claudia continued to perform. What is it about the dance world that makes a woman put up with this kind of anger and humiliation in order to dance? Claudia had a good answer:

> I love how it makes me feel. It makes me feel more womanly than I've ever felt. It makes me feel more elegant. It makes me feel all the things I never was. I was never daddy's little girl. I look at photographs of myself when I was a little girl, and parents naturally want to show off their kids, but I don't think I was that kid. . . . I was not naturally gifted and bright. I was tall and geeky and kind of pigeon-toed. My father didn't know I was alive until I was about eighteen years old and played piano for him. So this was a wonderful epiphany.

It is ironic that second-wave feminism has enabled women to afford the means to discover a stereotypically feminine side of themselves. Claudia had not grown up thinking of herself as feminine, and dancing helped her perform gender more appropriately than before. For this, she was willing to put up with shouting, although she was happier with her kind and respectful new teacher.

Audience Pleasures

Ballroom dancing first appeared on American television in 1952, with *The Arthur Murray Dance Party*, a popular show that continued for twelve years. Ballroom dancing was shown occasionally afterward but did not achieve the same mass audience as before, perhaps because audiences no longer dance ballroom, and they do not understand what they see. This has changed with the advent of reality television, particularly *Dancing with the Stars* and *So You Think You Can Dance*. Both shows have attempted to educate their audiences about ballroom and Latin dancing. *Dancing with the Stars* has Len Goodman, who won Blackpool in his youth and has been a teacher and coach for many years. On each show, he explains what the audience is seeing, and he often disagrees with the other two judges, neither of whom has a ballroom background. *So You Think You Can Dance*, which showcases many different types of dancing, uses experienced ballroom and Latin judges, who sometimes have to correct the mistakes of the other judges.[43]

Many students watched ballroom on television, especially on PBS, though some did not watch regularly. Jane was just starting to compete. She traveled a lot for work, but she made it a point to "watch any dancing that's on." She recorded *Dancing with the Stars* to watch when she returned from trips, because she saw it as "a good opportunity to see the professionals dance." Like most dance students, she was "way more interested in the professionals than the stars." A friend of hers had bought one of the costumes, which the designers sell after the show is over. In addition, she told me, "I went to the tour. I did enjoy it."

One of the reasons that dancers liked watching these shows was that it added to their knowledge of the top American dancers. Although most of the professionals on *Dancing with the Stars* are permanently retired from competition, a few move between the show and competing,[44] although this is difficult. Knowledge about top dancers is important to students, particularly those who compete. Wendy loved the TV shows but loved knowing the names and placements of top dancers even more:

> Tony Dovalani is doing a really nice job these days. He's won rhythm the last couple of years. I like Max and Yulia, who came in second to Andre and Elena. I don't like most of the Latin dancers. . . . I loved Ben and Shalene; I really liked watching them a lot. There were times when I liked Nick and Lena on the smooth stuff. I really liked David Hamilton and

Olga Foraponova, but he doesn't compete anymore. I loved Melanie Lepa-tin; she had such sass.

Wendy also prided herself on knowing the international stars. She had at-tended Blackpool, something many American students would like to do. She wanted me to know how much more important Blackpool was than anything in America:

> Bryan Watson and Carmen are obviously the kings, and the guys who dance at Blackpool are a whole other thing. . . . That's like going to the Olympics. It's just extraordinary. Max and Yulia won one of the dances the last time I was at Blackpool, and everyone was gasping because that's such a big deal [because they dance for the United States].[45] The Ohio Star Ball —Americans think it's a big deal but not in the international world.

Several things are notable about these comments. First, the frequent use of first names tells the listener that she had seen these people dance and had followed their careers. Second, the eastern European names were pro-nounced correctly, although the last names are often hard to pronounce for Americans. Third, Wendy indicated that she had superior knowledge, be-cause she knew that American competitions did not rank that highly on the world stage.[46] Finally, her knowledge went back a number of years to danc-ers who no longer competed, which demonstrated how long Wendy had been dancing. Wendy's current teacher had competed at Blackpool and had taken her there, because he still had reserved seats, so Wendy was perhaps repeating things she had learned from him.[47]

Blackpool featured highly on many students' lists of where they wanted to go, and a number had been there. Becky-Sue had been dancing a long time, and through her connections she had seen *Dancing with the Stars* re-corded live, but she really wanted to go to Blackpool:

> I buy a lot of the tapes of Blackpool, Slavik, and all of them, Bryan and Carmen and all those people. I've watched them, because I really do ad-mire them. Unfortunately, I haven't seen them dance in person. . . . I get to see some of them here. Michael Chapman brings a lot of them into his competitions for the professional show.[48] . . . My dream is to make it to Blackpool. My husband says he always wanted to go to the Masters, so I got tickets one year for his birthday. Then one year, he wanted to go to a professional heavyweight fight, so I did that for him for his birthday. So I

keep waiting for my turn to go to Blackpool. I have contacts, because I've been around so long, and I know a lot of people that could probably get me in there now. . . . My husband promised me.

Social dancers live in a different world than that described in this chapter. A few of them have been to local competitions—sometimes teachers organize a table there—and many more have watched the dancing on television. Most admire professional dance performance, although some told me they were not interested in performing. A few were hostile to the topic when I asked them about it. Vernon had originally learned to dance as an adolescent. He and his wife had started having lessons again when their children were grown, until his wife developed physical disabilities and had to stop. Vernon continued to take lessons by himself. He loved to dance and had performed in student showcases, but he called *Dancing with the Stars* "the worst of television," and he did not approve of professional competition:

> I think the professional dance world, as is available to me, is a real turnoff. . . . I respect that there's a skill to that kind of dancing, but it's not ballroom. It's way removed from ballroom dancing. . . . There's no intimacy between these professionals, who are out there in their exaggerated costumes doing these incredible—it's more circus performance. So I don't have any respect for it at all.

Vernon objected to the show aspects of competition dance. His comment about the lack of intimacy in the professional performances is at odds with what most viewers see. Most find competition dance "mesmerizing to watch," and they "love everything about it." Most students know they will never dance like professionals, but they find professional dancing inspiring to their own performance, and they love the idea that they, too, are part of this romantic and glamorous world. Vernon was less interested in professional performance than he was in his own dancing, and he made sure family and friends came to see him dance when he was in a student showcase. Furthermore, he valued his intimate connection with his teacher in the lessons he was paying for. This theme of paying for intimacy continues in the next chapter on the economics of ballroom, in which we shall see its many complications.

3

The Economics of Ballroom

MARK IS A successful pro/am teacher, taking students to about fourteen competitions a year. When I asked him how many students he typically took, he answered,

> Three to five or six at a time, when it comes to the local competitions . . . or as many people as I have space for. I'll have twelve to fourteen at Ohio Star Ball, since that's the pinnacle of our competitive calendar. Everybody wants to go there, because they know it's the end-all, be-all. . . . I try to put myself in the position where I don't have any overlapping in age categories and proficiency levels, because it's not fair to students. I feel like if they're coming to me and they want to be able to compete, they deserve all the opportunities that are available to them.

Competing with such a large group involved complicated logistics. The demand for Mark's services was high; students wanted to be part of his group and to dance with him. All his students competed with him, and he would not take a new student unless he had a space in the right age category and level. Mark explained,

> We're all in this together. We're a very supportive team, supportive of each other. All my students get along great together and with the other students in the studio. In the last four or five years, that harmonious balance has become more important to us than anything. We don't take on new students because we think they have tremendous aptitude, and we think they'll be great vehicles to show off our teaching ability, showcase our teaching talents, because we think they can be champions. That's not the issue. We take students that we think are great people and we think fit with our group. We are so honored that other students at competition are envious not that our students win but because we have such a close-knit group that's so supportive of each other. We have a great team, and that's something a lot of people recognize at the bigger competitions, before

they recognize that they all happen to be good dancers. We teach them to
be good dancers.

Mark realized that the quality of the emotional experience was as important to students as the dancing skills they learned. His students liked doing
well, but they liked being part of the group even more.

Mark's story illustrates how economics and intimacies intertwine.
Mark's students wanted to be part of a glamorous and intimate group removed from everyday living, a romantic utopia not confined to a couple.[1]
They quickly became friends, close to their teacher, and at home in the studio. Whenever Mark started a new student, she became quickly enmeshed
in the studio's warm and close-knit dance family. Even students who lived
in other cities and flew in for lessons felt included. Students' willingness to
pay to compete with a top, well-connected dancer shows that in the modern world, intimacy is indeed for sale.[2]

The Economic Underpinnings of Competition

Teachers such as Mark regularly win top teacher awards. Competitions go
to great lengths to attract such teachers, because they bring many students
and enliven the spirit of the event. Teachers' charges for competitions vary
considerably. Some teachers charge less than average, in order to increase
the number of students they take. Teachers who do this make a good living
but work hard in the process. Of course, most would prefer to bring fewer
students and charge more. One year, Mark counted how many heats he had
danced at the Ohio Star Ball: "from up to a minute and a half or a minute
forty-five each time, it was like eleven hundred and thirty dances in the six
days." Dancing at this intensity had taken a toll on his body. When I interviewed him, he had had "one knee surgery, two shoulder surgeries, and now
one more knee surgery" in five years. When I later saw him at a competition, he was scheduled for a third knee surgery.

In U.S. competitions, pro/am occurs during the day, and evenings are
left to amateur and professional pairs.[3] Students typically compete in a
number of different dances, and many also compete in more than one style.
There are five Latin dances, five ballroom dances, five rhythm dances, and
four smooth dances. In addition, pro/am couples may compete in extra
dances such as the hustle, the West Coast swing, and the salsa. Students
pay for each entry separately, so it is in the organizers' interest to have stu-

dents enter many heats and to have teachers bring many students. Heats are offered at several levels of difficulty, depending on the student's experience and competence, starting at prebronze for beginners, going through several levels of bronze, silver, and gold, and ending in open competition. Students may dance at two contiguous levels, for example, intermediate and advanced silver. Finally, students are separated into age categories that vary from A1 to C at large competitions. They are allowed to compete in their own age category and a category lower. As Mark demonstrated, teachers who take more than one student may dance many rounds, especially at large competitions where there are quarterfinals and semifinals. Eddie Ares, shown in figure 4.2, is a good example of a teacher who takes a number of students to many competitions. He works hard with his students while on the floor and hangs out with them off the floor.

To attract teachers such as Mark, competitions award top teacher prizes to those who dance the most heats. For the DanceSport Series, a set of seventy competitions nationwide, teachers accumulate points from those they have attended. The teacher with the most points wins top teacher of the year.[4] Students also accumulate points for participating in the Dance-Sport Series. The Ohio Star Ball hosts a dance-off for those with the most points, thus encouraging teachers and students to attend many competitions.[5] The same teachers win top teacher awards repeatedly. In 2008, the top teacher of the year was Rauno Ilo. Born in Estonia, Rauno immigrated to the United States with his wife and ballroom dance partner, Kriistina. They competed successfully in the United States but did not reach the top, and when they retired, they opened a dance school in Indianapolis. While Kriistina stays home to run the studio, teach, and raise the couple's two children, Rauno spends many weekends across the country competing with students.[6] At one competition, the 2009 United States Dance Championships (USDC), Rauno won the prize for top teacher overall and also won top teacher in each of the four styles. Since this is one of the most important competitions, prize money is generous. In addition to the fees his students paid to dance with him, Rauno's prize money for this one competition totaled $23,500.[7]

Sometimes a teacher and a particular student become recognized as a couple who regularly compete. For example, Alain Doucet and his student Beverly Moore win every event they enter together in the ladies C age category, a scholarship category for students age fifty-one and older.[8] In a 2009 interview, Doucet reported that they intended to enter nineteen competitions in 2010.[9] Each time they compete, they do so in three styles in open

Fig. 3.1. Competitors lining up for pro/am compose themselves into the erect position they need when walking out on the floor. 2010 Emerald Ball DanceSport Championships, Los Angeles, CA. © 2010 Jonathan S. Marion.

gold and in the open scholarships. Their picture can be seen in color plate 8. This is an ideal many teachers aspire to; however, there are a limited number of students with the means or desire to compete so much.

Men such as Rauno and Alain are at the top of the heap in pro/am circles; they raise the level of any competition they attend by bringing many students or by dancing with a student who is better than some professionals. In addition to top teacher awards, competitions frequently offer inducements to the most successful teachers, such as free and upgraded hotel rooms. To make these competitions attractive to well-heeled students, everything about them is taken seriously. Teachers and students look immaculate on the floor and even before they enter, as can be seen in figure 3.1, in which students and teachers line up to dance ballroom at the 2010 Emerald Ball.

Top competitions have entries in the thousands. For example, the 2009 Emerald Ball had ninety-six hundred entries, which at about forty dollars[10] per entry means the competition grossed around $385,000.[11] However, the expenses are considerable. The 2008 Ohio Star Ball's sixty-three judges all required paid accommodations in addition to compensation. In their program, I counted thirty-seven other personnel, including scrutineers, masters of ceremony, and administrative staff. Organizers must develop and maintain websites for advertising and registration and to report results.[12] Competitions often pay top dancers to put on a show that will attract attendees. Big competitions take a full year of organizing, so some people are employed full-time. However, most competitions are smaller than these. Some have as few as three thousand entries or less, and although their short durations lessen expenses, organizers still have to pay for judges and other essential staff.

There are two ways that professionals can become economically successful dancing pro/am: by taking many students, dancing many rounds, and winning top teacher awards, like Becky-Sue's teacher, or by competing extensively with one affluent student, like Wendy. Students like Wendy would rather develop a two-person intimate relationship than be part of a group like Mark's. Wendy did not want her teacher to take any other students with him, because she enjoyed his one-on-one attention and the introductions he made to other professionals at the competition. These made her feel like a dance-world insider, rather than just another student. Nor did she like him to compete with a professional partner at a competition where she was dancing pro/am. Although her teacher danced with other students at the studio, Wendy felt special being his only competition partner. This arrangement was expensive. Wendy was paying for her teacher's time and boarding costs by herself, and it was costing her around fifteen thousand dollars per competition. However, Wendy was successful in her career and could afford it. When her teacher began taking other students as well, she became alienated from him and switched to another teacher. Most professionals competing in pro/am do not have the luxury of choosing between these strategies. Because there is a limited number of pro/am students, teachers will often take whomever they can. Most teachers do not take as many students as they would like, nor do they compete as often as they wish. Their students may also limit the number of heats they enter, because of the expense. Most students go to a few competitions each year, and most professionals take only one or two students with them when they compete. Yet these students still expect a glamorous and emotionally intense experience.[13]

People outside the ballroom world may find it hard to follow this long description of its financial underpinnings. However, it is difficult to understand the pressures teachers feel to provide instant intimacy or the pleasures students get from receiving it without understanding the financial payout. Paying to enter a world of expertise is not unique to the dance world; this can also be had in golf tournaments where professionals and amateurs compete together.[14] However, unlike professional dancers, professional golfers do not train the students they play with. A dance student who does well enhances the teacher's reputation and encourages other top students to train with the same teacher. Dancing well is important, but, as we saw in Mark's story, the experience of entering the inner sanctum of the dance world is equally important.

Most pro/am students want to excel, but this is not always of utmost importance. Most know that they will not win, or even place, if the competition is a big one. If they enter enough events, however, they will likely do well in the less popular ones. Competitions maximize the number of students who win something, which encourages them to continue dancing. Furthermore, teachers provide access to a glamorous world and are highly motivated to make the experience of dancing with them enjoyable. Since there are more teachers willing to take students than students who can afford to go, emotional engagement is in the teacher's interest.

Careers in Dance

The arts are not well supported in the United States, and dance is one of the most financially difficult arts careers to sustain. According to the U.S. Bureau of Labor, dancers of all kinds had a median hourly wage of just over twelve dollars in 2008.[15] Annual earnings were not given, the Bureau noted, because dancers rarely work full-time. Although ballroom teachers sometimes make as little as this working for chain studios, their median hourly wage is typically much higher. Private lessons at competition or chain studios cost approximately $75 to $125 for either forty-five minutes or an hour, depending on location and the studio's prestige.[16] Independent studios, which hire dancers as staff, take a healthy cut of student tuition; dancers working for these studios reported making between twenty-five dollars and fifty dollars an hour. Independent teachers, who charge students directly and pay rent to the studio, make a higher hourly rate. However, these teachers have to market themselves and attract students through their reputations, which is difficult unless they are well known. Many studios supplement individual lessons with group lessons to work on issues, such as style.

They also offer group social dance lessons to students who do not want individual lessons or find them too costly. Group classes cost between ten and twenty-five dollars per student. Groups classes are often more profitable than private lessons, because teachers make up in volume what they lose in individual fees.

Although the opportunity to earn money from teaching makes ballroom a more lucrative profession than other types of dance, it comes at a price. In performance dancing, the audience is only interested in the beauty and skill of the performance. The dancer's personality and charm are not on display, except as part of the beauty and skill. As a result, any acting required of the performer will be surface acting at most.[17] However, as we have seen in previous chapters, successful ballroom dancers must dance with students in a way that makes them feel wanted and valued, helping them deal with their anxieties and nerves and socializing with them off the dance floor. During lessons, teachers must create an atmosphere of enjoyment. Popular teachers engage in deep acting for many hours each day with a variety of students, most of whom can afford to go elsewhere if they are unsatisfied with the service. This puts a great strain on teachers.[18] At the beginning of the book, I described a teacher who did not provide this support to his student. However, the business is notable for how few teachers lack these socioemotional skills; dancers who wish to teach must engage in this emotional labor, or they will not succeed as teachers, no matter how well they dance. A number of the professionals I interviewed asserted that personality is more important than dance skill.

Making a Living and Competing Professionally

Teachers who still compete with professional partners often feel conflicted about pro/am, because the emotional and physical effort involved can detract from their professional performance. Yet without pro/am dancing, they could not afford to compete. Many professionals take only a few students to competitions, in order to focus on their professional events. Indeed, some take no students to the most important competitions. Furthermore, top international dancers usually confine pro/am competition to the style in which they themselves compete. Pavel, a top Latin dancer, usually took three or four Latin students when he and his partner, Tsvetanka, competed. He enjoyed teaching and competing pro/am and would continue to do it even if he were a "multimillionaire." He saw professional, as well as financial, benefits:

> Financially, teaching pro/am is very good. . . . When I dance with Tsve-tanka, I have to learn this, and I have to learn that. With pro/am, I can keep my instinct of success and of dancing; this I like. I like teaching pro/am, because the more you teach, the more I grow up as a dancer. Then, the better I teach them. . . . There are often people in the business, they do pro/am just to make money, but I make the people, in Latin, dance good.

Pavel said it was difficult with beginning students, who, after learning the fundamentals, were confident. However, "once they learn more, they start to see how empty is their basket, and they start to lose confidence." At this point, they sometimes became so unsure that "they lose their character and the special thing that is in them." Fixing this, Pavel said, was like "building a puzzle," and this sustained his interest. Pavel was emotionally engaged in his students and received personal satisfaction from their success.

Immigrants such as Pavel can achieve financial security by moving to America to dance pro/am. Yet they do not always find it easy to teach, because language and cultural barriers make it difficult to attain an emotional connection with students. Many countries allow their amateurs to teach those younger than themselves, and in these cultures, dancing is serious business, and discipline is expected. When dancers come to America, they must adjust to new realities; they typically teach adults who dance as a hobby rather than as a potential career and who want to be liked and entertained in addition to being taught.

Peter is another example of a dancer who found economic stability by moving to America. A world-class Latin dancer, he had worked at various jobs in several countries to support his dancing career, as both an amateur and a professional. He had struggled to earn enough money to support himself and leave time for dance, until he was recruited to come to the United States to teach ballroom to a "multimillionaire's" wife. This man sponsored the competitive career of Peter and his partner, and for the first time, Peter found himself living comfortably. In return, Peter devoted himself to teaching the wife to dance. However, medical reasons caused the couple to move to a different city and to give up dancing for a while. Peter then moved to New York to further his competitive career; the coaching was better there because many top European coaches regularly visit

New York. When I interviewed Peter, he did not know his annual income, and he explained.

> If I knew that answer, I probably wouldn't be dancing anymore. The way it is, you just work on the situation at the moment; there's no budgeting. What you earn you put aside, and then you go and spend it. . . . I don't really keep that much of a track of it. I couldn't even tell you what I earned on my tax last year. . . . I wouldn't have a problem saying it, but I don't know. . . . All I can say is every time I go to England for three weeks—for competitions and lessons—I probably change about three or four thousand dollars over in cash, maybe more. I'm going to say five thousand dollars in cash I might change over. And that's not including money on hotels and rental cars and on credit cards to pay when I get back. So it's expensive.

Although he spent most of what he earned on dancing and basic living expenses, Peter was better off financially than he had been before coming to America, because he was able to earn money by teaching, taking students to compete in pro/am, and coaching young amateur and professional couples. Peter was used to doing without. As a child, his father had been a self-employed handyman who temporarily sold the tools he did not need each time Peter wanted money to compete. When he was a young adult living in London, every studio had "three or four champions, and then you're sort of just the junior member." Peter had been able to find a limited amount of teaching there: "eight, ten lessons a week for I think it was fifty dollars at that time." He had supplemented his income by performing at various studios on the weekends. Since it was difficult for his partners to earn as much as he did, he often had to help. In America, there were fewer top coaches, so his services were in greater demand.

Peter chose to limit the amount of emotional labor expected of him by students, because he wanted to focus on his competitive career. As a result, life was difficult, even in America:

> There's a lot more scope, a lot more work, a lot more range of work with the pro/am, and still with competitions and everything, the money's tight. . . . When you look at what you've spent and what you've earned, it's actually pretty good. . . . We're literally away for three months of the year. The amount we spend in those three months is the equivalent of two and a half, three months of work. So really what we do is maybe six months of work a year—the equivalent of—and then we've got to pay living

expenses here, normal sorts of expenses. . . . If we retired tomorrow and started concentrating on teaching, I could double my money, because I could add twenty-five percent to my income by not traveling and not using those expenses and another twenty-five percent because I could work during that time when I'm normally away. I'd probably add more to that, because I'd have more time to build a business. When you are away so much, you've got to have students who are understanding.

"Students who are understanding" meant students who would allow Peter's career to come before their pleasure, something dancers like Wendy would not tolerate.

Most dancers who lived in America and competed on the international circuit reported similar accounts of spending and earning. Though they spent everything they earned on lessons and competitions, they were financially better off in the United States than they would have been had they lived elsewhere. In fact, a number of professional international-style dancers told me that the decision to attend a particular U.S. competition depended equally on the desire they had to compete in that particular competition and on whether they had students who wanted to go.

A few top international couples do not compete in pro/am, because they are able to make a better living from performing. These dancers are well known in Asia, where they are invited to perform and to lecture for generous sums of money, plus expenses.[19] However, these couples are few and far between; only a handful of competitors ever reach that level. These dancers perform a type of emotional labor that focuses on achieving and performing an intimate connection with their professional partners in both competitions and exhibitions.

Except for these top dancers, who are known the world over, those who compete in American style tend to be better off financially, because they can take students with them to all their professional competitions, whereas international-style dancers compete largely overseas. Furthermore, the travel expenses of American-style dancers are lower, because they do not have to travel overseas for coaching. They are also more likely to own studios, because they are rarely away from home for more than a few days at a time, even if they compete often. Of course, since dancers living in the rest of the world do not compete in American style, these events do not have the cachet of international-style dancing. Furthermore, as we have seen, pro/am dancing takes an emotional toll on professionals who find themselves pulled in more than one direction. Mark was unusual in that he did not find this to be a problem. In fact, he said, he was as thrilled when his students did well as he was when he won with his wife.

Social Dance Teaching

Studios are able to charge the rates they do because of the popularity of pro/am and social dancing. In the Philadelphia area alone, a dance newsletter advertised fifty places to dance mixed ballroom and Latin; thirty places to dance salsa or mixed Latin; nine places to dance various types of swing, including West Coast swing and lindy-hop; twenty-one places to dance Argentine tango; and seven places to dance hustle.[20] All those who attend these dances need places to learn. Because social dancing has become so popular, most studios concentrate exclusively on social dance classes, with the occasional private lesson. Many offer a package for "wedding couples" who want their first dance as a married couple to exhibit some skill.[21] In social dance classes, students partner each other instead of a teacher, rotating from one student to the next each time they dance a set of steps. These types of group classes teach students many different steps and how to lead or follow a variety of partners, skills that greatly enhance their social dance experience.

Some social dance organizers do not have their own space and must rent. Janice had been teaching ballroom at a ballet dance academy, but ran into difficulty there:

> They were space-constrained, and they either had to invest a lot of money in a new location, or they had to cut something. They could make a lot more money teaching little kids preballet and ballet and tap and hip hop in a room than they can adults doing ballroom dancing. We took up more space. . . . So I took the whole program over to the YMCA. I formed my own company, renegotiated the contract with the Y under my company name, and because the Y is nonprofit, they were not interested in making money. I was more interested in getting the program going, so we lowered the prices from what we had been charging, and the program exploded. The Y was not space constrained at the time. . . . We have stuff going every day of the week there, and I have three or four teachers that work for me on an ongoing basis. . . . We were lucky back in the [dance academy] days to have six or seven classes running. Now we have twenty to thirty classes a week.

A Brief History of Chain Studios

In spite of ballroom's growing popularity, most Americans still do not understand the attractions of partner dance. Indeed, most have never experienced the pleasures of dancing as one; if they have, many lack the skill to have enjoyed it. Pro/am dancing is more puzzling, even though it is the formula used on *Dancing with the Stars*. Most Americans do not know that ballroom exists outside the television, and if they do, they may associate it with shady practices by dance studio chains, such as Arthur Murray. Since that organization's inception, it has had a reputation for aggressive sales techniques and has been the focus of a number of court cases involving older women flirting with bankruptcy after being persuaded to sign long-term dance contracts.[22]

The Arthur Murray studios opened during the 1930s heyday of the big dance hall and dance band, and from the beginning, business took precedence over dancing.[23] Arthur Murray changed his name from Murray Teichman during the First World War, to escape his German last name. While studying business administration, he supported himself by teaching dance. After graduation, as the dance craze grew, he founded a system of lessons which developed into the franchised studios that continue to this day. A second franchise chain, founded by Charles Casanave and Fred Astaire in 1947, competed with the Murray chain, and although it used to employ the same aggressive sales techniques, the Astaire chain has diverged somewhat from the Murray model. Today, both chains are shadows of their former selves. Douglas had started to teach at Arthur Murray's in Toronto in 1959. Two years later, they moved him to Philadelphia: "Downtown Studio was at Chestnut Street. It was a city block long. It had forty teachers. We had twelve Arthur Murray studios in the city. . . . My job was to train all the teachers and to run all the medal balls and to get them all certified and give them all their training and to coach."[24]

Patrick had also started teaching for the Philadelphia Arthur Murray studios in the late 1950s but did not advance as far in the organization. After high school, he did a stint in the Marines. When he came out, he saw a "'No experience necessary' ad" for Arthur Murray. He described the interview process as only concerned with "whether or not you were an extrovert." After he was hired, he was trained "five nights a week for six weeks, . . . from six to ten," after which he started teaching bronze-level dancers:

It was a monster. It had an elevator. They had a room for tango. They had a room for foxtrot and waltz. They had a main ballroom in the front and main ballroom in the back. Each room had a dial telephone. They were constantly running tapes in the back room, and if you dialed 1, you would get variety; if you dialed 2, you'd get all foxtrot. . . . In your free time, you went to silver classes and gold classes, and actually the original bronze was so difficult, half of the people dropped that started out. I mean, we were using muscles we didn't know we had, and they were aching, totally aching, but if I went the extra mile, I would learn it.

This rigorous training system was twofold: dance technique combined with marketing technique. "You only, maybe, got one or two" new students "a week, because they had this setup across the street." This setup consisted of "a phone room which would be calling people for lucky dollars," telling them that "they won a free prize and so forth, which was a sales pitch to get people to come in."

There are no Arthur Murray studios left within the city of Philadelphia and only three in the suburbs. There are ten in the entire state of Pennsylvania. These remaining studios have many fewer teachers than in Patrick's example. Fred Astaire studios have shrunk even more. From a heyday of huge studios in and around the city, there are now no Astaire studios in the Philadelphia area and only one in all of Pennsylvania.[25] These studios have, in part, been replaced by numerous independent studios teaching pro/am, social, or specialized dances such as Argentine tango.[26] The same pattern is true nationally.

The chains have always recruited untrained but promising teachers, and many professionals told me of their early experiences teaching at a chain, when they were only "one step ahead" of their students. Mark had started out teaching at a Fred Astaire studio, "for which," he said, "I am very thankful," because "they have the best system in the world set up to develop brand-new teachers." He added that dance is "a tough world for [teachers] to come into, if it's not one of the chains, where they are watched and nurtured and groomed."

At the chains, all teachers learn about selling. As Mark put it,

I was groomed, in the beginning, to run a business. That's the only shortcoming, in my opinion, of the chain system. They're in the business of doing business. It's not their priority to develop top, elite dancers, because it hurts their business. These dancers will leave and go somewhere else. . . . I was groomed to run a studio and do business for the chain, which, in turn, would do something for me, but at least as much for them.

Because Mark wanted to become "a top, elite dancer," he eventually bought himself out of the franchise.

Mark's story is typical. Almost every successful American-born teacher that I interviewed had started out at one of the chains. The main difference between the two organizations is that teachers and students at Fred Astaire have somewhat more flexibility. Although Fred Astaire runs its own competitions and encourages teachers to take students there, Fred Astaire students and teachers also compete in independent competitions. This practice is in contrast to that of Arthur Murray, where the current president of the company, John Kimmins, runs competitions focused on pro/am. He calls the professional competitions at these events "by-products."[27] For this reason, ambitious professional dancers or students often leave Arthur Murray to join independent studios, because they want to attend the more demanding competitions run under the auspices of the NDCA. At NDCA competitions, pro/am makes the money, but the professional competition is the main event. Kimmins often judges at NDCA competitions, but, except for a few top professionals, his students and teachers are nowhere to be found.

Teaching in the Chains

Arnold and his wife owned two Arthur Murray studios. They had met when he began taking dance lessons with her at Arthur Murray, after he got divorced. He was "very interested in her, and she was interested in" him, but nothing happened because the chain has a strict rule of "no fraternization." When he got a job in another city, they started dating, because she was no longer his teacher. They then married, and when Arnold was in his early fifties, they decided to open an Arthur Murray franchise together.

When I interviewed Arnold, he came across as a businessman who owned dance studios rather than as a dancer who owned a business. He was certified to teach up to silver level, and he had only competed professionally a couple of times, though he often took students to Arthur Murray competitions. His wife had not started dancing until she was in her thirties. Arnold believed strongly in the Arthur Murray rules:

The rules are pretty uniform. Like everything else, there is a certain range, but the range I would say is very narrow. I have students that I like a lot, but it is almost instinctive at this point where I don't really talk about my life. I will joke with them. I may relay anecdotes if we are in a conversation, but people will ask me about things, and I am very vague, because I don't want to talk about myself. Sometimes they get a little offended, like I don't like them or something.

Arnold worked hard to bring students to Arthur Murray competitions and took groups to both local and national events. While there, he and his wife spent time with the students on and off the floor, making sure that they were enjoying themselves. Teachers like Arnold and his wife perform emotional labor to focus attention on the student and draw it away from the teacher.

Another Arthur Murray teacher, Howie, had been a member of the swing-dance club in high school, and when he attended a small midwestern liberal arts college, he took some dance lessons. After graduation, he started work in a town with a large university dance team, so he joined the dance club and took more lessons. When he lost that job, he decided that he really wanted to be a dance teacher rather than, as he said, to "take another job I don't like." He did not know how to do this, so he turned to the Internet:

I had been a member of Dance Forums[28] for a couple of months. I posted a message to it saying, "How do dance students become dance teachers?" They said, "You usually go to a studio; pretty often they let you work for free, and they train you as a teacher." I said, "Okay, I can deal with that. . . . I'm going to have to move back in with my parents for this." I found all the ballroom dance studios and teachers in the area, made a short list of the ones I wanted to work for. . . . I set up interviews with each of them. I got job offers from three of them. I accepted Arthur Murray's. . . . I started with them as a trainee in June. Because of my previous experience, I was able to start teaching classes in mid-July, so only about after a month.

Howie had been "initially set against going to Arthur Murray," because "they don't have the best reputation in the dance community." However, even though there were "probably some studios where all they wanted to do was to sell you something rather than to teach you," hopefully, "those have gone out of business." Howie was impressed with the teaching and the syllabus, and while he knew he was "never going to train a world champion," he was hoping to "make a living doing this." He added, "While their pay scale is terrible, if I pay attention to what they do, I will learn how to make a studio financially solvent."

Howie was the "new student specialist"—he gave the first six lessons to students to get them started before passing them on to a more experienced teacher. He hoped someday to become certified to teach more advanced students. Right now, however, he was struggling to learn the Arthur Murray culture. A couple of times he had joked with a student who then complained about him to the management, so, he said, "I had to learn to modify my sense of humor." When he went social dancing at places where he might see students, he was not allowed to tell them in advance that he was planning to be there, even if asked. Although he was not teaching the more advanced students, Howie partnered them at the local Arthur Murray competitions, because he was the only male currently teaching at his studio. At the most recent competition, he had to dance with six different students.

Selling the Arthur Murray Way

When Howie described the Murray business, he appeared to use language learned in a course:

> I tell people I'm in sales, which I think is true for the most part. My main job is not teaching lessons; it's selling lessons. And teaching them is just a method to do that. . . . The first thing you do is you build rapport with your potential customer. You get to know each other, so you know where you are. You then find out what the customer needs. Somebody may come in the studio because they saw an ad for a free lesson. That's not why they come in. They come in because they want to be more active, or they might want to make their wife happy, or they have an event coming up, or they're lonely—that was my reason—or they want to feel pretty. . . . You then need to ask them, "What else?" There is never just one reason someone is there. . . . You then ask them, "Can I show you something that will meet your needs?" Get their permission first, so that they invite you. They always say, "Yes," because they know they are there for a sales pitch. Once you have people saying yes, they are going to keep on saying yes. . . . You also explain how the program is customized to meet their needs. . . . Finally, you have to ask them for a sale.

This description considers the "customer" a cultural dope.

Sociologist Erving Goffman divides public life into "frontstage and backstage" performances, and at Arthur Murray, the two seem never to intersect.[29] This is in contrast to many independent studios, where there is greater informality and students and teachers often become friends who socialize outside the dance studio.[30] In addition to John Kimmins's involvement in the NDCA and its sponsored competitions, Murray studios have other connections with the larger world of competition. Some top dancers are involved in the organization and come to coach at local studios.[31] Bill and Bobbie Irvine first came to America in 1965 to demonstrate and judge, and they were invited back to lecture to the Arthur Murray studios. This is how they described and defended the organization:

> In the United States, the Arthur Murray Schools of Dancing are something of an institution. People go there primarily to learn to dance but also for companionship, and quite a number of the pupils are not in their teens.
>
> However, this does not mean any kind of exploitation. Many of these women used to go dancing several times a week with their husbands; widowed they could be cut off from a source of real enjoyment—so they join the Arthur Murray Schools of Dancing. To many of them it is a way of life; it makes a focus of activity and entertainment, very well organized indeed and conducted with great friendliness on the part of the staff.[32]

In this polite description, Bill Irvine sounds almost like an anthropologist explaining the habits of a strange tribe. These schools must have seemed a far cry from the British dance schools the Irvines were used to, which taught competitive couples and emphasized the international competition circuit.

Howie's description of selling is different from that which Bill would have been used to in studios where the focus was on amateur and professional couples with coaches guiding their practice. In describing the students as "customers," Howie acknowledges that the exchange of information is, and should be, one way only. Despite the seeming friendliness of the experience, Arthur Murray shrouds its studios and teachers in an air of secrecy, and many students find the atmosphere not to their liking. In this way the Murray system differs from the independents as they are run today. According to sociologist Ann Swidler, modern adulthood involves an ongoing process of growing, and relationships necessitate "continuing mutual revelation."[33] The Murray model harks back to an earlier era, when adulthood was considered fixed once it was achieved and when obligations and commitments were more important than revelations. Based on this model, teachers are obligated to deflect attention from themselves, because the student is a customer, not a partner. This model can explain Arthur Murray's demise and its legal troubles, as today's adults expect and enjoy the mutual sharing of intimate information in their relationships. Independent studios are more in tune with this expectation, and teachers and students each talk about themselves in turn. Having grown up in an era of mutual disclosure, Howie found it difficult to behave according to the Arthur Murray rules.

The Arthur Murray model helps to refine the concept of instant intimacy and to show its development in the postmodern world. It assumes that students want to be courted and charmed but that this desire ends at the studio door and can never go further. The student is encouraged to talk about him- or herself but learns little about the teacher. What I am defining as instant intimacy goes deeper than this. It implies that one can reveal oneself to a comparative stranger, receive similar intimacies back, and create a deeper connection quickly. This works in a world of one-night stands, celebrities, Facebook, and television tell-all talk shows. Students want to feel special from the get-go, which necessitates mutual sharing and a feeling that the relationship is built on honesty and might go deeper. Independent studios, by and large, understand this. The relationship is based on commerce, as in the chain studios, but that does not mean it is never perceived as genuine.

Although Fred Astaire originally had a reputation similar to Arthur Murray's, those who work there now describe the Astaire studios as notably different. Anastasiya, a Latin dancer, and her husband, Aron, were Russian immigrants who had each been recruited to teach in America at a Fred Astaire studio, where they met, started competing together, and eventually bought a franchise. They were top Latin competitors, and they took students both to Fred Astaire competitions and to those overseen by the NDCA. In addition, they competed as professionals in major worldwide competitions. When I interviewed them at their large and airy studio in a new shopping complex, there was a friendly, open atmosphere and little of Howie's worry that one had to be careful not to overstep the bounds of friendship. When asked to describe the policy about relationships between teachers and students, Anastasiya answered quite differently from Arnold:

> In the studio, it's important when students communicate with each other
> and are friendly with each other. We try to give them as much as we can

in terms of time for them, and then listen if they have problems and give them fun. As you know, life is not that easy. Dancing is something—you can forget about your job, your stress. . . . Give them fun and smiles and hugs as much as we can.

Whenever Anastasiya and Aron competed professionally at U.S. competitions, loud cheers emanated from their students' corner. These cheers attest to their success in providing their students with feelings of intimacy and belonging and testify to students' desires to be involved in teachers' lives.

Spending Money on Dance

Although most teachers are not rich, we have seen that competitive dance is an expensive hobby for students. Expenses include individual lessons, teacher's time, travel, hotel entry fees, dresses, and other incidentals such as shoes, makeup, and hair. Students at every socioeconomic level acknowledged the expense in my interviews with them. Becky-Sue, one of several affluent students I interviewed, spent a lot of money on competitions; each cost about seven thousand dollars, and she attended approximately ten a year. Her teacher often won top teacher, and he danced from morning until night each day of the competition. When asked how much she spent a year, she said,

> I'm rounding it off here; probably around eighty to one hundred thousand. . . . That's including lessons, coaching, number of competitions, dresses here and there. My husband still pays for my lessons, but he got to the point that the competitions were just too difficult. What I'm doing right now is—I hate to admit it—I have a financial fund market account that I've been taking money out of. [My husband] started this a couple of years ago, because our business fluctuates . . . We have high season and low season. Because of the economy, we have some times where business is very slow, and we don't have money to do extra things with. So I am basically buying my own dresses and, with my market fund, pay for competitions. . . . I don't know how much longer it's going to last, because he already sees my account going. He's like, "We're getting down to a figure that I'm not real happy about." I go, "Well, there's nothing I can do. I have to use my account."

Even though finances were always on her mind, Becky-Sue had the security of a husband who, even if reluctantly, supported her decisions. Claudia had been left reasonably well provided for by her late husband, and she had a professional career, but she had to be careful with expenses. She loved dancing just as much as Becky-Sue but was more oppressed by the cost. She had taken out a loan to pay for a large package of lessons as well as occasional competitions, so she would not have to be constantly spending:

> I would give up everything and just do nothing but ballroom dance, if I could afford it, but it is out of my league financially. . . . The financial commitment is just very tough. My banker says, "Everyone carries a home equity loan. Everyone carries a little bit of debt, so you shouldn't feel too worried." Well, I am not of that ilk, so my program is going to come to an end fairly soon. I don't know if I'm going to re-up with a new program for the near future, because I wanted my program of lessons to last three years, and it turns out, so far, they're lasting just under two. . . . I have a lot of serious decisions to make.

If Claudia gave up dancing, she knew she would miss more than just the movement.

Stress over the cost of dancing was common. Many of the dancers I interviewed were dependent on dancing's pleasures and so continued to overspend. Even where there was no financial hardship, dancers often felt guilty spending so much. Gerald, an older dancer, and his wife competed many times each year. Though, he said, "We're not spending our last penny on this dance," it is "an expensive sport," which bothered him. He rationalized that "you can't take it with you," but the cost made him uncomfortable.

Some dancers were able to afford to compete by being careful. Hortense spent about fifteen thousand dollars and attended about five or six competitions per year. However, she competed in one style only, confined herself to few entries, and left as soon as her event was over. Since her teacher took other students, she did not have to pay all his costs. These strategies had helped minimize her expenses, but she still had difficulty paying for dance, since she was divorced and had children in private school. The costs, she said, are "exorbitant," adding, "I don't like the fact that it's a rich person's sport, but unless you're financially stable, you can't do it." Hortense presented herself as only interested in dance and not in the emotional connection. However, she was anxious to dance only with skilled professionals. Not long after our interview, she left her teacher for a top dancer, whose prestige she saw reflected in herself. The intimacy students receive from their teachers takes different forms, and teachers have to adapt as needed.

Making Dance Affordable

The belief that one must be privileged in order to compete had motivated Stephanie to leave the studio system and teach social dancing. She, too, had started at Arthur Murray's:

> There was nobody on earth that loved dancing more than I did, but I said, "I couldn't even afford the lessons that I was teaching." There's something wrong with that. Everybody should be able to afford to dance, because dancing was a human thing to do, not a rich person's thing to do. Only rich people, at that time, could afford it, and, to me, something was fundamentally wrong about that. There is a place for everybody. Everybody has their own style, and if it works for them and there are people that are willing to go with that program, then that's great, but that wasn't my program. I believed that it should be available to students to be able to come and learn, because to me it wasn't about the competitions and putting the ball gowns on; it was about being able to come in and gain confidence. . . . It's really important to me that teenagers can come in, because not everybody is going to be able to be good at sports. But maybe they can gain confidence by becoming good dancers and good leaders and good followers, and they now have a community of people that they can relate to who are purely in it for the enjoyment and the community activity and the social activity. I think there's more to be gained by that end of it than there is going to the Ohio Star Ball.

As can be seen in this comment, Stephanie understood that the pleasure of dance included the social relationships. Her social dance parties provided scaled-down versions of the intimacy and glamour purchased in competitions. The atmosphere was open and amicable, and regulars often brought wine to share over the dinner Stephanie provided for them to eat together.

Stephanie's studio was one of a number of places where dancers could feel welcome once they had mastered the basic steps. Dance halls have changed their meaning during the past century. In their early days, they formed part of the courtship experience of working-class youth; now they are places for older singles to congregate safely and without disapproval in the big city and its suburbs. These singles are paying for the instant intimacy of a commitment-free dance around the floor, a brief and friendly conversation, and a feeling of belonging.[34] In addition to providing social opportunities for singles, social dancing provides married people with the chance to dance with others in public, enjoying a brief, safe intimacy. The two people dancing together in figure 3.2 are each happily married to others.

Teachers like Stephanie charge little per student and make money by packing students into each lesson. Students at any economic level can learn to enjoy the pleasures of dancing in the arms of another, in time to the music. Stephanie's studio offered social classes for ten dollars and private lessons for sixty dollars, which was about the same as other social dance studios in the area and was cheaper than neighboring competition studios. There are many studios like Stephanie's. At the Atrium Ballroom, teacher Barbara Capaldi has many group classes per week where students learn steps and rotate so that they become comfortable dancing with a variety of partners (see color plate 6). In fact, the two types of studios shade into each other. Students at some competition studios do not all compete, and some students at social studios eventually move up to privates.

Although group classes do not provide the same degree of emotional connection as private lessons, those who teach group classes go to great lengths to give students a sense of belonging and caring and to ensure that students get to know one another. They communicate with their students via regular emails, organize trips to see dance competitions in the area, bring in top professional dancers for group coaching, and arrange special dinner dances on holidays, such as New Year's or Valentine's Day. Some studios invite students to attend dance parties together at another studio or even dance cruises to exotic places. Over time, students may become quite close to their dance teachers, even if they have only had group lessons. These activities create a sense of group belonging similar to that described by Mark. Social dance teachers must expend considerable emotional labor to make this happen.

As noted earlier, ballroom dance is a more lucrative career than some other kinds of dance, because of the opportunities for teaching and pro/am competition. In other areas of dance, teachers are typically part-time workers paid by the class. Because few Americans learn ballroom and Latin dance growing up, those who become ballroom teachers are frequently not skilled enough to teach top-level pro/am. Instead, they remain just one step ahead of the students, like Howie. There is a shortage of highly skilled pro/am teachers, especially men, which has enabled dancers from other parts of

Fig. 3.2. The pleasures of dancing with someone other than a spouse, demonstrated by Rachel Greisler and Nate Pincus. DanceSport Academy, Ardmore, PA, July 2010. © 2010 Jonathan S. Marion.

Fig. 3.3. Coming to America. Jean Paulovich, shown here teaching amateur Latin dancers Tirsa Rivas and Melzer Pinto, is one of many eastern Europeans who were able to immigrate based on their dancing skills. DanceSport Academy, Ardmore, PA, July 2010. © 2010 Jonathan S. Marion.

the world to immigrate to the United States as teachers. Teachers like Jean Paulovich, from Belarus, shown in figure 3.3 teaching a young amateur Latin couple, are in great demand to teach pro/am students as well as amateurs.

Immigrants often find American students puzzling. First, most Americans want to enjoy themselves.[35] Second, even the most serious competition students practice only a little. Becky-Sue, who said she now went through her routines on her own before she went to a competition, noted that she did not do this "for a long time": "I think a lot of students don't because it is difficult to practice alone." Likewise, Leanne, the top competition student described in previous chapters, labeled herself as "never one that just whips in the studio and practiced on your own." If she had just had a lesson and learned something new, she might go home and "run through in a little space or whatever," but that was all. This is a student with a winning record who might be expected to take dance seriously. Even students who claimed to practice often described less-than-stellar discipline.

Immigrant teachers do not understand this attitude, but they must learn to adapt to it. Otherwise they end up like the teacher I described in the preface, looking at everything but their partner and dancing with an expression that says they were intended for better things. It takes a particular personality to enjoy creating the emotional performance required of pro/am teachers on and off the floor. Those who cannot do this find it difficult to succeed, because unhappy students leave if their teachers do not make the lessons pleasurable or pay them enough attention.

In addition to teaching students from a variety of places, the most successful professionals, particularly those living in and around New York City, teach a population with the resources and desire to pay for dance lessons. In the Chinese-immigrant community, ballroom is highly valued. Many women hire top professionals to teach them, compete with them, and accompany them to parties. Lulu, a dancer in her early sixties, had learned to dance in America. From the beginning, she was interested in having the best teachers. She explained how the system worked:

> All those instructors from Bulgaria and from Russia, those young instructors, they can instruct us in their dancing. So they start out, you know, competitive dancing. Lessons, they want to get even better. We take turns to give dancing parties. . . . Our dancing party became from sixty to eighty to one hundred to one hundred twenty, and this is all private. We take turns giving parties. . . . Whoever likes to dance, we all invite them. . . . With our private dancing party, we are probably up to two dozen, three dozen, all professional, in the party dancing with us.

Lulu explained that the women learned routines with these professional partners. When the music started, they would rush out onto the floor to try and outdo one another. In addition, the women organized a more informal weekly party in a Chinese restaurant, where they would bring professional dancers with them to eat and dance the night away. The prestige of the partner a woman brought reflected on her own prestige. As Françoise, a young Chinese American, explained,

> A lot of the women and men who dance, of course they love it, but it's also a status symbol. There's a lot of glamour to it, but it's like, "Look at me. . . .

I can dance. I have the time to devote to it. I have the resources to devote to it, and I have the resources to get this type of teacher and to be able to spend this kind of money." The more experienced the teachers, the more expensive it is. Whether you get amateur or whether you get world finalist, it's going to matter. People are going to talk about you, especially, I think, in this Asian community. It's important who you dance with.

To dancers like Lulu, the prestige was more important than emotional intimacy. Although most Americans do not know how expensive pro/am dancing can be, members of the Chinese community in the United States could increase their status by dancing with a costly top professional. However, skill was important also. Like Hortense, Lulu competed to win, and she did not understand American women who were not always as competitive as she was.

This fashion for ballroom started in 1930s Shanghai when the Nationalist government was in power. At that time, Shanghai was the economic center of China, and the prosperous elite took up dancing as a sign of their success and Westernization. On the weekends, they would hold dances in their homes. During the week, young men danced in hotels with not-quite-respectable young dancers. When the Communists came into power in the 1950s, this practice ended. Many wealthy families moved either to Taiwan or to America. When dancing reasserted itself among the immigrants to America, it was usually the women who danced with professionals, and this time, it was quite proper.

The passion of Chinese women for dancing is not confined to the United States. Dancing is very popular in China, including Hong Kong, where pro/am dancing has taken off. It is popular in other parts of Asia also, particularly Japan and the Philippines. However, in America, the Chinese community is notable for a passion for ballroom. The wealthiest dancers spend large amounts of money competing in U.S. competitions. The importance of status and of winning in ballroom is exemplified in a 2006 Hong Kong court case. The head of private banking for HSBC, Monica Mimi Wong, sued for the return of an $8 million advance payment on a $15.4 million fee to be paid to Gaynor Fairweather and her husband, Mirko Saccani, for eight years of exclusive and unlimited Latin dance instruction. Fairweather was fifteen times world champion, and she had taught Wong, who was passionate about competing pro/am in the United States. Saccani became Wong's pro/am partner, but they fell out after he threatened her and called her a "lazy cow" because he was unhappy with her performance at a tea dance.

Wong was "humiliated and embarrassed in front of her friends" and suffered "severe emotional distress after the incident."[36] Saccani clearly did not understand the status aspects of dancing for Chinese students. He testified that he was trying to improve Wong's dancing. Wong was successful in her suit, and she remained committed to dancing with a new partner. "It's like winning Wimbledon,"[37] she said. "I will continue to dance and compete as long as possible. It's my passion."[38]

As discussed in earlier chapters, professionals who taught Chinese women often found them reserved and uncomfortable with the touching and looking that dancing entailed. This did not mean, however, that they did not want their share of attention. What they wanted, though, was not emotional intimacy as much as status and skill. Sometimes, when they did not do well, they would blame the teacher, because they did not typically develop the same bond with him as American-born students often do.

In this chapter, I have referred to the emotional labor involved in dancing. This topic is discussed in more detail in chapter 4, which covers the work of creating and portraying an emotional connection with a partner.

4

Feeling the Dance, Showing the Magic

THE DESIRE OF dance audiences to believe in the emotions portrayed by the dancers is underscored by the popular television show *Dancing with the Stars*. This desire is especially strong when audiences do not dance, and each season audiences speculate about the possibility of romantic relationships between stars and professional dance partners, when they know both are single. For example, during the spring 2010 series, viewers were obsessed about whether a romance was developing between ESPN host Erin Andrews and dancer Maksim Chmerkovskiy.[1] So intense was the speculation that a couple weeks after the show ended, there were over thirteen thousand posts about them on the network's online message board; most of the posts were speculations about their feelings. The thread about the couple had been visited over three-quarters of a million times. Readers not only speculated; they articulated their desire for a relationship:

> Please let them be more than friends. I don't need to KNOW for sure, I just want them to be a happy romantic couple off-camera, even if it's only private. I just freaked last night at the thought she was stringing Maks along. . . . But I do not want to see a crushed Maks again and I'm afraid right now for next season. Straddling the love bug line. (Post 9242)

> Hi guys . . . keep hope alive! Have faith in fate. Two broken people who found strength, hope for the future, friendship and love each other. That's a bond that can't be easily faked out. . . . Until they actually say NO WE ARE NO DATING WE ARE JUST FRIENDS . . . then there is HOPE ☺ stay positive for BOTH ERIN and MAKS! (Post 9151)

The show encourages speculation. In one episode, Erin and Maks danced a routine on a king-size bed. While most members of the audience do not read the ABC online message board, they clearly share the sentiment that a couple who dance like they are in love must really be in love.

Audiences for professional dance competitions know that the emotions portrayed are sometimes a performance. However, they too want to believe in a man, a woman, and love in the air, even if only for the moment of the dance. When a performance does not match this expectation, audiences are troubled. Ruud Vermeij tells the following story in his book on Latin American dancing:

> In 1991, I danced a duet to Mahler's 5th Symphony with Peter Townsend, as part of a lecture demonstration at the World Congress in Blackpool.[2] The intention of the lecture was to demonstrate how a change in the ingredients of the dance, i.e. the music and the dancers, affected the entire expression/meaning. While we were occupied with dynamic changes and spatial forms, the audience perceived a relationship between two *men* and some were disturbed by this to the extent that they perceived nothing else. The point here is that no matter how well we controlled our steps, our partnering, no matter how clear the choreography, we were two men looking, touching, gesturing, partnering one another, and this was the essential expression. The steps made no difference at all.[3]

Most of Blackpool's audience of dancers would have known that Vermeij and Townsend were a well-established couple, but the public demonstration of this relationship in the form of a Latin dance interfered with their understanding of what they were seeing. Although the dance is a performance, the audience wants to believe that the feelings portrayed could be authentic and that the feelings are heterosexual.[4] Unlike for other dance forms, in which characters are established and acting is expected, ballroom audiences are interested in the dancers themselves and in their emotions.[5] As Vermeij's story demonstrates, "authentic" means a man and a woman —not two men—even if they have strong and genuine romantic feelings for each other.[6]

Intimacy is only believable when certain cultural expectations are met. Otherwise, it is hard to believe even genuine intimacy. Given these expectations, how do ballroom couples learn to portray sex and/or romance? Do they need to share a romantic relationship in order to achieve authenticity on the floor? Some top couples I interviewed were not sexually involved with each other. Others were a couple off the floor, and these often believed that something special showed between them when they danced. They understood the artifice of performance but emphasized authenticity of feeling.

Portraying Authentic Feelings

Mark was a winning American smooth dancer with his wife, Audra. When I asked him if he thought that it helped to have a romantic relationship with his dance partner, he said,

> To succeed as well as ours has, yes. I think it has to be very close. We're fortunate because we're man and wife; we had a relationship before dancing. I really honestly don't know how the couples that are not romantically involved, or how couples that are romantically involved with other partners outside their own relationship—I can't even fathom how they make it. . . . Some of them are great. I can't even get my brain around what it must take to make that work, . . . can't even get across that chasm.

Here, Mark confirms the stereotype that real love is that which exists between a man and a woman and that marriage demonstrates its presence.

When Mark first began teaching dance at a Fred Astaire school, he had "just three or four" dance partners, and each of these partnerships was brief. He had competed with them at chain competitions, so these "were not really serious events." Since then, Mark had trained his wife, and they had been competing together for ten years. He met her after opening a franchise, where she applied to teach. She had only had a few dance lessons when he hired her, but he liked her personality and thought she would succeed. At the time, he was looking for a partner but did not think of her, because, he said, "I thought I was a much more experienced dancer, and I needed to look for somebody experienced. I would never dream of taking somebody new and training them from the ground up. That was way below me at the time." However, they began dating, and Mark quickly realized, "This girl needs to be my partner."

Mark believed that the dance partnership naturally followed from their strong and authentic feelings for each other. He noted, "People have always commented on how much we enjoy dancing together," and "they can see how much we love one another." Mark's partner had found performing emotion difficult at first: "like a lot of young girls, they haven't had the life experiences to draw on the character they need to be to produce top-level competitive dancing." At the time, they were not yet married, and Mark found that it was "not always the easiest thing" for him "to stand in the middle of the floor and let everybody in" to see his strong, private feelings of love for his partner.

Mark conceded, "It doesn't have to be between two individuals that are romantically involved, because I've seen brother and sister combinations do very well, even though I can't comprehend it." However, he clearly privileged what he viewed as authentic feelings. He thought the best way to portray an emotional connection on the floor was to let his inner feelings out:

> Ours was developed naturally. We feel that people see a genuine side of our relationship on the floor. I *do* have tremendous love and respect for Audra, and we *do* have a great relationship. Everybody else will tell you that, and I do feel we do a good job of showing that. I don't think it's anything we had to work at and be aware of: "This is something we need. How do we get it?" That developed naturally. . . . My biggest fault was how to look at her on the floor and allow everybody to see that aspect. . . . I'm not comfortable in showing it in myself, but I wasn't really comfortable allowing everybody else in to see what we had between the two of us.

Even a portrayal of authentic feelings takes work to produce. Latin dancers Nikolai Pilipenchuk and Natalia Skorikova show this in color plate 7. This couple had a personal relationship, now ended. However, they no doubt use that experience in the tender portrayal seen in the picture.

Paris Is Burning, an award-winning documentary about the drag-ball competitions held in Harlem, emphasizes "realness" in performance.[7] Contestants try to look as authentic as possible and to pass for the genuine article—for example, a supermodel or a businessman. As Judith Butler points out, "realness" in drag exposes all gendered acts as performances.[8] In Mark's story, however, we see a double consciousness. Mark believed that the expression of emotional connection was better for being genuine, but he found this difficult to do. It also took experience. Performers cannot produce the visible expression of a feeling unless they have a life of feelings to call on as needed. In Mark's view, his wife had found this difficult, until she was old enough to have experienced a variety of deep emotions. When I interviewed Audra, she did not volunteer this information herself. But Mark's comment was not in response to a specific question; he volunteered it as part of his explanation that he had taught his wife to dance, a statement with which she concurred.

Producing Authentic Feelings

Partners who were romantically involved commonly expressed the belief that their special relationship made their dancing more powerful. Usually, however, romantic relationships resulted from the dancing partnership, not the other way around. Dancers recognized that they had to work at showing emotions but also that it took considerable emotional labor to maintain dance relationships at all. Peter was a top Latin dancer from Australia.[9] Every romantic partner he ever had was also a dance partner, because, he said, "There's no time." Paul explained, "When I was in London, I was working a day job, and then having lessons, and then practicing until eleven o'clock at night, and then going home, and doing it all again. During the weekends, I was traveling to Germany for competitions." Peter saw advantages and disadvantages to romance with partners:

> For some people, it's a mistake, but I think it's actually quite normal, because they spend so much time in close proximity to each other, working, dancing, practicing, traveling. . . . The ones that actually last a long time, . . . it's the reason the partnership works: . . . parallel reasons—you enjoy doing it. . . . I've had a lot of relationships with my partners. . . . When I was with [my former partner], I was dating her for six years and dancing with her for seven. . . . I care a lot for her. We were quite close. Then one day, I don't know what brought the subject up, but we just sat down in the living room of the house we were renting and just decided that we're just together because we're together. That night I went up into the bedroom, moved into the spare room, and we continued on as normal, except there was no relationship. There was no awkwardness—we were good friends—actually shared a bank account together. . . . We were just mature enough to realize that it wasn't going to go any further, and we didn't lose anything.

When this partner left to pursue another career, the two remained friendly.

Peter had been in many partnerships, some including romance and some not, so he had a broad perspective on the issue of authenticity. One of the problems with close emotional relationships with a dance partner is that when things go wrong, it can "actually slow you down." It became very easy to "cross the line into the arguing side of things." Peter added that in order for a partnership to work, you do not need a romantic relationship, but you "have to have respect for your partner." Partners also had to have the same ideals and goals. This suggests that negative feelings must be worked through to produce the appearance of warmth and intimacy, lest they get in the way.[10] Although Peter believed in trying to avoid conflict, he thought that regardless of the type of relationship, "everybody is having these conflicts." To him, it did not really matter whether a couple was romantically involved. Intimacy could be portrayed irrespective of actual feelings, and the relationship was bound to develop depth over time:

> You're all in the same boat. You're all struggling with the fact that you are spending a lot of time together. Even if you're not dating each other, they might be sharing an apartment because it's cheaper and because you're traveling so much. . . . You're all having conflicts. Sometimes you're so nervous in what you've done yourself that day, or how your competition went, that as soon as you hear a criticism, which is really somebody trying to say, "Hey, we need to fix this," you take it as a criticism against yourself. . . . It's why we need coaches. . . . Being defensive is a habit, and we've got to do an impossible job.

When Peter taught, he was a master at instant intimacy, but he knew from long experience that professional dance partnerships move past this, independent of actual feelings.

When partners have complex feelings about their own abilities and performances, and when each member of a partnership has grievances against the other, it is difficult to portray the intense emotions that the performance requires. Furthermore, each dance has a different character and necessitates a different emotional display. If a couple is in love, it may be hard to portray the rejection that is part of the tango, for example, or the man's dominant posture in the paso doble. Sometimes, Peter said ruefully, "it's better to have a dictator, . . . a guy who's dictating, and the girl just shuts up and does it." He conceded that "it's not very happy for the girl" but argued that it is more efficient. Although Peter implied that either the man or the woman could be the dictator, he clearly believed that it was better for the man to be in charge. This constant reaffirmation of the view that the man is in charge on the dance floor undercuts the intense emotional labor both men and women must do in reality to make a performance appear authentic.

It is ironic that in spite of this stereotypical sentiment, Peter described his current partner, a woman who is both opinionated and independent, as the best relationship he had had, both personally and professionally.

Working together, they portrayed the character of each dance with intense feeling. They had each left another partnership before dancing together, and while they were still getting to know each other, they went to England for coaching:

> One of the comments was actually by [former ballroom champion and coach] Karen Hilton, when we were in the studio in London having lessons with [former Latin champion and coach] Shirley [Ballas]. We heard about it afterwards. She'd said, "They dance like they are in love." We were so happy to suddenly have this new opportunity. . . . Every practice was like—if she didn't feel something was quite right, I'd be like, "Wait. Wait. Let me see if I can fix it for you." And she'd be the same. 'Course that's changed, as it always does—honeymoon period's over. . . . The dancing's gotten better since then, but we may have lost a bit of that, because now we're busy with what's right and what's wrong, whereas, before, it was just a whole new experience.

Even though Peter privileged genuine feelings, he was aware that the emotional connection arose out of expertise. He quoted a saying: "Devotion to the motion equals emotion." What he meant was this:

> When you actually partner one another and you start synchronizing, start to do the same sort of actions, and you coordinate together, it brings out an emotion in both of you so you look like you are together. Helps if you like your partner too, of course. And the flip side of that, . . . you can see very easily if people are angry at each other or not very happy.

Peter understood that a partnership was something you "had to work at." He acknowledged that feeling involves a performance and that working together produces emotions, but he believed that genuine feelings helped and that it was not possible to suppress anger completely.[11]

Feeling Management

Arlie Hochschild writes in her book *The Managed Heart* about feeling management.[12] She argues that in the modern world, much of our work involves the production, or at least the appearance, of appropriate feelings. Dancers work hard to produce the feelings that they portray on the dance floor. They may portray emotions by being in love with their partner and letting these feelings show, like Mark, or they may work to bring their feelings in line with the emotions they are trying to portray. Peter recognized that feelings may be manufactured, but he also thought that genuine love showed through. He further thought that dance practice developed genuine feelings, and undoubtedly it does. In my experience, part of dance's pleasure comes from feelings produced by physical intimacy with another person to whom one might be attracted—at least a little.[13]

One way of studying emotion is to examine the work that people do in order to bring a feeling in line with a desired display.[14] Some dancers rationalized that their actual relationship was key. Others acknowledged that they were acting. However, the dance floor is not the only place where dance partners perform emotional labor. One of the top ballroom dancers in the world, Liliya, had become successful competing with a partner with whom she had a long-term romantic relationship. When I interviewed her, she was in an even more successful partnership with a dancer who was not her lover. Liliya told me that they were best friends. She described "getting along with the partner" as one of the most difficult things in learning to dance. Speaking from experience, she said, "You can create more problems with the romantic relationship." She said that in her current partnership, "the respect value is more." In fact, she believed that the earlier partnership had lasted longer than it should have: "The relationship was more important to me than the dance." Whereas she used to fight regularly with her former partner, she never fought with the new one. At the time of the interview, they had been competing together for about eight months, and Liliya believed their lack of conflict was due to the lower emotional temperature of the relationship, but also because they were older and more experienced.

What Audiences See

Although Liliya's second partnership was technically perfect, the first appeared to me to have had an emotional intensity lacking in the new one. Of course, as the viewer, I create meaning from watching an event. Reader response criticism was developed to examine the role of the reader, rather than the author, in interpreting literary works,[15] but it can be applied to other artistic endeavors, such as dancing. It is likely that a viewer who

Fig. 4.1. Dancing a romance. J. T. Damalas and Thomas Mielnicki look happy and loving in spite of their immense physical exertion. 2008 Emerald Ball DanceSport Championships, Los Angeles, CA. © 2008 Jonathan S. Marion.

knows whether a dancer is involved with a partner or not will see a different relationship in each case. The insider status of most ballroom dance audiences makes it likely that the dance will be viewed through the eyes of those who know whether the dancers' emotions are genuine—that is, whether they are romantically linked.[16] As we saw earlier, however, this only works when the partners are a man and a woman. Figure 4.1 illustrates this point. The emotions displayed by American smooth champions J. T. Damalas and Thomas Mielnicki are intense and sincere enough that the audience believes them, even though most know that theirs is not a romantic relationship.

Liliya had a pragmatic view of performance and did not see it as an authentic expression of love. In fact, this is how she described the most difficult thing about performing:

> It's like you come out every single time, and people expect the magic from you. It's very hard to give them the magic every single time. I think this is the most difficult thing, because sometimes you just have an off day. I don't mean dancing off, but it's more emotionally. Our dancing skill is now very good, so it doesn't really fluctuate, but emotions and the musicality —what we forget—that can make it difficult.

This is from a woman whose dancing always appears magical to the audience. Even though the magic appears to come from nowhere, Liliya understood the intense emotional labor involved. In ballroom, partners are always in closed position, and they rarely look at each other. The music and movement are romantic, but there is not the same display of emotional intensity found in other styles. However, their bodies must be synchronized, and their facial expressions must display the character of the dance: dreamy romance for the waltz, love and happiness for the foxtrot, or passion and fury for the tango. The use of body and face rather than looks to create emotional connection can be seen in color plate 3.

Liliya's view of dancing placed less emphasis on the man's leadership, unusual in a native Russian woman raised in a gender-conventional culture. When I asked her to define the man's role in dancing, she told me not to tell her partner her answer:

> I think dancing is fifty-fifty. I think the woman has to be smarter a little bit
> —for example, me being a professional for so long, and [my partner] just
> came from amateur. He's a great dancer and probably the biggest natural
> talent I've ever danced with, so I respect him for that. . . . I don't know
> if we have a leader actually. . . . Let's just say in official things and every-
> thing, I would say [my partner] is the leader. . . . [The woman's role is] to
> lead without people knowing it. The woman's role is to keep the peace and
> be smart.

Thus, Liliya had a complex understanding of the emotional labor required in dancing with a professional partner. She understood that sometimes dancers have to "produce magic" when they do not feel it. She also understood that there is a certain amount of subterfuge in the performance. The man has to look as if he is in charge, even when he is not. Even though men in the ballroom engage in a greater variety of emotional labor than other men do, Liliya appeared to support Hochschild's point that the emotional labor the woman performs is harder—women have to be a little bit smarter than men. This was especially true in the rarefied world in which Liliya lived, where she and her partner made their money performing, not teaching. Still, Liliya loved it when dancers could produce emotions easily, and she thought it important for partners to respect each other. She thought this increased with age. "The younger people are," she said, "there's no respect."

Surface Acting and Deep Acting

When Hochschild described emotional labor, she reported that many jobs require workers to detach themselves from their feelings.[17] Some workers, such as sales clerks, needed only surface acting—for example, producing a smile for an annoying customer while still feeling annoyed inside. The flight attendants Hochschild studied engaged in surface acting, but they also had to perform deep acting, particularly on long flights. In deep acting, one actively changes one's feelings by talking to oneself about how one should feel. Both kinds of emotional labor are called for in the dance world. Liliya preferred it when she and her partner could bring their love of dance to the surface and make the performance magical—deep acting—but sometimes they were only able to produce a surface appearance. Hochschild calls this burnout.

Sofiya had danced with the same partner for many years, and they had immigrated to America as a couple. They had danced as a married couple and, after they separated, had continued dancing for a while. During this time, Sofiya was angry at her ex, but this was not apparent when she performed. When I interviewed Sofiya, they had stopped competing. They were in the process of getting divorced and were also breaking up their dance business.

To succeed in a professional and romantic relationship, Sofiya agreed that "you have to believe in the same things." Furthermore, she added, "You have to have a relationship to be able to communicate with this person." When Sofiya first started dancing with her former husband, they "were nobodies," so they "developed this style together" as a jointly agreed on endeavor. Sofiya quoted Alan Tornsberg, a top Latin competitor, now a coach. Tornsberg had told her, "I was stupid trying out with girls on the dance floor." He explained, "If you saw this person before, you know what she can do." Instead, he said, "I should have been taking them out and spending time with them, and basically talking, finding out if you will get along together."[18] In other words, as long as the potential partner could dance, then personal compatibility was more important than dance compatibility, because the latter was easier to develop. To Sofiya, this was good advice.

Like Peter and Liliya, Sofiya was ambivalent about the benefit of a romantic relationship in dance:

> There is supposed to be two reasons why people get together as dancers. If you get together romantically because you like each other or love

each other, and that's why you're together, and then you dance together, it's a bonus. We know couples who succeed in this. . . . It's so nice to see them interact with one another, going on dates, and it's beautiful. So if you fell in love with this person, that's one thing. That is probably helping. . . . The other thing is probably with our case. We got together because of the dance. . . . It was convenient. I think it was more from [my ex-husband's] side rather than me. I fell in love, but that's what I always felt from him, that he was letting it be because it was convenient, especially in the beginning. I never felt he was interested in me romantically.

Sofiya and her husband had constant conflict while being coached or practicing afterward. Her husband was an intuitive dancer relying on feelings rather than cognition. She picked up new information very quickly, whereas he could not always understand what was wanted without a lot of questions. Dancers say the ideal is to leave conflicts on the dance floor, but this does not always happen, as Sofiya described:

We took it home big time. . . . We couldn't stay professional when we had a fight on the dance floor. The first thing [my ex-husband] will say after I wouldn't agree with him, "It's not working. I don't love you. I never loved you. I don't want to be with you. . . ." What the hell does that have to do with the price of beans? How did we end up talking about personal relationship if we're talking about natural frickin' turn?

Yet after their romantic relationship ended, Sofiya and her partner still performed with great warmth toward each other, almost as if they were sharing a private joke. Sofiya noted, "People are very surprised at us splitting up, because we always came out as a couple and as beautiful, no problem." She explained, "We're probably the same as a lot of dancers; we fool a lot of people. . . . We could easily get in the mood of this and perform." Sofiya used a combination of surface acting and deep acting. She projected romance on the dance floor, although she was unhappy with how the relationship was ending. And when they danced together, the emotion of the dance took over, and her feelings genuinely changed at least for the duration of the dance.

Janice, the social dance teacher from chapter 3, had competed earlier in her life and had yet another view about the dancing partnership. Her husband had never danced. She had danced pro/am before she quit her office job to teach, and all her partners had been friends, not lovers. Still, she noted,

> I think if you partner somebody for a while, you can't help but get close. There are partnerships that bring people together, and there are partner- ships that send people apart. There are some married people who can't dance together or compete together. . . . It can be a friends' relationship. I don't think it has to be a sexual relationship. . . . I don't really feel like danc- ing is a sexual thing. That's not true for other people. . . . I think ballroom dancing's a thing unto itself, just dancing to the music, two people dancing as one. It's such a great feeling, and it's got nothing to do with sex. . . . The most important thing is how you treat each other.

Producing Feelings in Pro/Am Competition

As we have seen, many students pay for the fantasy of romance. They want to believe in genuine emotions, and so teachers must give the appearance of enjoying time with them. Teachers become good at working on their emotions: they frequently told me with great sincerity that they were fortu- nate and had wonderful students who were rarely difficult and whom they were always happy to see. This often sounded like deep acting.

Yet, if the production of feeling is difficult with a professional partner, how much harder is it when professionals dance with students, and their intimacy has a recognizable commercial base? Mark explained:

> I find it difficult to teach things I find difficult for myself: relations between a man and a woman. I have that naturally [with my wife], but with my stu- dents is a totally different thing. There needs to be some sort of chemistry between partners, no matter what kind of relationship they have. That is really challenging for me, because I have a problem showing everybody the inner workings of my relationship with my wife. You can then under- stand how uncomfortable it might be for me to even try to create a façade of that relationship with my students. In order to produce the right look for the judges and give the spectators—and judges are also spectators—I have to try to give that to my students. That's definitely challenging. Where to put their toe, how much to turn their toe out, where to put their hand on their New Yorker, how much to drop their weight on the floor—those kinds of things—that's a piece of cake.

Fig. 4.2. Changing styles. Teacher Eddie Ares, dancing with longtime student Karen Angell, moves from sexy rhythm to romantic smooth, as needed. 2010 Emerald Ball DanceSport Championships, Los Angeles, CA. © 2010 Jonathan S. Marion.

Mark taught his students the importance of producing what Hochschild calls "feeling rules."[19] Sometimes students were disappointed with their results. Mark told them, "If you don't win, look as happy as if you did, and when you do win, look like you expected it." This man, who believed in the authenticity of feelings, also understood feeling management.

Hochschild argues that men who do emotion work are atypical; this is women's work in both the home and the workplace. This is one more way in which male dancers differ from other men. Both in their professional dancing and in their teaching, their emotional labor takes two forms. They create the kind of emotional connection—sharing information, looking after their partners—that we typically associate with women. They also engage in a more masculine type of emotional labor, by flirting and creating an erotic connection. Different dances require different emotions, and teachers work to produce these with students. Teachers sometimes find this difficult. For example, as figure 4.2 shows, teacher Eddie Ares, who competed in professional rhythm, was better able to produce a sexy look dancing rhythm than a romantic look in smooth.

Mark had found it difficult to stop being overprotective toward his wife on the dance floor. He had trained her to dance and to compete with him, and it took him a long time "to get over being her mother out there." It was even harder with students, because, he said, "I'm in charge of everything that's happening." He constantly monitored each student, understanding that different students needed different kinds of attention both on the dance floor and between rounds. In this situation, it is difficult to dance with the student partner as if there is an emotional bond.

Non-Western Students

When teachers had non-Western students, the issues became more complex, because many of these students did not know the feeling rules that Westerners take for granted. Ballroom dance is popular in East Asia, especially Japan and China; indeed, in Hong Kong, wealthy women pay top professionals to partner them at afternoon dances.[20]

Dance is also popular among Asian Americans, especially those of Chinese origin. Most Chinatowns in the United States have at least one ballroom studio. When European and American teachers have Chinese or other East Asian students, they often report that students find the dance relationship difficult. Pavel, a Latin dancer, described the problem:

> I teach a lot of Asian students, ninety percent Japanese, Korean, Chinese. They're very conservative. I have one student; she didn't want to look in my eyes. When you dance Latin, you look at the eyes. For years, she didn't want to look at me, and I tell her, "Listen, you're going for competition; you can't not look at me." She's like, "on the comp, I'll do it. I can't do it now." For four years, she wouldn't look at me. . . . I really had to convince her, and she really needed time to go around the competitions and see the good dancers dance. . . . I know she wants to do it, and I understand her culture, so I never get discouraged. Some people [have a] different personality. Because of the success and the high result they want, they are ready to do anything. Even if they feel shy—and in their culture they're shy—in the dancing, they will do what it takes, because they are hungry, to do well.

Of course, not all Asian students are shy, especially those raised in America.

Pavel had thought a lot about the meaning of touch, because his Asian and Asian American students found it difficult to be physically intimate in public, let alone with a married dance teacher whose wife frequently coached them. These students were not looking for an intimate relationship—they wanted to perform well—and they found the physical intimacy particularly hard because they interpreted it as sexual. In order to convince them that intimacy was safe and not erotic, Pavel explained it as follows:

> A touch and a touch is very different. If the touch is done correctly, from the right place, it's a pleasant thing like a conversation. If it's touch for the touch, it's different. Our main teacher, Hans Galke, when you work with him—he touches me, and he's a guy—and it feels great, because he does it right from the body, so it's not a sexual thing. . . .[21] If you do it to connect with the person, there is a ball of energy of the man and a ball of energy of the woman; it's just two energies together in one ball. You tune the bodies together. . . . If your energy's going into mine, it's like a conversation with the body. It's not really a touch. It's like a magical moment.

In this explanation, Pavel was also performing emotional labor, putting at ease students who feel uncomfortable in a world of instant intimacy by explaining to them that the physical connection of bodies does not have to be inappropriate. At other times, when he was dancing with American students or hugging me at a competition, he knew exactly how to be close and personal in the usual dancerly manner.

Emotional Labor for Women Teachers

The female teachers I interviewed had different issues with developing an emotional connection. Vilma, a former competitor with her own studio, had been teaching for about seventeen years. She had had one student so enamored of her that she had to go to court to get him to stop stalking her. She had learned to be frank when male students misunderstood her intent:

> I sit them down in the office, and I say, "I know it's confusing, but we're your dance teacher. We're not a brothel. The teachers are not allowed to date their students. It's confusing, because we touch you, and we hold you close, and we boost your confidence, and we do all the things that a

good girlfriend should do. But you have to understand that this is a dance
school, and if that's what you're here for, we would love to have you. If you
have other intentions, then maybe you should find another place."

In other words, students must learn that the teacher is performing, not
displaying authentic emotions, and that touch in dance does not mean the
same as it does elsewhere. However, Vilma was not above using student
crushes to her advantage. If the crush was not out of hand, she said that she
either "ignored it or worked the angle to get them to buy more lessons."

Vilma was realistic in her belief that partner dancing has a sexual component to it, and she understood that there is a sex-work component to teaching dance.[22] As one of her male teachers had described it, "We are all a little
bit prostitute. It's part of the game. You're not encouraging them. You're
making them feel good." Vilma added, "If flirting is part of making them
feel good, so be it. It's harmless and fun, and if they start to misunderstand,
that's when you lay off." Vilma explained, "We don't flirt to the point where
they don't get it."

Although Vilma found flirting easy when teaching, she found it difficult
to perform sexual passion when she competed. She "hated trying to be
sexier than the other women." She thought that the women were "plastic
and fake" and added, "Half of you is completely envious and jealous, and
the other half is disgusted." She called this a "crazy emotional rollercoaster
ride." She found it difficult to undertake the emotional labor necessary to
produce the performance she desired. She did not want to engage in deep
acting, and she hated it when her partner—who was also her romantic
partner—was "emotional" about it and became frustrated with her when
they did not do as well as he hoped. Vilma described the ideal performance
as gendered. She called it "a man/woman presence on the floor." To achieve
this, she said, "You need to work together." She added, "You need to create a picture, and, really, it's not the man's role or the woman's role. It's the
space in between that's important." She acknowledged that this is difficult
to do. She wanted the performance to look authentic, even though her own
experience had lacked a sense of reality.

Social dance teachers described a different kind of problem. Rather than
teaching students to perform with emotional intensity, they tried to teach
students to dance well enough to enjoy themselves on the dance floor, with
the confidence to enjoy the brief flirtation that each dance entailed. Often,
however, learning to dance made students tense, which precluded pleasure.

Teachers told horror stories about teaching married couples. Janice said couples are "always working on each other, instead of themselves." When she saw "a lady trying to fix her husband," she would say, "I'll work on him; you work on you."

In order to make lessons pleasurable, social dance teachers worked at enjoying themselves and encouraging students to feel the same way. In the modern world, where many people find that their leisure is at a premium, dance teachers, particularly those teaching group classes, become experts at producing instant fun. Hochschild argues that while we tend to discount commercialized niceness, such as the ubiquitous "have a nice day," we also value the niceness we pay for "as a form of needed reassurance that in the midst of many strangers we are safely out of harm's way."[23] Social dance teachers tried hard to make students feel safe.

Janice let students find their own comfort level. If a student only wanted to dance with a spouse, she would say, "Fine, don't rotate." She also recognized that bodily contact is difficult at first. Although she would tell them, "You need to get closer," if they were too far apart for a step, she understood that "most beginners feel a little more comfortable having a little space." Janice described what can happen when a student's former romantic partner was also in the class: "You don't realize what's going on until you're having people rotate, and all of a sudden you notice that somebody is never dancing with somebody. They're always standing out or skipping or mixing up the rotation, because what they are doing is avoiding one other person in the room, and that's a little difficult." Janice usually dealt with this situation by ignoring it.

Stephanie, whom we met in chapter 3, taught classes similar to Janice's. Her group classes attracted many students, and she had an open attitude toward touching and the emotional relationship on the dance floor. First, she acknowledged, not everyone came to dance: "They might be looking to pick someone up." She did not really mind this but noted that they soon left, "because this is not really the environment." She had heard "rumors at one point that [some teachers] were being inappropriate," so she "mentioned it to them," but "didn't take any action," because, she figured, "they are an adult." She made an interesting comment on how people handled close dancing with a stranger:

I thought it was fascinating to watch how people transition from the very first time they have to be in closed position, how their body language was.

They pull back. They draw their chin back. They're really uncomfortable being in contact with another person. It's probably the first time, for a lot of people, that's happened. Over time, their personal space starts to become smaller and smaller. I have no personal space at this point.

Women Students and Emotions

And what of the students? How do they find the physicality of the dance? How do they learn to perform dances of sex and romance with someone they are paying? How do long-married older students, who may have forgotten how to flirt, cope with dance studios? What about young singles who see flirtation as an invitation to dating or at least to "hooking up"?[24] Do students misinterpret the intention when teachers seem to become quickly involved with them? What do teachers do when this happens? Most people do not have Stephanie's lack of personal space, so how do students interpret what seems to be a violation?

Ellen, age fifty-four, had a demanding professional career, a husband, and a grown family. Although she had danced ballet as a teenager and had considered making it a career until an injury put an end to her hopes, she was uncomfortable with the touching that ballroom dance entailed. She first went to the studio with her husband, but he was put off, because "they're very touchy and huggy and kiss-kiss on the cheeks." Ellen found this "very awkward"; indeed it was "probably the hardest part in learning to dance." She and her husband had a longstanding joke over how difficult she found flirting, even with him. She became more comfortable when her teacher showed her how to control the level of physical contact with partners. She observed that it was difficult for her to move her core, because she felt uncomfortable if it came in contact with her partner.[25]

Teachers work hard to make students feel comfortable, as was noted in the discussion of the lesson depicted in figure 2.3. Another example of this is shown in figure 4.3, in which teacher John Larson is seen teaching the foxtrot in preparation for a showdance. Foxtrot is a notoriously hard dance to learn, and John is unfailingly cheerful as he encourages students to feel comfortable with the steps and also the syncopation.

Sometimes teachers encouraged students' crushes. Brenda was self-conscious about her weight. She had a successful career with a good income for someone in her early thirties, and she loved dancing. However, she said, "In my mind I'm always, 'You're too fat to be dancing.'" She knew that she

Fig. 4.3. Learning the foxtrot is fun. Teacher John Larson with student Beth Kephart. DanceSport Academy, Ardmore, PA, July 2010. © 2010 Jonathan S. Marion.

was good at it but felt that she did not fit. Her discomfort meant that "the physical proximity to another person" was the hardest thing to learn in the beginning. These insecurities made her vulnerable to the teachers, particularly one teacher, who constantly flirted with her and on whom she developed a crush:

> I've had a crush on a couple. The first one, it was more of a typical student-teacher crush, where it was a new experience, and it was exciting and intoxicating. I think it was less the teacher, more the experience. You thought you had a crush on the teacher, but what you really had was a crush on the dancing. . . . The next one was a more physical thing. . . . [The teacher] is good looking, he has a great body, he can dance. If you love to dance, watching a man like that totally enthralls you. . . . He's very flirty, and he likes hugging and kissing and touching. For whatever reason, he had this thing about my butt. It got grabbed three or four times in a day when I was there. I'm like, "Knock it off, will you?" Then I sort of started liking him. I realized, "Oh, he's cute." It was a gradual thing, because I couldn't stand [him] at first. I thought he was pompous and arrogant and had an ego out the wazoo. And then it was, "Oh, he's kind of cute, and he's a really good dancer, and he seems to like me."

The flirting finally ended when she sat the teacher down and told him to stop, because although she knew he was playing, it did not look that way to others.

Brenda was vulnerable to this kind of flirtatious teasing, but she noted that this teacher flirted outrageously with many students. Brenda realized that "he loves having women all over him" and that he competed with other male teachers to see who could get the most attention from students. She said, "The more women that they have fawning over them, it's like a status symbol with them." Sometimes, she told me, students had misunderstood the teacher's motives and had imagined that there was a real relationship. These students had ended up quitting. Brenda's description shows the emotional labor she put into redefining her feelings. In the first instance, she decided it was the dancing and not the teacher that she loved. In the second, she told herself that she would not misread the intent of a teacher who was such a flirt, so she got over the crush to protect herself.[26]

In contrast to the behavior of the teachers, Brenda's studio did not approve of students who "were not there for the right reason" but "were more there to hit on women." This made Brenda feel safe around other students, because she knew they were not going to do anything inappropriate. Furthermore, although the studio was independent, it had strict rules about students and teachers fraternizing. Brenda thought that this was "ridiculous." She could have a drink with her teacher when at a competition, but when she and another student were having a drink after the practice party and a teacher walked by, he was not allowed to join them even if invited. "Even if he were to come in and say, 'Hi,' he would get in trouble." This same teacher would have been hugging and kissing her goodbye a few minutes before. Although Brenda expected the studio to be an erotic place, she learned that this all ended at the door.

With all this emotional drama, how did Brenda become comfortable performing? She stopped having lessons with the teacher she had had the crush on, even though she considered him to be the studio's best dancer. She switched to "the second-best dancer," who did not "do some of the things the [the others] did, you know, with the flirting." This teacher was "an incredible gentleman," and when they danced, she felt they were more like partners than student and teacher. Brenda loved performing, whether it was at a competition or at the more informal student showcases that competition studios organize to give all students the chance to perform in front of family and friends. She described what she loved about going to a competition:

> The fact that it's a competition without being a competition. There's competition, but everybody there is usually so nice. . . . Everybody gets along, and everybody cheers everybody else on, even if you don't know them. You know they're out there putting themselves on the line just as much as you are, and you can't help but clap for them, and you generally make friends with people. Plus, it's nice to get to practice your craft in front of other people. . . . I've always found there's less pressure competing than there is doing showcase, because I don't know these people and am not going to see them again, whereas, with showcase, these are people you're going to see all the time. It's your family, even other people's family. They know me now, because this is my fourth year of showcase.

Brenda spent much of her leisure time dancing or in related activities. She took between three and five lessons a week and never missed a studio party. She had made friends with other students, going out for dinner or drinks with them. By now, she said, "I know their families. I've been to their houses." She also attended competitions with another student, just to watch. They would watch prestigious competitions such as USDC or Ohio because they could not afford to compete as much as they wished. Although Brenda was single, with a well-paying profession, the studio she went to was one of the most expensive in its competition charges, so she could not compete more than once a year. Brenda worried about her dance expenditures, but she felt like an important player in her studio, where she was connected to many teachers and students. At her job, everyone knew she danced, and they asked about it regularly. She liked the notoriety it gave her. She was a little wistful about some aspects, because although she suspected she was being exploited, dancing had become central to her identity, and she wanted to believe she was cared for at her studio. Her story perfectly exemplifies the costs and benefits of the purchase of intimacy.[27]

Managing Male Students' Emotions

Although Brenda's experience was an extreme case, flirting was something that most women students experienced. Studios typically have a level of flirtatiousness not found in everyday life, but they are careful to mark the limits. The women teachers I interviewed were more careful with male students than the male teachers were with their women students, because the men found it easier than the women to place limits on the behavior of their students. When a woman student got out of hand, which happened occasionally, the men knew how to put the brakes on, just as in the outside world. For the women teachers, the situation was more fraught.

Sally, a dance teacher in her thirties, described two different occasions when she "had someone who became inappropriately enamored." She blamed herself as much as the students, because she "did not draw a boundary when it needed to be drawn." This had happened because she "either didn't see it or was so busy trying to be the perfect teacher." In one case, the situation had cost the studio quite a lot in refunds, and in the other case, the student was told not to come back. In both cases, Sally had experienced "real angst" and had since learned to be more careful.

Even when teachers were careful, male students sometimes fell hard, and when they did, they were difficult to control, because men are used to taking the initiative in courtship situations. In addition, whereas most women know that men's flirtatious behavior may mean little or nothing, men feel free to interpret that same behavior on the part of women as a sign of interest.[28] Daniel had never been married and would not reveal his age, although I estimated him to be in his late fifties. I was puzzled by this reluctance at first—he was the only respondent who demurred—but the reason quickly became clear. He saw himself as someone still active in the relationship market and had fallen heavily in love with a much younger teacher. He had imagined that they might have a future together. When I interviewed him, the relationship was long over, but he still dreamed of getting back together.

Daniel had done a little dancing some years earlier but not seriously. About four years previously, a serious personal relationship ended, so he decided to "get back into dancing." He called three dance studios near his home, and only one picked up the phone. The young woman who answered became his instructor. He liked her, but she left to pursue a professional partnership elsewhere. Daniel was not happy about this:

> I had just signed a new contract, and you pay this money up front, and it was many thousands of dollars. A week later she was gone, so I was pretty upset about that. At that point, Natasha was given to me, and it wasn't until probably my first lesson with her when I realized, "This isn't so bad after all, 'cause I'm learning a lot more." . . . Keeping in mind that Natasha is a Russian and really just learning to speak the English language, so there were initially some communication problems. . . . I saw this strange little girl from a foreign country. Her hair was not beautiful like it is today. It was all wetted down or something. I got to know her better. We just started to laugh a lot. . . . When a beautiful young woman says, "I like you," that's encouragement.

Daniel believed that he and Natasha had something special. He joked about what a good lesson was: "when I am hugging Natasha." And he explained that developing an emotional connection with her was "really easy." Natasha had told him, on their second lesson, that developing a connection "was something very important that few people understand fully," but she was going to teach him like he was "something special." He had difficulty, however, with the general physicality of the studio:

> It's actually gotten better. I don't think about it as much that way anymore. . . . I don't feel comfortable dancing with a married woman, because I feel that dancing is very intimate. It's a little sexual. . . . I always dance close connection. . . . Dancing's very romantic, very sensual, sexual, and intimate. I'm an affectionate guy. Like I will put my hand around someone—I

know them well as a friend—but there's a limit, and I don't like to do that to a woman I'm not attracted to.

In order to become comfortable with dancing, partners have to be comfortable with body parts touching often in intimate ways—legs between legs and pelvises touching, for example. Dancers become quite blasé about this. They are explicit that they find it pleasurable, but they do not read anything into it. Daniel was never able to reach this point. He appeared to be a man who read the intimate touch of dancing as touch is read generally in American culture. He could not make the transition to the physicality of the dance world, and when he was dancing with a partner, he misinterpreted the meaning.

Daniel was especially enamored of the physical closeness of dancing with Natasha, and he read more into it than was intended. When they first started competing, he was ecstatic with the results, but problems soon began, and his description sounded like that of a jilted lover. He described an example of how badly Natasha had treated him:

> We were dancing the tango, and unfortunately it was the end of our day. Her foot furthest from me, supposedly I stepped with my heel on her big toe. It split her toenail in half, so she ended up having to pull off half her toenail, and it was very painful. . . . I think we had three or four more dances, and in that sense, she was a trouper. . . . I felt horrified, and she was blaming me for this. I don't remember stepping on her. . . . I got the silent angry treatment for about three hours, and I was sitting out in the hallway. She did not even want me at the table. . . . This female instructor came by. . . . She said, "I saw who stepped on her toe, and it wasn't you." So here I was being blamed—I got the cold treatment that night at dinner, and it was miserable. . . . I spend all this money—and we're talking thousands and thousands of dollars for this competition—and this is the disrespectful and immature way I get treated. I mean, it hurt; it hurt very much. Those were embarrassing—no, not embarrassing but just humiliating and hurtful, because I cared so much about her, and I tried so hard.

Had Daniel not been so enamored of Natasha, he probably would have simply changed teachers, but instead he went and talked to the studio owner about his problems. The owner told him that these things happen with a competition partner; they were bound to "get close." Looking back, Daniel felt that the owner had encouraged him to fall hard. He complained that "there were antics and things that were done that were maybe inappropriate," which put him on an "emotional rollercoaster."

Inevitably, the day came when Natasha left the studio. This had happened some time before my interview with Daniel, but he was still devastated. When he had signed up for the lessons, he told the owner that Natasha was part of the package; she must never leave. The owner promised him this, even though such a promise cannot be made. Daniel had seen other teachers come and go at the studio. Although he was outraged by the violation of his feelings, Daniel did not feel obliged to apply appropriate emotional boundaries to the teacher who replaced Natasha:

> She's really bent over backwards, been a real sport about it, knowing what I've gone through, and, in fact, has worked really hard. She knows I have made not necessarily derogatory remarks about her but not necessarily positive comments, because I felt like when I was dancing with Natasha, I was dancing with a Ferrari, and now I was dancing with a pickup truck, for want of a better description. . . . I didn't mean to be hurtful. I didn't say it to her. . . . On my first lesson with [the new teacher], it was very hard. I had to pull her aside and explain to her I was not sure I could do it. At that point, I broke down and was crying for like two minutes. I was just shaking all over. It was like two or three days of just pent-up emotion and hurt and disappointment. . . . I think [the new teacher] understood. She could see how close we were. Everybody could.

Daniel had organized his life around his dancing. He told almost no one at work, regarding it as his big secret. When people looked at him, they did not know of his other life dancing with a beautiful young woman. Furthermore, he wanted to be able to walk out without disapproval when he had a dance lesson, even in the middle of a meeting, by explaining that he had an appointment. He had lessons almost every weekday, and when he went home afterward, he sat watching the tapes of him and Natasha at competitions. He loved dancing but loved the emotional and physical intimacy even more, buying into the common cultural myth that romance is not commercial.[29] Even though he was spending about forty thousand dollars a year on dancing, he had been able to delude himself that his relationship with Natasha was genuine and had no commercial basis. When she left, he felt that she had left him, not the studio.

Two dancers dancing as one involves various types of emotional labor, from learning to display genuine feelings to summoning feelings up for display even when they are absent from the heart. It also involves learning to manage student-teacher relationships, to police inappropriate feelings, and to sustain the desire for dance.

In the next chapter, I turn to appearance work. Appearance is central to dance; some dancers would argue that it is almost as central as technique and choreography. Certainly, as we shall see, dancers put a great deal of effort into it.

5

The Tan, the Hair, the Makeup

Embracing the Look

THE PROFESSIONAL BALLROOM competition at any major event is a sight to behold. The men wear tail suits with hair slicked straight back in the manner of Rudolph Valentino. Their hair must stay motionless for the entire event. They keep it shiny and glued to their heads with a wet gel blow dried with lots of hair spray. Although a dark tan is not as important as it is for Latin competition, men's faces are tanned, often with a matt makeup which makes the skin appear translucent and without blemish. Tanned faces and bodies make dancers stand out better on the floor, because the bright lights can otherwise make a person look ghostly. Practically everyone uses fake tan, which is easier to control than the real thing. Shoes are immaculate and usually black, as is the suit.

These handsome men each frame a gorgeous creature. The women's long dresses are in every color of the rainbow. Designed to move with the dancer, they flare out from the bottom with each move. Additional scarves of the same color hang from arms or shoulders and are often attached at the other end to the skirt of the dress, increasing the appearance of movement. Dresses are embellished with hundreds and even thousands of contrasting-colored Swarovski crystals, glued by hand. Earrings, bracelets, and necklaces in matching stones add to the look. Shoes are typically flesh colored—this is said to make the legs look longer. The women's backs are bare and tanned, and faces are elaborately made up. Hair is long, swept up, elaborate, and perfectly smooth, often entailing the use of hair pieces. Bodies are in top condition, the result of diet and exercise. There might be more than fifteen couples all dancing at once, and the effect is visually overpowering. The lights, the movement, the music, and the color are a feast for the eyes and ears. Audiences have come to see the dancers, and in addition to technical perfection they expect to see a show.

I loved the experience of dance from the first lesson, but it took me a while to appreciate a scene like the one just described. When I first became serious about dancing, I declared that I would never compete, because I could not imagine wearing the clothes and jewelry commonly seen on the competition floor. The skimpy Latin dresses looked even worse, but both styles appear tacky to the uninitiated.[1] In addition, the elaborate hair and makeup were unappealing. One's aesthetics change quickly with experience.

Learning Body Work

Most of the immigrants I interviewed grew up dancing and found nothing unusual about the clothing worn in ballroom dance competitions. From the beginning, they reported loving the work involved in creating this appearance, especially as glitter and shine appeal to most little girls. They understood early that appearance work is an essential part of being a dancer, over half of what it takes to succeed, according to Maximiliaan Winkelhuis in his advice for ballroom competitors.[2] Tsvetanka started dancing when she was four years old and switched from ballet to ballroom in kindergarten. Although dancers often look quite ordinary in daily life and must work hard to become extraordinary when performing, Tsvetanka is beautiful off the floor as well. She described the effort she put into creating and maintaining her look, long before a competition. Noting that "in dancing, appearance is one of the most important things," she took gyrotonics[3] classes twice a week in addition to several hours of dance practice a day. In the beginning, she had worried that she might get too bulky from the exercise:

> When I first started, I only went for my back, because it was hurting. Then we started to find the changes in the body. They explained to me that you would not get muscles but that the muscles would get leaner. Also, you would have more connection through the body. . . . My body became longer, more stretched. When I was nineteen, twenty, I was a bit chubby —not chubby-chubby, but my thighs were bigger. After I started to do gyrotonics, everybody said to me, "Wow, there is a big change in you." . . . I think that elongation of the muscles created more elegance.

Tsvetanka was also careful about diet. When she was younger, she and her partner would "eat whatever," but now they had a nutritionist, and they had learned "what is good and what is bad, . . . how to eat for energy."

In addition to the work on her body, Tsvetanka spent hours planning her costumes. She had had many offers from dress sponsors but was afraid to say yes, "because you have an idea for a dress, and that idea, through development, happens to be totally different at the end of the process." If you had a sponsor, this could be difficult, "because it's just not what you imagined." Instead, Tsvetanka and her partner spent considerable time and energy planning the ten or so new dresses she ordered every year:

> I have at home this little board I created many years ago. Everything I like, from the Oscars, from the Grammys, from the red carpet, I cut from the newspapers and magazines, and I put there. I make sure every day I go through it. . . . Every year, the routine is the same. You go to Blackpool, you go to the U.K.,[4] you go here and there, so you kind of know what the room looks like, which colors are good.[5] We make sure that when we are at the competition, we check other dresses. Sometimes we get inspired by what other dancers wear as well. We know the colors. We decide three months, probably, prior. We say, "This is going to be the look we are going to have." Based on that look, you do the hair; you are going to have a bun or a pony tail. Based on that, you decide what kind of makeup you are going to wear. So everything fits.

Work on the dresses did not stop with the design, however. While Tsvetanka had, as she put it, "a lady who sews for me," she economized by doing the laborious work of stoning her Latin costumes herself. This takes hours to do and is part of the reason that a fully stoned Latin dress would cost around three thousand dollars and even more for a ball gown. Jewelry adds several hundred dollars to the cost. Dresses without stoning cost several hundred dollars.

On the day of the competition, appearance work intensified:

> You put your tan on—that's the first important thing. Your dress, of course, is ready. Then it's the makeup part. I do my own makeup. You put the eyelashes and everything, and then, at that particular moment, you look in the mirror. . . . I am very bad at my hair, so [my partner] does it, since we were little kids. He used to do, actually, my makeup as well, because he was very good at that. . . . I help a little bit with his hair and sometimes the makeup.

Tsvetanka and her partner were compatible in looks, and she believed that this was important. She told me, "I've seen couples where both man and the lady are very, very good, but for some reason, the body structure, it's not as great." Having compatible body structures was "very important," she said, "if you want to have a great success." She and her partner are tall and slender with longer than average legs, and Tsvetanka believed that having similar shapes helped their dancing as well as their appearance. They coordinated their clothing to accentuate the similarity. Pavel wore made-to-measure pants and a shirt open to the waist. These cost him several hundred dollars because he knew where to get them made inexpensively. Otherwise, they would cost close to a thousand dollars. Tsvetanka's point of view was clearly echoed by two couples: Gherman Mustic and Iveta Lukosiute in figure 6.3 and Nikolai Pilipenchuk and Natalia Skorikova in color plate 7. In both cases, the women's bodies show gleaming, tanned muscles, and their height matches that of their slender male partners.

Romance and Appearance

In our culture, appearance is key to the portrayal of intimacy and connection. In movies, for example, romantic couples—particularly the women—are beautiful. When viewers speculate about romance on *Dancing with the Stars*, they speculate about handsome couples. The two couples about whom rumors spread during the spring 2010 season—Maksim Chmerkovskiy and Erin Andrews, and Cheryl Burke and Chad Ochocinco—fit this bill perfectly. Both men frequently displayed their tall, well-built bodies, and each woman represents a different type of glamour: Erin is tall, slender, and blond, and Cheryl is dark, curvy, and exotic. The seminudity and close proximity of flesh titillates the audiences, who cannot believe that these gorgeous people can resist each other. I also suggest that each couple carefully encourages speculation about the nature of their relationship, by appearing on talk shows together and allowing themselves to be caught together in public.

Ballroom dancers say that the quality of the dancing should be the most important part of competition, but they recognize that the appearance of faultless beauty helps judges and audience believe that romance is in the air. The appearance work involved in producing this illustrates the argument that the body is now part of a "self-project," which individuals shape according to their needs just as they shape other aspects of themselves—"a changeable form of existence."[6] Latin dancers such as Tsvetanka exert great discipline and control to achieve bodies that look naturally libidinous. Vigilance can never stop. In addition, the cultural mandate of thinness, particu-

1. World champions Yulia Zagorouitchenko and Riccardo Cocchi show physical and emotional connecting while dancing the rumba at the 2009 United States DanceSport Championship, in Orlando, Florida. © 2009 Jonathan S. Marion.

2. Shoes at the San Diego DanceSport Championships, San Diego, CA, 2010, and jewelry at the Desert Classic DanceSport Championships, Palm Desert, CA, 2010. © 2010 Jonathan S. Marion.

3. Glamour on the dance floor. World and Blackpool champions Katusha Demidova and Arunas Bizokas show a range of emotions at the 2008 United States DanceSport Championships, Orlando, FL. © 2008 Jonathan S. Marion.

4. Rita and Garry Gekhman performing their silver robot showdance at the 2006 United States DanceSport Championships at Hollywood Beach, FL. © 2006 Jonathan S. Marion.

5. Jive is an opportunity to show technical perfection. Maria Manusova and Eugene Katsevman perform the jive at the 2009 United States DanceSport Championships, Orlando FL. © 2009 Jonathan S. Marion.

6. Barbara Capaldi teaching a group dance lesson at the Atrium Dance Studio in Pennsauken, NJ, August 2010. © 2010 Jonathan S. Marion.

7. Natalia Skorikova and Nikolai Pilipenchuk. Genuine emotion, perfect bodies. United States DanceSport Championships, Orlando, FL, 2008. © 2008 Jonathan S. Marion.

8. Two ways of aging gracefully. Beverly Moore and Alain Doucet at the 2010 San Diego DanceSport Championships, San Diego, CA. © 2010 Jonathan S. Marion. Joan Goddard and Chris Johnston at the 2010 Emerald Ball DanceSport Championships, Los Angeles, CA. © 2010 Jonathan S. Marion.

larly for women, is exemplified on the dance floor.[7] However, whereas ballet dancers are expected to be wraithlike, with no perceptible curves, Latin and rhythm dancers are expected to be curvaceous but slender, with long legs.[8] Ballroom dancers, ideally, are more delicate than Latin and rhythm dancers are, although some American smooth women are tall and shapely. The women are not as slender as ballerinas, but no one reveals an ounce of extra fat. The appearance work that Tsvetanka performed, both as a regular routine and right before a competition, was about the production of pleasure, for the viewer, the dancer, and her partner. A desirable appearance is understood to be the product of rigorous behind-the-scenes discipline, a "calculated hedonism"[9] that dancers understand.

Aesthetic Labor

The body work described by Tsvetanka is a form of aesthetic labor, a term developed to describe the appearance work undertaken by employees whose attractive looks are part of the services sold.[10] The dancer must not only work on feelings; she or he must also work on the body to produce a look that enhances the dance. Not only are the workers' emotional labors commodified; so are their skills at creating the right look. In many industries, good-looking employees make the employer look good.[11] For dancers, the competition functions as the employer; competition organizers know the importance of beautiful professional couples and go to great lengths to attract them to their events.

Like models, creating the look that sells is essential to the dancer's job. However, whereas models try to look as if they live the life they portray, by attending fashionable parties and clubs wearing the right clothes, professional dancers are more concerned about their appearance on the dance floor.[12] Although they frequently extend that look to the area beyond the floor, most of what they do off the floor has the performance in mind.[13]

Appearance work involves considerable backstage effort. Exercise and diet help to produce the youthful, slender body idealized in our society. Professional Latin dancers, in particular, unabashedly display their bodies in outfits that are unforgiving of bulges. This is especially true of women's costumes, which have become skimpier in recent years, but the men typically wear tight clothes with shirts open to the waist. Appearance work also naturalizes gender, making it visible and obvious.[14] Formal clothing for women in Western societies is designed to show skin and to indicate the trim, sexy body of the wearer.[15] Tsvetanka's comment about compatible looks did not mean a lack of gender difference. It implied a man and woman who look as though they belong together, idealized bodies of the sort we do not see in everyday life. Such bodies are the stuff of romantic dreams and facilitate the audience's desire to imagine romance. Ballroom audiences are more knowledgeable about dancing than are television audiences, but they still respond to gorgeous couples. One way a couple can make this happen is to dress in clothing that shows they are a matched pair. In figure 5.1, wearing silver outfits studded with rhinestones and showing bodies without an ounce of extra fat, Nazar Norov and Irina Kudryashova, a young Latin couple, have only their hair color as a counterpoint to their otherwise matching appearance.

A Short History of Dance Dresses

The dancers' clothing is even more important than the bodies they transform. Clothing, more than anything else, signifies glamour in our culture.[16] As a young woman growing up in Britain in the 1950s, I used to watch the television show *Come Dancing* with my parents, who were avid fans.[17] At that time, the clothing was less revealing but harder to dance in. In ballroom, the men wore tails, and the women wore full dresses with many layers of net underneath, so that the skirts stuck out on all sides. In Latin, the women wore shorter versions of the same dress, sometimes with a longer overskirt for ballroom that they could take off when they needed a quick change. These dresses had appeared in the early 1950s, contrasting with those worn in the 1930s, when Ginger Rogers held sway in dance movies wearing long clinging dresses that floated when she moved.

When the women wore such full skirts, couples had to be careful, because the front of the woman's dress could easily bunch between the man's legs. Instead of the woman coming into the man, as happens now, he had to come into her so he could push her dress away with his body to move in closer.[18] Furthermore, the dress bounced up and down rather than flowing with the couple's movements.

Ball-gown designer Deirdre Baker claims credit for the revival of what came to be called the "Ginger Rogers gown." Deirdre, a dancer from Australia, started her dress business in London in 1977, while she was still competing.[19] Although lifts are not allowed in competitions, she and her husband performed in shows where lifts were common, and the stiff ball

Fig. 5.1. Perfection. Irina Kudryashova and Nazar Norov, a Latin couple on the way up, are careful to coordinate a perfect appearance, including bodies, clothing, and hair. 2010 Emerald Ball DanceSport Championships, Los Angeles, CA. © 2010 Jonathan S. Marion.

gowns made them difficult. Deirdre was asked to make an old-fashioned Ginger Rogers gown first for amateur ballroom dancer Sue Potter, then for Helen Stuart at the U.K. Closed Competition at the beginning of the 1980s.[20] Helen's dress was a sensation. Immediately after the competition, all the dancers who had ordered dresses from Deirdre for the U.K. Open canceled their orders and asked for Ginger Rogers gowns instead, similar to the one Ginger Rogers can be seen wearing in figure 5.2.[21] Within a couple years, everyone was wearing the new style.[22]

In addition to allowing the man to invite his partner to come into him, which made for a more graceful beginning, the new dresses allowed more use of the upper body, more fast spins, and more long gliding motions. They also created the appearance of a more intimate connection, because the couple was physically closer, and as the man guided his partner around the floor, the dress accentuated their movements. This can be seen by comparing video of two former World and Blackpool champions dancing the foxtrot: Bill and Bobbie Irvine in the 1960s,[23] and Mirko Gozzoli and Alessia Betti in 2009.[24] Clothing styles for men dancing ballroom have barely changed since the 1930s; men still wear tail suits. In the first video, Bobbie Irvine wears a bright red dress about as wide as it is long. The skirt ends at her knees, and she dances demurely around the floor with her slightly bent knees showing clearly.[25] She has a beautiful top line but looks quite stiff underneath. Of the two, Bill takes bolder steps. The dress is pushed between them and flows around the sides of his body as he attempts to get closer. Bobbie dances gracefully, and her connection with her partner transcends the dress but is hampered by it. In contrast, Alessia Betti, in a long turquoise dress that moves with her, spins and turns, dancing with her body as well as her legs. She and her partner dance closely with legs intertwined, something that was impossible in the older style of dress. Alessia's dress is reminiscent of Ginger Rogers dancing the foxtrot with Fred Astaire in the 1930s.[26] It is hard to imagine why dancers such as Bobbie put up with such stiff dresses for over twenty years, when they were so difficult to dance in.

In *The Dancing Years*, Bill Irvine describes how he and his wife rose to the top of ballroom competition.[27] It is interesting to contrast his description of their appearance work with that of today's dancers. No mention is ever made about diet and exercise, except to note that Bobbie thought she gained weight when they took a rare two-week vacation. There are descriptions of some of the dresses she wore and an amusing story about their trip to Japan, where dresses occupied most of the tiny hotel room. The Irvines used to drive everywhere in Britain, rather than taking other forms of

Fig. 5.2. Ginger Rogers and Fred Astaire in *Swing Time.* © Bettman/CORBIS.

transportation, because the dresses took up so much room. Photographs of the couple show Bill as a well-dressed man with a bald head and the kind of teeth that scream "British working class." Unlike top professional men today, he saw no reason to fix his teeth. Bobbie looks immaculate, although little is said about her appearance in the book, other than occasional comments about the beauty of her dresses. Even when she was at the pinnacle of her career, she was buying her own clothes and doing her own makeup. Her hair is never mentioned, nor is her slender body or her remarkable eyes. The couple can be seen in figure 5.3 with Bobby in a typical dance dress. The Irvines were apparently more concerned with how they danced —of which there are many lyrical descriptions—than how they looked.

Fig. 5.3. Bill and Bobby Irvine receiving the Embassy Trophy from ballet dancer Beryl Grey. © Hulton-Deutsch Collection/CORBIS.

They describe none of the day-to-day appearance work that dancers engage in now; "work" meant dance practice. Now, as Jonathan Marion notes, "to assume that it is only in motion that dancers express their dance would be a mistake as their costuming . . . is itself communicative of the underlying mythology."[28] He appropriates the term Roland Barthes applied to wrestling, a "spectacle of excess," and finds it equally appropriate for the world of competitive dance.[29] Ballroom dance harks back to the Hollywood movies of the 1930s, which presented a life of effortless everyday glamour.

Dressing and Performing

Liliya provides another illustration of how little girls are socialized into the glamour of dance. Her earliest memories were about clothing. In her first ballroom competition, she wore "one of those little short skirts where you can see the underwear—it was yellow, in the polka dot." Liliya added, "As far as dancing, don't ask me. I don't remember." This admission from one of the world's top ballroom dancers that her appearance had been more important to her than her performance starkly contrasts with the Irvines' account.

Liliya's childhood passion for clothing and glamour had fueled her love of dance. Asked which competitions she most remembered, she quickly turned to appearance work:

> I think all of them is exciting, because I loved competing. I loved getting ready. The little girl is probably in it. That's how you get in it. You love to put the dress on, do the makeup, because at this age you're not allowed to do the makeup, especially in Russia at that time. To school, we had to wear uniform, no makeup, no jewelry, no nothing.

Now that she was an adult, who competed in all the major competitions and performed in numerous shows each year, Liliya's dress routine had become less exciting and more routinized—just part of the job. However, she still paid careful attention to clothing, and she always looked lovely:

> It takes me probably about three hours. I'm pretty good at doing my hair now. I can almost do it in fifteen minutes. . . . The major competitions, I have a hair stylist, and when she's around, she helps me a lot. Most of the time, if we're in Japan or anything, I have to do my own hair: hair, makeup,

get everything ready. I try to get in about half an hour of yoga before the performance. You warm up, and the rest is all wonderful things. . . . I have a sponsor in Japan, and they make me probably forty dresses a year. I always have the pick of what I would like to wear. It depends on the music. I always joke, but for the major competitions, I pick my dress up on the day of the comp, because it all depends. If you decide to wear red, and this day you just wake up and you do not feel red—because the red dress is the red dress, you have to feel great in it. Like Blackpool, I had about six, seven dresses. Everybody's laughing at me, but I have to do that. I have to feel right in my dress.

Liliya and her partner always checked each other's appearance, and because each was so experienced, this did not lead to tensions. Sometimes they wanted "to portray something in particular" in a performance, and then they would talk together to see how to evoke the mood. Because they danced ballroom, Liliya's partner wore a black tail suit and had few decisions to make. Occasionally for a show, he would wear a dinner jacket instead of the tails and sometimes a black tie or even a black shirt.

Liliya's current partnership was new, and they had been practicing more than usual. As a result, she had cut out some exercise:

Not even Pilates and yoga right now. I need that time off for my body to recover. . . . I still probably do twice a week. If I am away, I can do yoga. I can only do Pilates if I'm here. . . . If I go to the city, I actually prefer gyrotonics to Pilates. It's more three dimensional. Where I am right now, I have a Pilates studio right across the street.

In addition to the exercise, Liliya did not smoke or drink. While she was not overly concerned with her weight, she remained careful. She described the way she ate as "healthy enough," explaining that she tried to eat fruits and vegetables. Her only food sin was coffee: "I cannot live without the coffee," she said, waving her cup at me as she spoke.

Critiques of Appearance Work

On the face of it, these stories exemplify what Juliet McMains calls "Glamour addiction."[30] McMains, who has been a competitive dancer, makes her stance clear in the heading of her book's preface, "Confessions of a

Glamour Addict." After admitting to being "in love with the flow of energy between two people, fixated on the physical mastery, attracted to the spotlight, and driven by competition," she adds, "it was Glamour that pinned me to the wall, that kept me hooked long after commitment and dedication had hardened into obsession and compulsion."[31] McMains argues that the ballroom industry produces Glamour[32] (a word that she always capitalizes) as a desirable object, which is "simultaneously visible and inaccessible"—a state that increases desire and encourages dancers to spend more money for more lessons, outfits, and competitions in the elusive hope of obtaining it.[33] Unfortunately, McMains never differentiates victims from exploiters; she describes a world where each actor preys on the next and where no agency exists. Viewing Liliya's attention to her appearance as an addiction belittles the genuine pleasure that she got from looking beautiful on the dance floor and underestimates dancers' complicity in appearance work.

Part of the explanation for McMains's disapproval of bodily projects is that Western society positions the body and desire as in opposition to society, technology, and reason. Desire is suspect and seen as disruptive of civilization. Yet this is a false dichotomy; reason is as much a social construct as desire is. Dancers celebrate the body and take pleasure in its display. They often do this somewhat furtively, since hedonism is suspect in this culture, even among those who love dance.[34] A review by *New York Times* dance critic Alastair Macaulay was headlined, "Ballroom: More Sexily, Less Strictly." The subheading continued, "A Once-Refined Genre Adds Lifts, Splits, and Exposed Flesh."[35] Macaulay expressed outrage at the performances in ballroom show dance, particularly the clothing, which he described as "women wearing elaborate versions of the bikini and men with shirts open to their navel." This critic prefers the asexuality and lightness of ballet to the earthiness of ballroom and Latin dance. He regularly decries what he views as exhibitionism and laments his inability to distinguish eroticism from porn on the Broadway stage.[36]

Gender and Appearance

Gender scholar Susan Bordo, in her book *Unbearable Weight*, describes a culture in which slender athletic bodies have come to represent the ideal woman in control of her appearance and destiny.[37] From this perspective, women are logically responding to the culture when they go to great lengths to monitor how they look. Yet this pressure combines with the power women experience from looking beautiful. The history of American beauty culture "has never been only a regimen of self-appraisal and surveillance."[38] Women use clothing and makeup for many purposes, including a declaration of adulthood, of sexual allure, and of the ability to define themselves. When Liliya was a child, part of her pleasure in appearance work was the temporary adult status it conferred on her as well as the sense it gave her of being special, in a country where few opportunities for uniqueness existed. Dancers dress for themselves as well as for audiences, and for those of us for whom glamour is not a dirty word, the brightness and glitter of the dance floor proclaim its devotion to the pleasures of looking.

By the 1990s, men were also being socialized into the joys of presenting oneself as a desirable object.[39] How do men in the dance world respond to the pressure for appearance work? They relish their embodiment of traditional but glamorous masculinity—either the elegant gentleman or the Latin lover—yet many feel obliged to make their partner the focal point of the performance.[40]

Boris, a ballroom dancer who competed with his wife, exemplified the view that men showcase women. He described the man's role as "to present the lady and to take care of her," adding, "I think it's the same as the role of the man in normal life, not much difference at all." This paternalism, common among male dancers, especially immigrants, maintains a heterosexual masculinity even as men spend their days with women. In describing the work of preparing for a competition, Boris's emphasis was on his wife's appearance:

> Besides the quality of your movement and choreography, you must look right. That's the dress, hairstyle, makeup, and also all the things—schedule, we order the food, the drink. . . . We always discuss, make design, make sure the dress is ready for the competition. . . . It doesn't matter your quality of dancing; if you don't look good on the floor, judges don't mark you.

In addition to Boris's showcasing his wife on the dance floor, he ironed all her dresses (as many as five for a show) and often did her hair. Although he considered the woman's appearance most important, Boris acknowledged that the man's looks also matter. He felt disadvantaged in this, because, he said, "I'm not very beautiful. I know there's much more beautiful men, so they have a big advantage." As a result, he thought, "I have to dance better, basically, to beat that, because some people are really handsome at all ages." In past competitions, he remembered comments such as, "Oh, your techniques are superb, but he's so handsome." This meant, unfortunately, that "they give them priority because of the look, the image they create." While women worried about their weight, they never described themselves as "not beautiful." Boris tried to make up for his plain appearance by looking immaculate. "The hairstyle, the makeup, the tail suit, and the dresses, shoes, all matters," he explained, and "all should be high class, expensive." Boris was spending around two hundred dollars for each pair of shoes he bought—and they wore out fast—and his tail suit could have cost fifteen hundred dollars or more for one that was made to measure, with shirt and tie costing extra, although he no doubt knew where to get them made more inexpensively.

Pavel, who has appeared in earlier chapters, was Tsvetanka's husband and partner, and he was interested in their joint appearance. Partners, he said, "have to match well, and they have to look beautiful, and they have to match the bodies." To accomplish this, Pavel worked on every aspect of the body and its presentation. He did not want to be too "chubby" or too skinny, and he was careful about his diet. In addition to practice and the many hours he spent coaching and teaching, he took gyrotonics classes, had a Pilates machine at home, and trained at the gym with a personal trainer. In addition, he designed dresses for his wife:

> I will have ten ideas, and I really don't know at the end which one. . . . I will sit at dinner and say, "Now, Tsvetanka I tell you ten dresses," and when I start telling her, I have fifteen really. Then I close my eyes, and I say, "Okay, which was my first? Which one I feel really open about?" Then I design what I want. This is a good thing, because it's very creative, but it's sometimes very distracting.

Because dance relies so much on the woman's appearance, men who wanted to do well wanted to control this aspect of the performance as much as the choreography.

Pavel had a complicated routine before every competition:

> You sleep longer. You go to have breakfast or lunch, and then we drink coffee. Then I do a little exercise, like stomach exercise, push-up. Then I shave. Then I make Tsvetanka's hair. I like to do her hair. Then I do my hair. Then she starts to do her makeup, and I'm looking at her, what she's doing, and I tell her, "Do more of this. Don't do that." Normally, before, we fix some costumes, if something has to be done or we want to experiment

something new. Two hours before the competition, we are ready, and then we warm up together. We listen to some music. My iPod has certain books. We listen to some nice things, and we talk. . . . In the beginning—when we didn't know how to dance so good—because we always dress well, we always did good. . . . Sometimes you go to practice, and you see very good couples, and you're like, "Wow, damn, they're very good." Then the competition starts, and they wear crap. The girl has such a gorgeous body, and she puts so much stuff on her, she looks like a Christmas tree. . . . When you compete, you have to impress the people with your appearance and look before you dance.

Pavel added that clothing should show dancers' best features and hide those they do not want attention drawn to.

Pavel was so concerned about the appearance of the couple that he did not like dancing with students who were overweight. He used to have "chubby" students but wanted "elegant, skillful" ones, thus implying that fat students could be neither. He was now happier with his students, telling me, "I have good-shaped ladies" with whom to dance pro/am.

American Masculinity and Appearance

American men who competed were also concerned about appearance, but they talked about it differently than did immigrants, possibly because American men do not typically think they should be too appearance conscious. Mark, whom we met in chapter 4, always looked immaculate on the dance floor. He competed with many students as well as with his wife, but he described his appearance work nonchalantly, declaring, "We always try to present ourselves the same way when we're out there with our students." When he and his wife performed, he "might put on a different, slightly newer suit," but little else changed in his appearance.

Like the immigrant men, however, Mark paid attention to his wife's appearance:

I was involved in the dress designs, for the most part. I had this picture and this vision of what I wanted my partner to produce as a woman. I do feel responsible for her persona, because of the style of dresses she always chose in the beginning. I had a large hand in that. She has very strong features. She's very curvy. She's got a fabulous figure, and every single dress she put on looked great on her. She always had great taste when it came to dresses, but as far as the styles, I enjoyed having a hand.

Mark's description is typical of the way American male dancers talked about appearance work. They were interested in their partner's appearance but left it up to her to put it all together.

Matt was an exception. He viewed himself as more interested in appearance because he is gay. Like the immigrant men, he paid attention to every aspect of his partner's appearance. Two of his professional partners "were blond and had light eyes," which contrasted with Matt's "dark eyes and dark hair and darker skin." He thought hard about how to make the difference work, asking, "What colors will work best with the partnership?" and "What designs will work on each of our bodies?" He exercised avidly, took great care with his grooming, and made sure that his costumes were perfect, because, he noted, "You are being judged on your appearance."

However, Matt went even further. Many male professionals became somewhat involved in their students' appearance, helping them select clothing and advising them about hair and makeup, but Matt really pitched in:

> Sometimes I help them put together a costume they can compete in, especially when you get a dancer not willing to make the investment of a really expensive dress. So we'll modify a dress. We'll rhinestone it—what pattern, where to rhinestone it, which colors work best for their body. . . . If they bring me something with a straight hem, where it needs cutting on the bias, when they bring it to their seamstress, I'll tell them where to cut it.

In addition to Matt's help with dresses, he said,

> I'm a little bit different from a lot of the teachers because I can help and assist the students with hair and makeup, which I'll do lots of times, especially if they're new students and not familiar with how to do that for themselves. . . . Sometimes you have a student with very little makeup, and all of a sudden you have to have stage makeup, and you have to have stage hair. I'll spend lots of time with them early in the morning, wake up early and go to their room, and we prepare: get them into their costume, get them made up, get their hair done, whatever it takes.

In constructing himself as a gay man who danced, Matt had become the perfect gay friend to his partners.[41] In helping them with every aspect of their appearance and in spending time with them perfecting the look, he fitted a comfortable stereotype of gay men who know and care about these things.

Appearance and Consumption

In Phoebe's story in chapter 1, we saw how far students will go for the perfect dress and appearance. Some students, however, spent much more money than she did and bought many more dresses. Becky-Sue bought a new dress each year, "sometimes two," and she bought them from expensive dress designers such as Chrisanne.[42] She had been dancing for fifteen years and was constantly trying to sell her old dresses. Becky-Sue explained, "Everyone has to be a certain size, and it has to be the right color, or they don't like the style of it or whatever, and dresses do go out of style." Becky-Sue owned "at least twelve or fifteen dresses," which she divided according to the uses to which she put them, including "free-style dresses" and what she called "my scholarship dresses, which are generally my nicer, more elegant ones." As a result, she was able to change clothes frequently while competing.

Becky-Sue's teacher was demanding about appearance, which Becky-Sue appreciated, although she believed there was no substitute for her own judgment:

> He takes pride in the fact that his students are well groomed, and we do ask his opinion with dresses. It doesn't mean we like it or respect it or even we'll do it. . . . I have a pretty good idea of what I look good in on the floor. I'm an older lady. I'm not going to go for the short little things. I try to keep it very classy, sexy but sophisticated, and that's kind of my look, or what I think my look is. [My teacher], he's kept it like that. He insists we get our hair and makeup done, and he wants approval of the dress. . . . He would not let us go out in something that he would find inappropriate.

Some dancers get their makeup and hair done by professional makeup artists at the competitions. Although a few professional dancers may use professional makeup artists, most of the makeup artists' business derives from students. Working on half-hourly appointments, makeup artists can be found on the competition websites of all but the smallest events, and students call ahead for appointments. Competitors with long, thick hair almost always need help putting it into the complicated upswept styles popular in DanceSport, the name often used for competitive dancing. In addition, students are not used to applying stage makeup, even if they wear makeup every day, and most do not know how to attach false eyelashes. Sometimes makeup artists work in pairs, sharing the expense of a room and turning students over to each other when one is booked for the desired time.

At big competitions, the makeup room will be a hive of activity, with two dancers in the chairs and two more waiting. The dancers are typically about to compete against each other—because hair and makeup are done just before competitors are due on the floor—yet the atmosphere is friendly. The television is often blaring with some sort of "women's show" such as *Montel Williams* or *Live with Regis and Kelly*, and the women in the room may make comments back to the television; often this consists of the sort of "girl talk" that indicates that men cannot be trusted. Because the dancing may start as early as seven a.m., and many beginning dancers need help with their appearance, appointments may start as early as three thirty or four a.m. for the bronze-level dancers who are first on the floor.

The hotel room is brightly lit, and the beds are covered with the extras that might be needed: eyelashes, hair ornaments, hair pieces to make thicker buns or longer pony tails, and extra makeup for sale. Each makeup artist brings his or her own makeup, and after inquiring about the color of the dress, the makeup artist gets to work. The air is sticky with hairspray—each hairdo must be absolutely firm and last the entire day (or several days for elaborate dos). Women bring dance dresses with them if time is short or if they need help getting into them. Appointments are by the half hour for either makeup or hair—it takes an hour for both—and appointments cost around $60. So a woman having her hair and makeup done two days in a row may spend around $240 plus tip.

Makeup artists are drawn mainly from the ranks of former or current professional competitors. Having learned how to do their own hair and makeup, they then begin working on other women as a supplement to incomes. I talked to one such former dancer. While still competing, she was recruited by another makeup artist to provide backup. This woman taught her a great deal more than she already knew, and they now work together at the larger competitions and take turns doing the smaller ones, so that each gets some weekends at home. The dancer told me that she would be going to twenty-one competitions during the year, so she would be away from her family for many weekends. Sometimes she worked almost the entire week at big competitions lasting five or even six days. Everywhere she went, she carried heavy cases of materials with her.

Outside the dance floor, at most competitions, there are several top designers selling clothes. Because dresses are designed to move with a dancer's body, the fabric stretches, and dancers of different sizes can get into the same dress, sometimes with minor alterations. Each designer hangs his or her dresses in a designated space, where women move from one designer to another, trying them on in makeshift dressing rooms. Once a woman has selected a dress, she then goes to one of the jewelry counters to choose matching jewelry. Some women get carried away and buy more dresses than they are going to use, seduced by the brilliant fabrics and the excitement of it all.

When women and men first start competing, they have no idea how well groomed judges expect them to be. Teachers talk to one another about students who dance well but have not yet learned that hair must be completely smooth and makeup should look like a mask; normal attractiveness is insufficient. This is sometimes quite difficult for students to understand. Furthermore, students do not always like the sleek look that is considered glamorous in the dance world. Coming to terms with all this is part of developing a dancing identity.

Wendy, the dancer from chapter 3, had always worn heavy makeup, so when she competed, she said, "I just shove it up to an uber level." Still, she had to pay someone to put eyelashes on for her, even though she hated wearing them, and she had to get her hair done because her teacher insisted:

> [My teacher] is like, "Is your hair smooth?" I mean like plastered to my head with gel. I don't particularly like my hair that way, but I don't care because I don't like my hair off my face. Once I'm into the thing where I'm going to do the hair, then what does it matter? It's not going to make me happy anyway. . . . I often don't like the way they do the makeup on me.

Wendy had resisted her teacher's desire to pick her dresses, preferring to design her own with the designer's assistance. Her teacher kept telling her to increase the stoning to make the dress more decorative, but she is five feet three inches tall and has large breasts. As she put it, "I'm pretty much decorated standing naked, so we don't need to put a lot of extra stuff on me." Although Wendy thought she was good at designing, she conceded, "there are some costumes I have had made that have not worked at all." However, others had been "spectacularly fabulous." Wendy regularly changed her dresses, working hard to sell those she tired of, and she bought two or three new dresses a year.

In spite of weight training and Pilates, Wendy struggled with her weight, which tended to balloon if she was not careful. She found this frustrating and considered it to be part of the "aging pile of crap." She also understood that dancers' appearances are frequently subject to judgment. Pro/am students are typically more svelte and youthful looking than the average American is—as can be seen in the pictures in this book—which is not surprising, given the amount of exercise and appearance work involved in dancing and the vigilance dancers exert. Only the occasional dancer may be seriously overweight, which Wendy certainly was not.

Some dancers who did not have Wendy's wealth were fortunate in finding a dress sponsor. Leanne was one of the top pro/am students, having won many first places in different styles of dance at her own age level and a level below. She was tall and slender and told me her only problem was "being underweight." She described herself as having a "fast-food lifestyle," adding, "I can go all morning without eating and then four or five o'clock in the evening have a fast-food meal and then at ten, eleven o'clock that night eat cookies and ice cream."

Leanne was divorced and lived in a small house, which looked as if she was hardly there. She danced with a top teacher, and her money went on lessons and the many competitions she attended. She had an interesting story about how she managed her thick hair and her makeup:

> I've been doing it for so long, it's become routine now, but a lot of things have been trial and error over the years, of what works and what doesn't. Where it used to take me two hours to get ready, it takes me forty-five minutes now. I don't do anything really special. I just know the makeup's got to go on. I do my own hair. . . . That was one of the reasons in the beginning I cut my hair off, just so I didn't have to go to those terribly early hair appointments. They weren't for me. . . . The more that you can have not to stress about on the day that you're dancing, the better off you are. For the most part, I know how I'm going to wear my hair. I know how I'm going to wear my makeup. I know which dress I'm going to wear.

Leanne's sponsorship was the result of her skill and her tall, slender shape, which showcased dresses beautifully. Sometimes she would only get to wear a dress once before somebody bought it. She was now working for a dress sponsor, going to events and selling dresses even when she was not competing. This provided her with income and also paid for some of her competition expenses.

Most of the amateurs dancing pro/am whom I interviewed were not as fortunate as Leanne, and many had to be creative about clothing. A young widow who had to pay all her own expenses from her human-services salary, Claudia, competed when she could afford to. She loved the appearance work, which started long before the competition:

> I diet like crazy beforehand. . . . I try my costume on, probably fifty times. I am very meticulous how I lay everything out in my bedroom when I check in the hotel. I carry everything with me on the plane, which is a challenge. I carry hair pieces. I carry hair ornaments, anything I think I might need, and dresses and foundations and stockings and God knows what else. When I went to Emerald,[43] I must have packed six pairs of fishnet stockings, just because, "What if I should rip a hole in one, then another one, then another one?" Then shoes and your shoe brushes.[44] Part of the fun is all the accoutrements. . . . I love getting dressed up in these costumes. It's hilarious, but I love it. Look at me sitting here in this business suit. . . . I really like getting dressed up. I like putting on makeup. I like putting on jewelry. I like putting on sparkly things. I love looking sexy. I think it's fabulous, and why not? I love to see guys getting all dressed up, get their hair all slicked back and put on their costumes and everything.

This comment illustrates both the pleasure women had in transforming themselves and the complicity with which they accepted the cultural norms that all women want to be beautiful and that being beautiful means being sexy. This was rational behavior because, as we have seen, dancing intimacy is more believable when these requirements are met.

Part of Claudia's preparation work resulted from her careful financial calculations. Most of what she lugged on the plane, in fear of losing her luggage, could be purchased at the competition, but Claudia did not want any unexpected expenditures. She was also careful about purchasing dresses. When she first started competing, she had bought two dresses directly from a designer for some of the top companies, whose prices were lower if one bought directly. She was careful about what she wanted, instructing him in her "trouble areas," such as her stomach, and telling him she did not want a lot of skin showing. She did not want "to look clownish." When the dresses arrived, she was delighted with them, telling me that her "legs have never looked so good" as they did in her rhythm dress.

Claudia also bought clothes to wear to lessons and studio parties: "ordinary stuff I can buy in Ross or T. J. Maxx or Dress Barn." These had spandex in them, so they worked well for dancing. Her newest ball gown was even less expensive than the first two. "A woman in Ohio" made the dress and altered it when it did not quite fit. The woman did enough of the stoning for Claudia to see the proposed pattern, and Claudia glued on the rest of the stones herself. The dress cost a fraction of what it would have cost if bought at a competition. Claudia was more resourceful than most dancers were about saving money on appearance, but others used similar tactics.

Social Dance and Dressing Up

Even though social dancers do not spend as much on their appearance as competitive dancers do, they care about how they look. At a typical practice party or social dance, most of the women are well dressed, in skirts and dresses that flip out as they move. Some wear clothes that sparkle. The men are more casual in pants and shirts, but they look like they have made an effort. Most dancers have invested in dance shoes with suede soles, making it easier to glide across the floor. The social dancers I interviewed spent money on clothes for dancing and liked to look nice when they went out dancing. The men wore what they described as "nice slacks," meaning that they thought about appearance. The trouble they took over their appearance heightened the sense that dancing was glamorous and romantic. A typical example can be seen in a group socializing at a studio party in figure 5.4.

Dance instructors teach appearance work to their students. In one issue of the *Delaware Valley Dance Spotlight*, editor Vivian Beiswenger wrote a column on dance etiquette.[45] First on the list was "Dress for Success." In this section, she noted that dance is a "social activity that involves sharing your personal space with others." She advised students to take special care with personal hygiene, to use mouthwash and mints, and to take a mint if offered, as it could be a hint. She also advised on shoe and clothing fashions and extolled the virtues of dressing up occasionally.

The social dance teachers I interviewed made an effort with their own appearance. They dressed attractively when they taught lessons or ran

Fig. 5.4. Social dancers get dressed up for a studio practice party at DanceSport Academy, Ardmore, PA, July 2010. © 2010 Jonathan S. Marion.

dance parties because they wanted students to feel that these were special events. Sometimes teachers had to learn how to do this. Doreen was an older dancer who had started teaching straight out of high school:

> I went five nights a week, and I always got dressed up. . . . At that time, paisley and minis were coming in. . . . I was still a Catholic girl—I was definitely old-fashioned. . . . I didn't color my hair. One of the girls was a hair dresser, so she totally redid me. She taught me how to put on makeup and made me wear padded bras. They all later told me they really liked me, but I was dressed like a dork. My mother made my clothes. . . . I had exactly two weeks of clothes to wear.

So critical were the other teachers that they told Doreen she should burn one of the dresses that she had really liked up to that point.

For women who want to have an intimate, romantic experience, the world of ballroom dancing holds many attractions. We should not be surprised that their purchase of intimacy goes hand in hand with the over-the-top look of glamour that dancers try to achieve, particularly in competition circles. When Eva Illouz analyzed advertisements from middle-class American magazines promising romance, she found that they were directed toward what was portrayed as "the good life," in particular to clothing, makeup, jewelry, hotels, and travel—all items that figure prominently in the life of a competitive dancer.[46] Along with liquor and cigarettes, these were the markers of romance and affluence. When her respondents were asked to describe romantic experiences, many of them described luxurious and exotic activities and places outside their normal milieu. Ballroom, whether on the competition floor or simply as a Saturday night out, provides this sense of glamour and romance to both single and married people. That sense can be put away when the user returns to the everyday world, and it is ready to be brought out again as needed. This association of glamour and desire is particularly marked for women.[47] Male dancers reinforce this association by focusing on their partner's appearance rather than on their own.

It should not surprise us that women who dance do more appearance work than do male dancers. Many writers have noted that women associate looks with romance. Indeed, in an earlier study of women who had been diagnosed with breast cancer, I found that the appearance changes associated with surgery and chemotherapy had a negative effect on women's sexual desire.[48] Women are the main consumers of cosmetic surgery and beauty products in general. The dance world differs from other worlds in the level of attention that men pay to women's appearance—attention that can be affirming as well as judgmental.

Appearance work is important is developing the identity of being a dancer. Perfect posture, for example, goes with a dancer at all times. The dancing identity involves more that simply appearance, however, and it is to this topic that we now turn.

6

Taking the Lead

The Male Dancer

JAMES, A HANDSOME and charming American-born dance instructor in his early forties, co-owns a studio in a southern state and is a regular fixture on the competition circuit. When I interviewed him at his studio, we were interrupted by students who told me how much they liked him and what a wonderful teacher he was.

James's journey to becoming a dancer was a long one. He "grew up in a little bit of a rough neighborhood" and had thought that he might become a police officer. He easily passed the exam, but they were going to place him in vice, and he "didn't want to do that." In addition, his "uncle had a [dance] school right outside of" a large naval base. James explained, "My uncle's about five feet seven, and I'm now like six feet. We used to get a lot of navy pilots with their wives, and he needed a taller teacher, so he got me in."[1]

James spent two years learning to dance before teaching, and at first he resisted. His friends gave him a hard time about it, partly because they assumed that only gay men danced. Even now, James acknowledged, "If I'm in a rough bar, I won't tell people what I do." He added, "I was the worst student in the world, 'cause I didn't come in wanting to learn to dance, so I didn't put in as much effort as *my* students do." He danced, he explained, to help his family.

His reservations are typical of many American men. Dance has long been understood to be something women do. Men who dance put their gender into question.[2] This negative portrayal goes back at least three hundred years in the West.[3] Sociologists Candace West and Don Zimmerman describe such threatening feelings as a result of what they call "doing gender."[4] In our culture, they argue, we learn to actively perform gender in line with accepted configurations. Furthermore, we police ourselves for behavior that others might see as gender inappropriate, lest we be called to account. This starts in the school playground when boys get named as "fags" or "girls" if they are caught appearing or behaving in a manner deemed feminine.[5] Similar accusations are commonly made against male dancers.[6]

As James acclimated to the dance world, he became comfortable with a variety of gender and sexual identities. In our culture, men carefully police masculinity and heterosexuality in others; both are closely associated with appropriate gender performance.[7] In many American high schools, boys view dance as an activity that qualifies a boy for "fagdom." In one study, boys described a boy who danced well and swiveled his hips as "disgusting," because they saw his ability to dance as an activity engaged in by girls.[8]

The idea of gender as a performance was developed by Judith Butler.[9] She calls this "performativity," the repetitions and rituals of performance that naturalize gender and render it normal. It is only during transgressive moments, such as drag performances, that gender may be understood to be manufactured rather than natural. In some ways, American men who dance can be seen in a similar light. Men who dance widen the allowable markers of masculinity, yet this creates a dangerous tension for many male dancers and makes it imperative that they work hard to develop a "natural" masculinity both within and outside the dance world. Figure 6.1 shows Peter and Alexandra Perzhu dancing rhythm. In this picture, although Peter is wearing a sparkling shirt, one that most masculine or heterosexual men might not wear, he is clearly performing a scene of male dominance.

How did James make the transition from a tough-guy masculine performance to that of a ballroom dance professional comfortable spending hours teaching women to dance, taking them to competitions, helping them select dance dresses, and worrying about their appearance? In other words, how did James learn to create the kind of emotional connection that many people see as women's work, while at the same time retaining a strong masculine and heterosexual identity?[10] Is this still doing gender "as we know it"?[11] James and other male dancers embody the type of man that Susan Bordo describes as typical of 1930s movies: "a man a woman could have fun with"[12]—that is, a "woman-made man" of whom Rudolph Valentino can be considered the archetype.[13] Becoming a male dancer is a "particular kind of project" involving the integration of seemingly contradictory identifications.[14] In examining how James undertook this project, we can see that he integrated his masculine identity into his dance identity in three ways. He continued to embody elements of hegemonic masculinity acceptable in the larger culture; he tailored a version of this masculinity for the dance word; and he developed elements of masculinity more acceptable in the dance world than outside it.

Fig. 6.1. Dancing like a man. Peter Perzhu dancing rhythm with his partner, Alexandra Perzhu, at the 2009 United States DanceSport Championships, Orlando, FL. © 2009 Jonathan S. Marion.

Masculinity varies by social class.[15] While many working-class men base their sense of manhood on physical labor and the ability to fight their way out of a tough situation, many middle-class men rely on economic success to demonstrate manhood. In becoming a dancer, James made a social class transition away from toughness. Yet he did not transform himself into a typical middle-class man. James learned how to become the man Bordo describes, something not class specific: "a man women can have fun with."

The identity of a professional male dancer is multifaceted, but one must dance so well that other dancers consider one to be an insider. This takes hours of practice, and it is through this practice that the professional dancer separates himself from the pack. Most students do not have the stamina or ability to repeat combinations of steps for long hours by themselves; yet this is essential for professional success. These hours of practice are especially important for American men, who do not usually start learning until their late teens. This reflects the hard-work-leads-to-success values of middle-class masculine culture but in an activity not in itself seen as masculine.

Several men, including James, told me that it was difficult to learn to dance, something they would not perhaps have said about more masculine endeavors such as skateboarding or shooting pool. James reported bad posture and difficulty in holding his frame correctly. He had to develop musicality, because, like most men of his social background, he had never had music lessons. However, in learning to dance, James was able to use his experience playing many and hard and dangerous sports. He had grown up on the coast, and he had been an avid surfer:

> [Learning to use my core] wasn't so hard, I think, because of surfing. And as the time went on, from surfing and motor cars and skiing, that wasn't too bad, but at the beginning it wasn't easy. . . . I think my flexibility was okay—I've done a lot of martial arts, and the martial arts helped that. . . . It's different, because with dancing you breathe up or soften the knees. I think I'm not as flexible as some of the other people. . . . [Learning to move fast?] I'm not too little. You had to make sure your body was in the right place. I think, because of the sports I did, it wasn't that hard of a thing for me as it would be for some. Yet I know there's a lot of people who are faster than me. . . . Surfing helped me, because it taught me where my center of balance was. . . . I didn't have a problem with strength.

Athletic success is based on superior force and skill, which had led James to a secure masculine identity.[16] Furthermore, the sports he liked emphasized physical ability and daring. Historically, male dancers have used their athletic prowess to demonstrate that "real men" can dance and not be sissies.[17] Once James started to view dancing as yet another athletic endeavor, he became more comfortable. He came to this understanding by seeing connections between his sports activities and dance:

> Dancing can give you a feeling that nothing else can give you. I mean, I've raced cars, I've surfed and skied and all that kind of stuff, and I enjoy that because it's physical. But there's something about moving around with another person and moving at the same time and doing it well. This is the only team sport I know, and it *is* a team. All the other things I do, that's by myself.

Dance is more than a sport. Furthermore, team sports are places where both homophobia and sexism are rife, while dance is a world where both are at least muted.[18]

Professional competition is another way that male dancers can solidify a dancer identity congruent with masculinity. Professional competitors —particularly the men—are the most admired dancers in the American ballroom.[19] Competition is something that most men recognize as an appropriate activity. It takes the dance to a higher level, because the hours of practice increase and the physical demands intensify. James had competed in American smooth with four different partners, starting around 1984, at his uncle's urging. At his first competition, he came third in the Rising Star, adding ruefully, "The only reason I came in third is just because there wasn't anybody to beat me. . . . It wasn't because I was that good." As time went on, however, James's standing rose as a result of hard work. He had his best results with his final partner, placing highly at the national competition and at Ohio—much bigger and more important competitions than his first had been. His success marked his place in the hierarchy of professional dancers.

Professional coaching from successful former competitors also helps cement the dancing identity. James solidified his insider status by rattling off names of top dancers and coaches he had worked with. These included well-known overseas coaches as well as Americans: "David Osborne, Joan and John Knight, Judi Hatton. I had Rosendo [Fumero] come in, Paul Holmes. I worked with Robert Richey and Glennis Dee, and even Pete Taylor helped us out a little bit."[20]

Male dancers gain further acceptance by taking students to dance pro/ am at competitions. All but the most successful professional men try to do this, because it pays for their own dance training and performance and because after they retire from competing, it is one of the most lucrative activities available to teachers.[21] However, as we shall see, this complicates the portrayal of masculinity.

Leading, Not Following

While dancing may seem feminine to outsiders, the view is different from within. Men make most of the decisions in dance; they lead, and women follow. This can be traced back through dance history. Partnered social dancing dates back to the 1600s, but the dances that we know today began to appear in the 1800s with the waltz. This was an era when men were the household heads, and women were subordinate. Although dance manuals today acknowledge that "it is difficult for many women in this day and age to identify with the words *lead* and *follow*," they add that "if both partners tried to be the leader, then dance would never work."[22] Leading is harder work than following in many respects, because the man "not only has to know what his own feet are going to do, he has to lead the lady through the figures."[23]

This idea of the man as leader is important in supporting both a masculine and a heterosexual identity. In ballroom dancing, the "capital crime" for a woman is "anticipating a move," whereas for men it is "hesitation."[24] Knowing what comes next reinforces masculinity, and even though James viewed dance as a team sport, he saw himself as in charge of the team, saying, "When I was taught the man's role in dancing, it was very old style." He explained this by noting that he was "trained by European coaches" who believed that "the man was supposed to be ninety percent responsible." He described what this meant: "Every time a mistake happened, it was my fault. Yeah, it was my fault, my fault, my fault." James added, "It was good in a way. It kept me working."

James acknowledged that times were changing and that "they're asking a lot more of the girls." Now, "the ladies have to dance their part instead of the guys leading so much, especially at the higher levels."[25] However, James liked to stay in charge. Many students learn routines to dance with their professional partners, so that they know their steps in advance and can be more proactive. They also learn to dance by themselves rather than in closed position for at least some of each routine.[26] James told me, "Most of my girls dance freestyle. They don't have routines." This meant that the student did not know what steps were coming next in the performance until James made the decision and indicated his intent. To accomplish this, he noted, "I train them only to dance with me." This made it difficult for students who went social dancing—something James disapproved of his students doing—but it kept James firmly in the driver's seat.

In contrast to James, American champion rhythm dancer Jose DeCamps, seen dancing with his student Natalka Cap in figure 2.1, expects each student to learn the choreography for herself, something Natalka does well. Yet, as can be seen, this in no way takes away from the gendered nature of Jose's performance.

James loved competitions, because this enabled him to spend time with other men like himself—men who had integrated dancing into a masculine and heterosexual persona. In this way, he was similar to George in chapter 1. When these men talked about their closest friends, they described other men who danced. When they were together, they joked about masculinity and sexuality, most likely because they knew it could be called into question elsewhere. The jokes served to verify that each was a man among men.

James was more macho than many of the men I interviewed, in his desire for control and his reluctance to let his students learn choreography. Yet he also needed to become a ladies' man—at least in the dance world. In his private life, he told me, he had no time for dating, because competing took him away frequently and he spent most of his evenings teaching. At competitions, however, James carefully looked after his students in ways most men in the nondance world would consider stereotypically feminine. In the evenings, James could often be seen drinking or dining with his adoring students, and when they were not dancing, they would go sightseeing together. His students did not buy dresses without consulting him, because they trusted his eye. If they wore something he did not like, he would ask them to take him shopping. James did this because he wanted them to "feel pretty," so they would "dance better." When they were competing, he said, "I like to have fun, and they're there to have fun. And if they lose me, they're not going to have fun anymore. So I give them a little bit of space, where I can take care of them in case something happens." His students enjoyed attending competitions with him and felt safe performing with him. James's caretaking behavior is typical of men who dance and is accepted as masculine in the dance world, even if it would be questioned elsewhere.

This caretaking behavior can be seen clearly in figure 6.2, in which teacher Scott Lazarov instructs a relatively new student, Linda Brajer, in the correct footwork. Both teacher and student are carefully focused on the

Fig. 6.2. Caring is masculine in the dance world. Scott Lazarov teaches student Linda Brajer at DanceSport Academy, Ardmore, PA, July 2010. © 2010 Jonathan S. Marion.

lesson, and Scott's friendly demeanor puts Linda at ease. Teachers such as James and Scott do this on a daily basis.

Dancing as a Boy, Becoming a Man

The story was different for men who started dancing as children. Colin, one of the world's top-ranked ballroom dancers, grew up in a working-class neighborhood in England. He was in his late thirties at the time of the interview but had started dancing around age five. He suffered from serious asthma as a child, and his doctor suggested he start swimming or dancing. His mother wanted him to dance. She knew someone with a studio, and she took him to Saturday-morning classes. Unlike James, Colin loved it from the beginning. As a little boy, he did not know any better, but as he grew older, he learned never to tell anyone he danced:

> I left school at sixteen. I would have left school at twelve if I could have, because in England at that time it was not cool to dance, and they didn't

know the difference between ballroom and ballet. The insinuation was always that I was a ballet dancer, and if I was a ballet dancer, the insinuation was that I wore pink tights. The problem was that because I was having a lot of success as a juvenile—I was actually ranked top junior in the country—I was in the paper. I had to go to competitions, and every now and then the school would ask me to do something that would present me. Like they would hear I had an award, and they would make an announcement at assembly. It was absolutely terrible. I used to, of course, not say a word. I had one serious friend, and he knew, but every now and then somebody found out. It was hell for me in school.

Colin's identity development was different from that of James, because he learned to think of himself as a dancer while still a child. By happenstance, his local dancing school was run by a couple who trained many top dancers. They quickly recognized his talent and, as he became more experienced, brought teachers in from London to coach him. Whereas James had difficulty learning to dance and was saved by his athletic ability, Colin's only problem was his poor health:

The only thing I can think, off the top of my head, that was a little difficult was the stamina part, . . . just because of the asthma I had as a child. I had to deal with that in dancing rounds. . . . I knew my basics. I think I was pretty good at learning the technique. . . . I've always been a bit shy. I would never say one word on a lesson. The teachers always thought I was the cutest thing, but I was just so respectful. . . . I just used to listen. . . . My biggest problem was, as a child, when you dance, your arms feel like they are going to drop off, because you are too young. I just remember the excruciating pain.

Colin could not remember much about life before dancing, and his mother considered his dancing to be paramount. As a result, he did not have to work to develop a dancing identity, as did James. Indeed, Colin never thought of himself as anything but a dancer. School was difficult, because his masculinity was frequently called into question, but as soon as he got home and went to dancing class, he was happy. When he reached the minimum school-leaving age, he had little idea about the future: "I just knew I was going to dance." He had known this for some time—his "first consciousness was about thirteen."

Whereas James had to bring dancing in line with his well-established gender identity, Colin had to heal the wounds that dancing had caused to his sense of himself as a man. He did this by establishing a different life for himself than that of his classmates. He moved away from home, became a top dancer, and traveled the world. He also dated the kind of glamorous women that the men in his hometown could not hope to interest. He now lives his life entirely for dance and is comfortable with his masculinity, surrounded by men like himself. Looking back on his difficult school days gave him satisfaction:

> The funny thing was—that's the old cliché. The cool guys when I was in school—the normal ones—now when you see them, they're not doing anything. They're the ones that don't have jobs or anything. It was so funny, going back to my hometown sometimes. These guys are the ones that are still in the hometown. . . . It was actually about two years later once I left school and I started to dance. I started to see those people later on. I still wasn't comfortable telling them I dance, but they knew I still danced, and it was about two or three years later where I actually felt I'd made the right decision.

Whereas most men would be conscious that it was a woman's body pressed against them, Colin had danced in closed position so long that he took the physicality for granted:

> I've got some girls—as people they're a little reserved—and you're sort of bumped in.[27] You can't dance with somebody that doesn't want to touch you. She's doing the wrong form of dance; go learn hip hop or something, 'cause ballroom you've got to be touching my right side. In order to dance, you can't just touch—it's not wood on wood—you've got to feel muscle. You've got to feel each other. I normally say to the person, "Can you touch me? Can you feel my skin?" They're touching, and I say, "You're touching me, but actually you are pushing me away. You're resisting me. You're not inviting me into your body. . . ." For me, I'm just like, "Boom." I just want to feel. That's second nature to me.

When Gay Men Dance

Like most Latin and ballroom dancers, Colin was avowedly heterosexual. Some writers have made claims to the effect that nearly half the men dancing Latin are gay,[28] but it is impossible to imagine how such an estimate could be derived. Since no documentation is given, these estimates seem little more than guesswork.[29] Dancers agree that gay men are more common in Latin than in ballroom, but given the influx of heterosexual eastern European dancers into the West, my informal estimate is that most Latin dancers in America are heterosexual.

Furthermore, sexual identity aside, the performance is resolutely heterosexual.[30] Most coaches go to great lengths to depict the relationship between partners as that between a man and woman who are romantically or sexually attracted to each other. This has changed somewhat with the advent of same-sex competitions, such as the annual Liberty Dance Challenge in Philadelphia, where the rules dictate that the partners must be of the same gender. Same-gender dancing has been allowed in collegiate competition also, but in most national and international competitions, partners must be a man and a woman.[31]

Although most members of the dance world know gay men and describe themselves as comfortable around them, the close dancing friends of heterosexual male dancers are typically heterosexual. Indeed, I was struck by the number of jokes heterosexual teachers made about being gay.[32] After observing one of these joking sessions, I later commented to a participant that I thought it interesting that men who dance go to such pains "to come out as heterosexual,"[33] because, in academia, heterosexuality is assumed, and only gays and lesbians feel the need to publicly declare a sexual identity. Overhearing this comment, another professional, who is gay, explained, "That's because, in the regular world, straightness is assumed, but it isn't in dancing." The pressure on male dancers to assert their heterosexuality was also found by Helen Wulff in her ethnography of ballet companies.[34] Heterosexuality is privileged in the ballroom dance world,[35] but it is not as hegemonic as it is in the larger Western culture, and some top competition organizers and judges have openly acknowledged a gay identity.

Because men's sexual identity is always at issue in the dance world, the appearance of heterosexual masculinity is maintained through symbolic practices. First, men ask women to dance. Sometimes, women do the asking, and although nothing is said if this happens, it can make people feel a little uncomfortable. Many women find it difficult to ask men to dance unless they are already close and intimate. Second, the language of leading and following symbolizes power and acquiescence. Finally, as we have seen, the look of the dancers is strictly gendered.

There are other norms less obvious to the outsider. For example, James's comments in the preceding section mark the dance world as one where second-wave feminism has had no impact on language. Men are men, and women are girls, no matter their age or status. When professionals describe a competitive couple, they often refer to the man's name only, as in, "Ricardo decided not to dance Manhattan. He did it last year but took a break."[36] Furthermore, choreography is usually done by men, either the man in the partnership or a professional coach. This is changing somewhat, as women's dancing has become more assertive and as some women coaches—such as Shirley Ballas—have become prominent, but choreography is still largely a masculine endeavor, with women staying in the background and assisting only as needed. As one male dancer explained, "If I am to lead the dancing, then I have to create it. I cannot lead what I am not comfortable with, and women do not have the experience of leading."

In a world where men are quick to assert their heterosexuality, what of gay men? How do they adapt to dancing heterosexual passion or romance? Issues of gender and the dancing identity are different for them. Matt, who grew up in a working-class suburb of New York and started to learn ballroom dance at age eighteen, had no problem thinking of himself as a dancer. In fact, in his gay social world, dancing was considered glamorous. He first began to envision a dancing career in high school, and he wondered how he might achieve it. No one in his family danced; it was just something he thought he would like to do. A big fan of Madonna, he dreamed of dancing in her show:

> I had my high school English-class instructor. He wasn't my official guidance counselor, but I would go to him basically for guidance because he was wonderful. He said to me, "I'm going to give it to you straight, because in all of my years as a teacher"—he'd been there for maybe thirty, thirty-five years—"one person has come up to me and said they wanted to be a dancer. Well, now he strips. That's the kind of career he has." He said, "My secretary here is actually a dancer." She said, "Yes, I'm a kick girl—on the kick line. . . ." He did actually give me some encouragement. He said, "Really, go for it, but just don't turn into a stripper."

Now, a decade after he had started, Matt was glad he had followed the teacher's advice.

Most people discouraged Matt with an "Oh, sure," when he told them of his plans to dance for Madonna. His father was concerned not about gender but about whether he could make a living as a dancer. With no one to show him the way, Matt started looking in the want ads and found one that said, "Dance instructors needed—No experience necessary." He had been taking jazz-funk dance lessons and karate for a year or two, and he thought that constituted experience, so he answered the advertisement. Matt's account of the audition is similar to that of other American teachers:

> I walked into this ballroom dance studio. I'm there with a T-shirt and baggy jeans and combat boots—very jazzy hip-hop look—and that's what I planned on doing. I walked in . . . with everyone in a shirt and tie and the girls in blouses and skirts. I thought, "I'm in the wrong place." They had about eight of us there, and they gave us some basics: "Here's a box step. Add rise and fall to it. Add hips to it." They hired myself and one of the girls on the spot.

Although this was not what Matt had envisioned when he answered the ad, he was happy as long as he was dancing. He described himself as "just fall-ing into it."

After Matt began competing, he developed a different perspective on dancing and gender than that of straight men. First, Matt said that he thought there were fewer gay men in the ballroom world than in other forms of dance. Then he added,

> There's still a lot of stigma over a gay man and a heterosexual woman or any woman for that matter. After all, two heterosexuals may not get along or be very close. It's fake then, and the whole connection between two people. . . . In the middle of the rumba they have to turn it on like they're hot and heavy for one another, and it's all in the dance. The few times when the woman is a lesbian dancing with a heterosexual male, and the judges know it, they prejudge. I think it's becoming less and less common, but there are still people who are very conservative.

Matt added, "If you have a connection to a partner, that's easy; if you have a partner who can emote back to you . . . I like to perform, and I find it quite natural." Matt clearly viewed the emotional intimacy displayed in dance to be a performance. Since it involved acting, not feeling, he believed that he could perform romance with a woman just as well as a heterosexual man could. As we will see in the next chapter, though, women students did not always view it that way.

Suspicion about the ability of gay men to act like they want a woman is common in American society. In a Newsweek.com article about this topic, writer Ramin Setoodeh describes gay actor Sean Hayes as "wooden and insincere" in his portrayal of Kristin Chenoweth's love interest in the Broadway play *Promises, Promises*.[37]

In the beginning, Matt was careful about revealing his sexual identity. When he was learning, he often had to dance with a male instructor in order to learn the woman's steps.[38] When this happened, Matt worried what the other man would think if Matt inadvertently revealed his sexual identity. This was a particular problem in ballroom, in which the dance is always performed in closed position. During those moments, Matt told me that he worried that he might get an erection. Now that he was well established in the dance world, he was more comfortable being out. Still Matt was careful, especially around new students. As he noted, "It's not something like, 'Hi, I'm Matt. I'm gay.'" Coming out to his students happened gradually. Matt explained, "Dancing is such an intimate thing, so you often share personal details of your life, someone that you're involved with, somewhere you've gone. I share those things, so eventually it will come out." Here Matt displayed his comfort with nonromantic emotional intimacy, since the student knew no sex was involved.

While Matt had to deal with a certain amount of homophobia, he never doubted his identity as a dancer. Looking back, he could see how much he had learned before he deserved this label. However, most of his friends were gay and not from the dance world, and he never hesitated to tell them that he was a dancer.[39] He found that most people were "elated" when he told them. Many of the people he knew thought of it as something they had always wanted to do. This is in marked contrast to the experience of most heterosexual male dancers, especially those who grew up in the English-speaking world. Gay men generally feel comfortable dancing, having internalized our culture's assumptions about sexual identity and dance.

Dancers from the Former Soviet Bloc—Where Men Dance

For male dancers from the former Soviet bloc, the story is again different. These men experienced relatively little discrimination as boys who danced because when they were growing up, it was a common activity for both boys and girls. They grew up in the Communist Soviet bloc, where dancing was one of the after-school activities offered to all students. So these boys could dance without gender dishonor, which meant that most eastern European professionals started dancing very young. Almost all of those I interviewed started out competing in ten-dance—that is, in both ballroom and Latin. It was not until their teens that they decided to specialize in one or the other, often after a number of years competing as amateurs.

Bernandas, for example, had been dancing for over twenty years, starting in the former Soviet Union when, at age seven, his mother took him to a dancing club. He did not enjoy it at first because the classes were long. Whereas an American child might have argued about doing something he did not particularly like, Bernandas did what his mother wanted. He never hesitated in telling people that he danced because, he said, "So many boys were dancing, I never felt like one of the few boys." The rewards of dancing started quickly:

> After a few months, we had a small competition in the school, so I became a competitor right in the beginning of training. . . . In my first competition in another city—it was the Soviet Union, but still there were couples from, I think, Poland and other republics of the Soviet Union, so we can consider it being international. It was when I was twelve. . . . My first trip was to France. I was fifteen then.

By this time, Bernandas had decided to make dancing his career, so he studied dance at university. He and his longtime partner reached the top of the amateur ranks in ballroom, and he was able to move to America, turn professional, and dance with a top dancer. At the time of my interview with him, he was supported not only by the many shows he and his new partner were asked to perform but by the many sponsors who wanted to be associated with them.[40] Dancing provided him with a way to get ahead in the world and gain recognition and rewards, so he had a firm self-identity as a good dancer. In addition, he had not had to make the social class transition that many American dancers make. He believed that he could go to the top in dancing and recognized the opportunities that it had given him. Dancing enabled him to leave an impoverished country and succeed in the richest country in the world. This made it entirely compatible with manly success.

Other eastern European dancers told similar stories. Pavel had achieved success as a dancer in America in spite of his father's fears that this would not happen. While he was still competing in his home country, he had the opportunity to compete in Germany, where he saw all his male idols, such as Hans Galke and Bryan Watson, men who danced full of power and passion like real men. While Pavel did not appear to have gender insecurities about dancing, when performing, he wanted to look "like a man" on the dance floor. This was a common concern expressed by male dancers. They saw the performance as highly gendered, and they worked hard to achieve this look. Pavel believed that "in Latin, the man has to create the woman." This point is underscored by Juliet McMains, who argues that male dancers feel the need to make sure that their movements appear masculine.[41] Masculine intent can be seen in figure 6.3, in which Gherman Mustic dominates over his professional partner, Iveta Lukosiute. Immigrants such as Gherman appear comfortable with this role, as do their partners.

Now age thirty, Pavel believed he still had his best dancing ahead of him. Pavel was typical of eastern Europeans, with few apparent concerns about meshing a masculine identity with a dancing identity. Pavel and his wife ranked highly in Latin competition, and their lives revolved around dancing. They certainly did gender in their daily lives—he was in charge of choreography, for example—but it took a back seat to dance. In addition to choreography, Pavel spent a great deal of time thinking about and designing costumes for his wife to wear. He was also an attentive and nurturing teacher. Pavel spent most of his time with women—his wife and his students. In this way, his life was not typical of most men. However, he had a masculine obsession with winning—something his wife did not share. He spent many hours each day practicing and then more hours weight training and doing Pilates and gyrotonics. He saw his devotion as compatible with masculine competitiveness; he wanted to be the best.

Married Men Who Learn to Dance

Whereas many women students told me that their women friends envied their dancing, men frequently had to justify dance lessons to male friends who did not understand. Given that most men in America would not place dance lessons high on the list of things they would like to do, what makes some men decide to learn dance?

Some men learn dance as a social activity to engage in with their wives, often because they know it will make their wives happy.[42] Others dance in order to have a social life and to meet women.[43] The married men I

Fig. 6.3. Traditional masculinity as performed by Gherman Mustic with his partner, Iveta Lukosiute, at the 2007 United States DanceSport Championships, Orlando, FL. © 2007 Jonathan S. Marion.

interviewed were typically older, with grown children and long-established marriages, so they did not feel that dancing affected their masculine identity. They were used to spending time in the company of their wives and saw dancing as something that enhanced the emotional intimacy of their existing relationship.[44] As a group, however, many reported that male friends were somewhat threatened by their dancing.

Gordon was a retired physical-education teacher in his early sixties. He had met his wife on the college gymnastics team, where he had taken some required dance lessons. Later, they used to dance at weddings and other social events. About fifteen years before my interview with him, Gordon's wife had asked him to take dance lessons with her at the local YMCA. Since then, they had made dancing a big part of their social life. They took lessons three times a week and arranged vacations to places that provided opportunities for social dancing. This is how Gordon described the reactions of their friends:

> There is a fellow across the street, and his wife wants to dance so bad she can taste it. His comment is, "No way." He's not going to do it because it's not something that guys do. . . . I have a friend whose wife wanted to dance, a fellow I taught with. We were at his house, and dancing always comes up. Talking about what you could do—an easy dance—I said, "If you can walk, you can waltz." We did a little bit of waltzing in his living room, just basic steps. His wife started making noises like, "Well, next Friday, why don't we come with you?" "Sure you want to do that? Great." I am looking at him, and he got a panicked look on his face. . . . Three days later, we got a call from his wife. He hurt his back, and he thinks it's from the waltzing, so he doesn't want to go dancing. When I hung up the phone and told my wife, she started laughing. There was no way he was going to do it.

Experiences such as this reinforced rather than challenged Gordon's sense of masculinity. He had been a successful wage earner supporting a wife and family. His grown children were now independent, and he and his wife of long standing liked spending their leisure time together. Gordon viewed himself as more secure in his masculinity than other men are because he was comfortable dancing with his wife on the ballroom floor.

However, Gordon found dancing difficult to learn, and he worked hard to be the one in charge. After telling me that the man's role was "not arguing with his wife," he added that it is to be the frame and to lead the woman. This is difficult for many amateur men. Leading keeps the man firmly in charge, but many women complain about the poor leading skills of the men with whom they dance socially. Conceding that his leading skills were not strong, Gordon explained,

> The only time we argue is on the dance floor. . . . She doesn't feel the lead. "Dammit, I gave you the lead." Often I will give her a step, and I will not be in a proper position to start it. And as a result my step is thrown off, and it fouls her up royally. And it's got to be her fault—now come, it's not my fault, . . . but she comes right back at me.

In order to stay in charge on the dance floor, Gordon had several rules that he followed religiously. Although he danced with other students in group classes, because partners rotate, he did not always enjoy it; indeed he grumbled that sometimes it was like "moving a sofa around the floor." He described himself as having "a total absence of desire" to dance with anybody other than his wife, and he would dance with no one else when they went out social dancing. This is frowned on in dance circles, because there is typically a shortage of men. Husbands who can dance are expected to make the rounds of unattached women and only dance some of the time with their wives.[45] Gordon's reasons for his behavior were twofold. First he described sticking with his wife as giving him a "comfort feeling," explaining, "If I make a mistake, she is likely to be less judgmental, and Lord knows I screw up enough." In addition, if he was planning to dance a step he was unsure he could lead, he would tell her what was coming. Since she was used to dancing with him, Gordon was able to maintain the illusion of leading without having to put his skills to the test of dancing with someone who could not anticipate his every move.[46] It was easier to be the one in control when the follower knew what to do.

Gerald also danced to please his wife, but whereas Gordon never competed and had no desire to do so, Gerald and his wife went to numerous competitions each year, dancing pro/am with each one's own teacher. This was a man who had not wanted to learn to dance, and he told an amusing story about how he started:

> My wife had tried golf and tennis, scuba diving, rappelling, and snow skiing. She tried all of the things I like, and then she said, "Would you try just one thing that I want to do?" I said, "Okay, anything that you want to do, I'll do." And she said, "Dance." And I went, "Damn." So I said, "Okay, I'll

take dance lessons, but I'm not going to enjoy it. I'll do it for you." I was [still] working, and she would make an appointment for a lesson, and I would always have reason to cancel. Then one night about seven thirty, she said, "How are things going? Do you have anything happening?" "Nope, nothing happening." She said, "Good, we have a lesson in thirty minutes." We took our lesson, and we went from there. I guess I was tricked into it, but I enjoyed it.

Gerald is a man's man, whose buddies were surprised to learn that he danced. Like Gordon, Gerald saw himself as more comfortable with his masculinity than were other men he knew. Once again, these friends had different views than did their wives:

> Most of my golfing buddies—the question originally was, "You dance?" with a big question mark. . . . The women find out we dance; a lot of them wish their husbands would dance. The husbands say, "For God's sake, don't tell my wife that you dance, or she'll want me to." I tell them, "It's really making a commitment, putting in time. It's nothing more than walking to music, and you can learn to dance. If you're not born having a voice, it's hard to sing, but if you don't dance, you can learn to dance." I've done it mostly for my wife, because it's something she's always wanted.

In Gerald's view, real men made their wives happy, and this was why he danced.

Dancing did not come easy to Gerald, and his difficulty learning was a roadblock in the formation of a dancing identity. He described himself as having "no natural talent" and complained, "It's disgusting to see the little nineteen- to twenty-year-old girls come in, and they got it like that. I think there's a direct correlation between age and how fast you learn and probably intelligence too. So I lose on both ends: I'm male, I'm not intelligent, and I'm not graceful." Gerald had worked hard to overcome these disadvantages, practicing almost every day and putting in more time on his dancing than he did on golf. Like other men, his experience competing in sports helped:

> It's like the other sports you get into. You play tennis, and then you decide, "Well, I need to do Pilates to be a little more flexible." Then "I need to lift weights to be a little stronger." Dance, you get into it, and you realize, "I

don't really have a good core." So you do your crunches for your core, and then you stretch.

Gerald reported no hang-ups over telling people he danced. He had been an athlete all his life, and now he wanted to do something to please his wife of many years. When he was working, he had traveled much of the time, leaving her alone with the children, and he felt an obligation to her. Both Gordon and Gerald were long married and enjoying retirement. Rather than challenging their well-established masculinity, dancing enhanced it. Furthermore, they saw it as a new and enjoyable activity for a married couple to do together, something that kept their marriages alive. These accounts fit Eva Illouz's descriptions of romantic episodes as taking place outside everyday life. These men were making that happen even after many years.[47]

Single Men Who Learn to Dance

The single men I interviewed who danced had a different set of motives. Dave was age fifty-two when I interviewed him and had been dancing for about eight years. He had never been much of an athlete; he was a sickly child and had not danced in his youth. He started lessons after being talked into getting out on the floor at the company end-of-year bash, which he had greatly enjoyed. While he was dancing at the party, he said, "In the back of my head, I'm going, 'I want to do something about this. I don't feel good about not knowing how to do this.'" When he would go out for pizza in his neighborhood, he often walked past a sign advertising dancing, and he wondered if they taught ballroom:

> I went in, and I tried to register for the ballroom. . . . They said, "Well, you can register now. There's a dance tonight." I went to the dance that night, and I met [the teacher]. She's very prominent in the area as far as for dance. I introduced myself. I said, "I live in the neighborhood. Is there any way you can teach me how to dance . . . ?" They were playing a waltz. She said, "Let's do a waltz right now." There was nobody there. I was early. . . . She is a wonderful dancer. I was just doing the box step, and she was very nice. . . . At the end, she said, "Dave, do you play an instrument?" I said, "Well, I play the piano." She said, "I can tell, because you are right on the money as far as the music. You have the ability to keep the music, the timing."

Dave said learning to dance came easy to him. He had no difficulty learning new steps, and he discovered that whatever dance he was doing, he could "take on the personality of the dance." His teacher emphasized the importance of dance frame and taught him how to lead. He was aware of the things that he needed to work on—strengthening his core, improving his flexibility, spotting when he turned—but he had become so devoted to dancing that he took many lessons and had branched out into Argentine tango and club salsa. Most of these were group lessons, because he had limited funds, but much of his life revolved around dancing.

Dave liked to tell people that he danced because he thought it made him interesting. His family did not live close by, and although he had told them about it, they "did not take it in." He had recently gone to a family wedding:

> They were playing hard rock music, and I thought, "Well, okay, I'll dance." They were just amazed by the fact that I was dancing so musically, and I was using my body with the music. My nieces and nephews said, "Dave, everybody is coming up and saying, 'Who is that guy?'" . . . My family is going like, "Man, Dave, I had no idea you could dance so well." I said, "This is not what I do. You should see me do tango. You should see me waltz."

Some of Dave's male relatives had told him not to tell their wives he danced.

Dave worked long, stressful hours handling complex customer problems for an insurance company, but he viewed himself as an artist and incorporated his dancing into this identity. He loved playing the piano and continued taking lessons, but it did not provide him with a social life. In dancing, reinforced by a teacher who encouraged him to think of himself as talented, he had made new friends and was much in demand as a partner. When I interviewed him, he was working on two performances, one a waltz and the other a tango. His two partners were romantically involved with men who would not dance, so they were happy to partner Dave and to share the cost of coaching sessions. Furthermore, when the teacher who taught him held special parties, she made sure Dave and another man were there to dance with the single women. Here is how Dave described the way dancing had improved his social life:

> I used to always religiously go to the dances every Friday night. It got to the point where I was expected to dance every dance I could. When I wasn't dancing, [my teacher] said, "Well, Dave, would you like to dance?" I got the gist of the fact that when you go to the dances, you've got to ask

people to dance. I was coming from a background—I'm an artist: I paint and draw. I was mostly inside. I never was really out with social things. I mostly had to deal with the fact that I had to be more outgoing. . . . When I was starting to dance, . . . I was meeting people . . . that were very kind to me, and they would let me dance with them. . . . They would encourage me, and they would help me feel like, "Oh! Oh! I'm starting to get better, because I'm dancing with so-and-so, who's been dancing for years. . . ." I fell into the ballroom scene from being really removed from it. We are in a small town. There weren't that many people coming to the dances, so I got to know a few people, and I got comfortable. That's how I evolved into the ballroom scene.

Dave transitioned from a man who viewed himself as a somewhat isolated artist into a popular and competent dancer. One version of masculinity in American society is the socially withdrawn man, especially around women. Dancing developed Dave's self-confidence as a male dancer who is "pretty good and clear in leading" and able to distinguish between those who "follow really well" and those who do not. In the latter case, he added, "I simplify things, so that they can." He never told dance partners that they were not following properly, because he wanted everyone to dance and not to feel discouraged. Dave told me that he sometimes teaches Argentine tango, and he eagerly listed the names of ballroom teachers he had taken coaching sessions with, adding that they are "world champions." Dancing had turned him into somebody. Like the male dancer shown in figure 6.4, Dave enjoyed taking the lead.

It was not uncommon in my interviews for older single men to say they learned to dance with the hope of finding romance and friendship. Most were like Dave; the social and artistic aspects of ballroom dancing were the most important. They hoped to meet a special someone, but in the meantime, the instant intimacy of social dancing sufficed. A few were more interested in romance than in dance, becoming romantically interested in their teachers and finding in dance a way of getting close to a young woman who would not have looked at them otherwise. A story of this type occurred in chapter 4. The student, Daniel, an Irish American from a strict Catholic background, was still unmarried in his fifties and was ambivalent about learning something he considered a "girlish thing to do." He believed that "men are not supposed to make some of these movements." However, a "fairy-tale relationship" he was in had ended, and to help him get over it, he decided to try dance lessons. When he called a studio, the young woman

Fig. 6.4. Taking the lead in social dance. Atrium Dance Studio, Pennsauken, NJ, August 2010. © 2010 Jonathan S. Marion.

"was very sweet on the phone and very enticing." He was hooked. He became besotted with a second teacher and was heartbroken when she left his studio. Still, he was the exception.

In the next chapter, we turn to female dancers. Women do not have the gender-identity problems that men have, nor do they lack the practice at emoting, but they face a different set of issues in becoming dancers.

7

Beyond the Glamour

The Female Dancer

LAURA HAD ALWAYS been a show-off. As a child, she produced shows using her brothers as props and remembered "forcing them into doing things," such as dressing them up and doing their hair and makeup. She never had dance lessons, although all her friends did and she "wanted them desperately," because her parents did not consider lessons useful to her future. In high school, Laura joined the theater and loved it, but this ended when she graduated and had to earn a living. Her first job was at a southern-food chain, where she quickly rose to manager. She hated the job and complained about it constantly:

> One of the guys I was dating at the time said he was tired of hearing me gripe and threw the want ads in front of me. . . . I saw an ad in the paper that said they would train you and pay you to learn to dance, and I showed him. He picked up the phone and dialed a number and stuck it in my face. By that point somebody was on the line, and I had to talk to him. At the tender age of eighteen, I thought I was fabulous and I could dance myself silly and could beat anyone else out there. I went in and did an interview, and I think I borrowed from all of my friends' experiences in tap, ballet, and jazz, mine having been only as a spectator. Got into the training class —I was training for about a week and a half. Walked in one day for training; the manager came and told me I didn't have any time for questions because I was teaching in three hours. I said, "I have no idea what foxtrot and cha-cha is. . . ." She said, "Don't worry about it. I'm going to teach you what you need to know to teach them." My teaching started from that point forward. It was at [Fred Astaire Dance Studios].

As this story shows, Laura had few career goals. When she applied to teach dance, she did not realize how difficult it would be. She started because a boyfriend made the connection for her, and at that point in her life, boys were important to Laura.

Laura said she thought of herself as a professional as soon as she got her first paycheck but still did not think of dancing as a career. She was young, and she wanted to have a good time:

> I'm not sure that the thought of [a career] ever occurred to me. It was just something that I really loved. I enjoyed dancing. I enjoyed getting dressed up. I enjoyed doing something that most other people did not do. I was always kind of an attention grabber. I always loved the spotlight. I don't think I really thought about it until I saw my first Ohio Star Ball on television. I looked at that, and I looked at the girls, and I looked at the dresses, and I was like, "Oh, my! That's what I want to do!"

This desire to live in the present, rather than to plan for the future, is typical of many working-class girls, even today, when other young women attend college and plan professional futures. Laura's story exemplifies the lack of pressure toward a career that many such women feel, because they expect their lives to follow their mothers' paths.[1] Even though Laura needed to make money to support herself, she saw these jobs as something to do until then.

While teaching at this studio, Laura became engaged, but her fiancé was unfaithful, so she broke it off and went with a friend for an extended vacation to Florida. They liked Florida and decided to stay there, finding jobs in the food-service industry. After about five months, Laura started to look for work teaching dance. Using her former boss as a reference, she began at an Arthur Murray in Florida. Another dancer there suggested they compete, and she agreed; they competed together for the next six years.

This was a crucial period in Laura's life. Her increasing devotion to dance transformed her from a girl marking time until marriage to a woman serious about competition. This meant putting marriage plans on hold, because competing and marriage are usually incompatible unless women marry their professional partners, and many do not. It was also an unusual pattern of behavior for young women from Laura's social background.

After she and her partner split, Laura moved around Florida working for different studios and developing her dancing skills. She became serious about competing and received a lot of encouragement from her various teachers. Arthur Murray allows teachers to compete only in their own competitions, and teachers must take students with them. When Laura outgrew these, she moved to an independent studio and began competing at the most difficult competitions in the country. Such competitions are independently run but registered with, and adjudicated by, the National Dance Council of America (NDCA). When Laura got the chance to dance with a professional partner in another state, she moved there. She changed states again to dance with her final partner. When she retired from competing, she continued to teach and work in the dance world. She was now in her early forties and enjoying her postcompetition life.

Like many dancers, Laura had lived an unsettled existence, moving from partner to partner and living in places where she "knew no one." She had never lived anywhere for more than a few years, until she stopped competing. Even now, she traveled to many competitions every year, supporting herself by working in the dance industry. As she put it, "I think my whole life has been a series of interesting events along the way. Nothing was ever planned—everything in my career has been, 'Oh, stumble into this!' and 'Oh, stumble into that!' It's been fun." It is hard to imagine a male dancer making this comment with the same equanimity. Most men feel pressured to develop a serious job. Laura was now engaged to be married and was excited to be finally planning her wedding, but, she added, they had decided to have a prenuptial agreement to protect their individual businesses.

Laura had started dancing as something to do until she settled down, but dancing had made settling down impossible. Her parents were bemused. They kept asking her, "When are you going to get a real job?" Even though no one suggested that dancing was an inappropriate activity for a young woman, her family thought she needed greater economic security, particularly since she did not seem to be getting married. Even after she became a successful competitor, her parents remained ambivalent. Laura's mother explained, "You're so passionate about it and to know that the potential for you to get hurt is so great because it's so like Hollywood." Laura was as much attracted by the glamour of dance as she was by the dance itself, and it was this attraction to glamour that worried her mother. Like Victorian mothers, she feared that dance would lead her daughter astray.[2] Laura's mother feared that her daughter had been caught up in the success myth of American culture, which envisions ordinary people becoming stars if they have enough desire, talent, and luck.[3]

The glamorous aspects of ballroom led Juliet McMains to title her book about the ballroom industry *Glamour Addiction*. She calls "Glamour . . . the machine that powers American DanceSport and the industry's primary commodity."[4] While not in the same critical mode as McMains, Sally

Peters also acknowledges her own attraction to ballroom's glamour, something which helped to hook me also.[5] Laura's love affair with the appearance aspects of dancing led her to compete in rhythm and even Latin for a while. She described this choice as resulting from her desire "to be that hot, sexy little thing on the floor." Eventually, she began to dance American smooth, which is where she had the most success. However, this was not her original choice:

> I was dragged into smooth kicking and screaming. I didn't want to go, didn't want to go, didn't want to go. I said, "There's way too much material in the dresses. I couldn't possibly wear them." They didn't care. They said I was built for smooth, that I was nice and tall, and I would look great on the floor. I rolled my eyes. I went, "Okay, fine."

As we saw in the chapter on appearance work, here the desire for glamour —in the form of sexiness this time—supersedes the desire for dance.

In a longitudinal study of Americans who grew up during the Great Depression, John Clausen invented the term "planful competence" to describe those who were able to achieve success despite a difficult start in life.[6] As children, they kept their future goals in mind and planned each step. Clausen does not discuss the outliers, but Laura's path to success was not planful. She fell into each opportunity as it arose rather than thinking it through. Although she had a successful career, she may have gone further had she started earlier, been more focused, and received more encouragement. She never ranked high enough to have a dress sponsor, for example, so finances were always tight.

We can see Laura's behavior as one type of "doing gender."[7] She grew up with a traditional set of gender expectations, which changed as she fell into dancing and developed a commitment she had not anticipated. This encouraged a shift from a femininity oriented toward home and family to one oriented to performance and glamour. It necessitated developing independence and, as we will see, a critical eye about gender relations in the world of dance.

Laura's story takes us beyond the gender divide. It shows that the social relations expressed in a category such as gender diverge deeply for individuals.[8] Dance is consistently appropriate female behavior. In this sense, the concept of "doing gender" fits the dance world. Yet the behaviors of individual women are far from uniform, a result of the variations in the relationships between individual and social practice,[9] as well as in the social context of women's lives.[10] However, for all women, the specific context of dance both challenges and reinforces the performance of femininity.

Laura found performing to be the most appealing part of competing and the easiest skill for her to learn. The hardest part was being taken seriously as a knowledgeable professional in a world dominated by men. Although she had a spontaneous career path, Laura was serious about her skills on the dance floor. This led to conflicts, particularly with her final partner:

> I don't want to say it was a flexing of muscles—I had been in the business a lot longer than he had—he may have been trying to assert his knowledge so as not to feel like a little puppy. Typically in this industry, the men become very aggressive, and they feel the need to teach their girl, no matter how much experience they have. They feel the need to coach her as opposed to working together. This is not just my partner; this is something you see across the board.

To survive, Laura argued, the women had to be strong: "You cannot be this little frou-frou thing, or you're not going to make it."

As Laura learned, not only are the steps "initiated and controlled by the man," but the language of the steps is labeled from the man's point of view: in a right turn, for example, only the man turns right, while the woman turns left. In smooth, the basic steps involve the man moving forward and the woman backward, and it is his job to show her off.[11] No doubt, Laura's less-experienced partner took literally his mandate to be the one in charge. However, men's and women's dancing is so different that "even when learning a given dance, say the foxtrot, what a man and woman learn, practice, and experience as the foxtrot is not the same."[12] For this reason, although professionals learn to teach the parts for both genders, Laura's partner could not have known what she needed to do as well as she herself did.

Because Laura could not make much money teaching dance in a studio so focused on competition—the kind where most competitive dancers teach—she struggled to make ends meet throughout her competitive career. Laura found it difficult to pay for coaching and the cost of competing. She would buy one dress at a time and change it for another after using it for a while, and she always bought discount dresses, so she never owned anything she considered to be really beautiful. After a while, Laura started making dresses herself. Even while she was competing, she sometimes needed to work second jobs outside of dancing.

Laura's account of her dancing identity is different from that of men in a similar position. While dancing was never incompatible with the gender identity of women professionals, they found it difficult to be taken seriously as dancers, which challenged their dancing identity. This reflects low expectations about women's careers; the idea that a young woman would sacrifice everything for dance—husband and children included—did not sit well with their families.[13] Furthermore, unlike the many men who take students to competitions, Laura could name only two women who had competed as smooth dancers and who had lots of male students wishing to compete with them.

Good Girls from the Former Soviet Bloc

Anastasiya started dancing in Moscow when her mother signed her up for lessons at age six. She started by learning rock-'n'-roll dancing, which is popular for children in Russia, and she was soon traveling and competing.[14] She got to wear "beautiful dresses and some heeled shoes," novel things for this little girl. She switched to ballroom at age eleven, and she said she immediately knew that this was what she wanted to do in the future. By the time she was fifteen, Anastasiya was traveling around the world to important amateur competitions.[15] In contrast with Laura, Anastasiya's mother traveled with her always and was her main supporter. She drove Anastasiya for coaching, and she encouraged her every step of the way. Anastasiya's mother had never learned to dance and was shy. She was determined that this would not happen to her daughter, and she took much pleasure in Anastasiya's glory on the dance floor. Anastasiya, now in her late twenties, was an accomplished performer, and her mother was proud of her role in making this happen. Anastasiya's success constitutes one version of a successful gender performance.

Anastasiya came to America when she was recruited by a Russian dancer already living here to be his partner and to teach at a Fred Astaire studio. Although she had a little teaching experience—mostly group classes to children—her serious teaching started in America. She started competing in ballroom but switched to Latin when she lost her partner and had to get a new one. Anastasiya married this partner, and they were still competing when I interviewed her. She did not appear to have the same partnership issues as Laura did. When I asked her what came easiest to her in learning to dance, she said she learned choreography quickly and then added, "I will say partnership between man and woman. That's easy for me. I don't have to think about it." She had not had the partnership struggles that Laura reported. When Anastasiya and her partner dance, his moves are powerful and dominant. She looks delicate and feminine, with curly hair framing her sweetly smiling face. Dancing this way is something they worked on a lot, she said, because "it's very, very important as dancers."

As a little girl, Anastasiya had been swept up in the excitement and glamour of the dance world. She described her first competition:

> I was so excited; I couldn't sleep the whole night. Even my parents, my grandma, and my grandpa came to watch. . . . The most what I remember is it was my first beautiful dress. I was so excited to put it on. We were number three. I was so happy and surprised. My parents were happy too, but what I remember is probably the dress. That's what's the most important. You're a girl, and you see those beautiful dresses with stones or big skirts. It was all about that in the beginning, instead of the competition.

Even now, with many competitions behind her, Anastasiya loved the dresses, telling me that she always took a couple with her when competing. When they got there, she would go and look at the ballroom to see which one would look best. However, she added, "The most important thing is how I feel in that dress. If I feel that that dress is *the* dress, and I look beautiful, then I'll wear it. If I feel bad, then I know the dress is going to be bad too. I need to feel good about myself, what I wear, that stuff." Like Laura, Anastasiya was taken with the glamour of dance, but unlike Laura, she remained starry eyed. Figure 7.1 perfectly illustrates the glamour of dance; it shows Anna Mikhed, an immigrant from Belarus who has danced ballroom with several of the world's top men, dancing with Giampiero Giannico. Almost as soon as they started dancing together, the couple made the final at Blackpool in 2010.

From the start, Anastasiya was more career oriented than Laura had been, due to her earlier serious training and greater family support. Laura had always cared about her appearance but had struggled to find the resources to look her best. Anastasiya owned many beautiful dresses supplied by a sponsor. It is easier for Latin dancers to get sponsors because they compete the world over, and the sponsor's dresses are seen everywhere. Laura's gender portrayal was of a good-time girl, whereas Anastasiya's was the loving and obedient daughter who became the loving and obedient wife. Though not true of all eastern European women, especially those not married to dance partners, a number of those I interviewed said they

Fig. 7.1. The glamour of dance. Blackpool finalist Anna Mikhed with her partner, Giampiero Giannico. 2010 Emerald Ball DanceSport Championships, Los Angeles, CA. © 2010 Jonathan S. Marion.

danced because they were married to men who wanted them to. Marriage increased the economic stability that coming to America had given them, and these eastern European women practiced a traditional femininity of supporting a husband. For Anastasiya, dancing and competing with her husband were an integral part of this support.

Anastasiya's take on performing was also stereotypical. The man, she said, "has to present the woman." The goal is for everyone to tell the man, "Oh, my God, your woman looks amazing on the floor." The woman in turn should "follow the man, listen to the music, look beautiful on the floor, and show that he is in charge." Whereas other couples do not dance in such a gendered way, Anastasiya believed that Latin was "all about the man and the woman." She regretted that this was changing and looked back longingly to "about twenty years ago," when dancing was "real," meaning highly gendered.

Anastasiya's story was similar to that of other eastern European dancers, for example, Lena. Lena's mother had a friend whose daughter was dancing at school. When Lena was seven years old, her mother took her there to see a performance: "I walked out of the class, and I told my Mom, 'I want to do what that girl was doing.'" Her mother started her in dancing class:

> My mom actually met her friend, and she's like, "What are you doing here?" "I brought my daughter to ballroom dancing class." She's like, "Get her out of there. . . . It's addicting. Once you do it, there's no turning back." I liked it a lot. I didn't have a partner for a while, 'cause I was little and I was always in trouble with boys. Not that many boys wanted to dance. . . . Eventually I got a partner, and then I started competing locally in Ukraine and then traveling to Russia and doing a bunch of competitions.

Lena had become involved in gymnastics before dance, explaining that everybody "was involved in some sort of activity" and that a girl "obviously has to do dance or gymnastics."

Lena's route to America was different from Anastasiya's. Her family was Jewish, and they came here as religious immigrants when Lena was twelve. They arrived when restrictions on Jews leaving the Soviet Union ended. Although the ostensible purpose of lifting the ban was to allow Jews to immigrate to Israel, the majority preferred the United States.[16] The family settled in a Russian-immigrant community. One of the mothers decided to open a little school where the neighborhood children could learn ballroom and reproduce the homeland experience.[17]

Lena had been worried about her dancing in the move to the United States, because she had "heard, in America, kids weren't that involved in ballroom dancing." However, many Russians settled in communities of people like themselves, so Lena remained relatively isolated from the larger American society. Soon after she arrived, she heard that a young male dancer was coming here from her hometown in the Ukraine. Their mothers arranged for them to try out together, and they had been partners for fifteen years at the time of the interview. They practiced at a studio owned by a Russian Jewish immigrant and supported themselves by teaching the children of immigrants like themselves. Lena had recently become engaged to a man who did not dance but who came from her same ethnic background.

Like Anastasiya, Lena's gender performance was different from that of Laura. First, she was deliberate in making plans. One of Lena's frustrations was that Americans were not properly respectful of dance success. After graduating from high school, she followed her partner to the same local university. They had done well in amateur competition—much better than most Americans do—because they had a European view of their career trajectory, which meant winning many amateur competitions before turning professional. After winning an important competition as juniors, school got in the way:

> We're like, "Oh, my God, we either going to take this seriously and achieve something in this department or don't bother, because people put their heart and soul and time into it." We went to our university, and we talked to our professors. We're like, "Listen, we're traveling. Can you give us a break?" They would be saying to us, "Well, you're missing school. We're a pure academic school, and you have to make sure you stay in school. Otherwise your professors will fail you." We went to the dean, and we explained what we do and that we can make up the work when we travel to all these competitions that we get invited to. They are like, . . . "You have to talk to each professor individually." . . . We spoke to our parents, and our parents were totally against it in the beginning. They're like, "You have to go to school." But then they came around.

With parental permission, Lena and her partner dropped out of school and devoted themselves to dance.

Like Laura, Lena had a strong female identity, but she viewed herself as different from American girls. She reported that she "never had a problem with discipline," explaining that in the former Soviet Union, "if you're told to do something by your teacher, you automatically do it," because "there's no such things as 'something hurts' or 'I'm tired' or all those things that kids tend to do." That this continues to be the case is illustrated by a *New York Times* story about young Americans training at the Moscow State Academy of Choreography (the Bolshoi's school). One such student is quoted as saying, "The work ethic is such in Russia that there is no room for failure, there is no room for laziness, there is no room to be nice when it is not appropriate to be nice." In her opinion, "Russia is the best, because there is this demand for excellence that there isn't in any other part of the world."[18] Even though the children Lena was teaching were immigrants like her, she thought they were too Americanized and "not willing to put in the hard work." Lena added disparagingly that they just "like traveling, putting on nice dresses, things like that." Sometimes, she said, "you just want to smack them really hard." In other words, the longer girls lived in America, the more they wanted to have fun, like Laura, instead of being obedient, like Lena.

Lena applied her disciplined attitude to her relationship with her partner:

> We grew up together. We went through all the stages, the teenagers; we went through everything together. We've always shared this one goal. We loved what we do, and we loved doing it together. That was always our forefront. Everything else was not as important, not relevant, and therefore, that was a driving force. We were able to deal with everything and be true friends—true great friends who can honestly say, "What you're doing is stupid" or "That is extremely clever." Very honest—that's what I think kept the relationship together.

Lena had been fortunate in making her way. Her middle-class parents had sacrificed to support her. Her studio had covered all her dance expenses while she was an amateur, in return for teaching children. This was something only available to dancers living in a Russian community with a critical mass of children wanting to compete.

"Everyone Should Learn to Dance"

American women dancers I interviewed who could not make a living on the competition circuit often taught social dance groups. None of the professional men I interviewed made a living this way because they were able to teach individual women and take some of them to competitions. Like Laura, Stephanie had started by teaching at Arthur Murray's. However, the outcome was different because her career trajectory took a different turn:

> I was actually looking for a job while I was going to college. I was doing a lot of waitressing work, and I happened to be looking through the paper to see if I could get some work over the summer. . . . I just happened to watch that same afternoon *Dirty Dancing*. . . . I had always been trying to explain to my family how in love with dancing I was. . . . As I am looking through the paper for a job, it said, "Do you want to dance like *Dirty Dancing*?" They were training for ballroom dance teachers at Arthur Murray's. I went for the audition, . . . and I think they hired maybe two or three of us. I thought I had gone to heaven. I couldn't believe that people actually paid me to teach dance.

Stephanie was so thrilled with this job that she almost left school, but her parents thought she was crazy:

> I have a wonderful . . . working-class family, not into the arts at all. . . . They thought I would get over this dancing thing once I got my degree. It was always like, "No, you should be a teacher. It's got good benefits, and you know what your hours are. . . ." They could never understand. They used to call it the gypsy life. I said, "That's great. I love that."

Stephanie provides another example of an American woman dancer whose version of femininity was the good-time girl with stars in her eyes —a girl who did not settle down to marry and raise a family, as her parents expected. Stephanie's parents envisioned a daughter who would graduate from college prepared for a safe and reliable fallback career, if needed, after she married. In college, Stephanie had almost switched her major from history and education to dance, but the thought of it upset her parents, who saw college as an investment in financial stability. Stephanie, in her midforties at the time of the interview, had never married, and nobody was in the offing. It was hard to meet anyone because, she said, "our social life is so tied to our dancing life." In contrast to Laura, Stephanie expected dancing to lead to a career from the get-go. Perhaps her college education made her more career oriented.

Stephanie's career followed the gypsy existence her parents feared. She moved to an independent studio after a few years at Arthur Murray but could not develop a big enough base of students. She then worked for several places simultaneously, but her "big break" came when she started teaching salsa at a hot nightclub in the city. She then got an opportunity to teach another salsa class at a popular suburban ballroom, "and it was a huge success." Stephanie decided she needed to expand:

> My salsa business really grew tremendously. I was renting out space and kept getting moved around. I said, "Okay, it's time. We need to get our own building. . . . " I felt like the people that had been following me through my career deserved a place of their own, a place that was ours, and nobody could change our schedule and tell us to leave, whatever their agenda. . . . Ever since then, we've added other programs, and teachers who are independent have a little niche of their own, like the Argentine tango and R&B line dancing, West Coast swing, and hip hop. I had to expand to accommodate those programs while I was teaching the salsa and the ballroom.

By the time Stephanie bought a building on the outskirts of the city, her father, who was a building contractor, was sufficiently supportive of her goals to coordinate the plumbers and electricians fixing up the building and to do much of the carpentry himself. Her loyal Italian American family, though they had been unsettled by Stephanie's choice of career, helped her achieve success.

Stephanie was happy teaching social dancing to groups of students in her own space and preferred this to the private lessons at Arthur Murray. "I think everybody should dance," she said. Although she never taught high school history, Stephanie saw herself as a teacher with the same goals of improving the world that a history teacher might have. She loved all the hugging and touching involved in teaching dance and considered flirting to be a healthy activity. She described herself as the best party giver in town—a good-time girl through and through—and most of her friends were people she had met in the business.

Stephanie rarely got the opportunity to dance with a professional partner, and this was what she most missed about competing. She described the pleasures of connection on the dance floor:

> There is nothing worse than dancing with someone who is really just a bunch of steps, and they're not really paying attention. It's really the chemistry, the conversation between two partners during the dance that makes the magic. . . . If a man's able to do that, if he is paying attention to the

woman, and he's giving her a good solid frame, and he's allowing her to be creative, a lot of the woman's personality can really blossom out of that, her sexuality, her playfulness, and his as well.

Stephanie's description shows that professional dancers are as capable of enjoying the pleasures of instant intimacy as students are. Unfortunately, she had to put up with her share of social dancers who were "just a bunch of steps," because steps constitute the content of social dance classes.

Pro/Am Women: Managing Husband and Teacher

Many of the women students I interviewed were competition devotees. Phoebe, whom we met in chapter 1, scrimped and saved in order to compete, and she was not alone in this. However, many women who competed were either successful professionals spending their disposable income or wives of affluent men.

Becky-Sue was spending her husband's money. She had helped him build a profitable business, and now in her midfifties and retired from this task, she considered the money she spent on dancing to be her payback. She was seduced into starting dance lessons through a flirtatious come-on:

I have always been a social dancer. I was out celebrating my best girl-friend's birthday with several friends. We were dancing, and a young gentleman came up to me and asked me if I danced. I said, "I'm dancing now." He goes, "Do you have any dance training?" I said, "Not really. I have a little tap, that's it. I've just always loved to dance." He said to me, "Well, you should try ballroom. . . ." My perception of it, at that point, was it was really for older people. . . . He says, "Well, rhythm and Latin are very similar to what you like," so I went for a complementary lesson [with him].

Although Becky-Sue remembered that her parents loved to jitterbug, there had never been money for dance lessons. Becky-Sue described herself as a tomboy who loved sports and building tree huts. However, once she started having dance lessons, she quickly became enthralled. Although her dancing resulted from an instant attraction to a charming young man, her relationship with her current longtime teacher was complex. She described their relationship as "love-hate." As she explained, "There is no way you can be around someone about fifteen years and not have some kind of emotional connection with one another." In fact, she compared it to "being with your husband every day." In both cases, she noted, "I know what he says before he opens his mouth, and he knows what I'm going to say, and we know each other's looks."

Becky-Sue entered the ballroom through instant intimacy. As can be seen, this often develops into something deeper over time. However, although Becky-Sue was the client, her teacher was clearly in charge, and his approval was important to her. Even when women appear to have power in a situation, they seek approval to a greater extent than men do.[19] Her reaction contrasts with that of the men in the previous chapter. Men who danced were concerned about the reactions of other men both off the dance floor and on. Women also defined themselves through the eyes of men. Becky-Sue described her teacher as giving her "a hard time," like her husband. She worked hard to please them both. For example, her teacher complained if she did not go to an extra evening class, while her husband demanded that she stay home. "There's constant conflict" with her teacher, she said, adding that he yelled at her a lot and spoiled her good time. Her ideal teacher differed from any she knew. "If I had my way," she said, her teacher "would be somebody that would stay calm and be positive." However, she added, "We all know that [men] can't do that. It's ingrained in them. They learn to talk to us like this, and they also declare things: 'Keep your hands where I tell you.'" Becky-Sue believed in a world where men are from Mars; they push women around. However, it was men she strove to please.

Becky-Sue had been having lessons for so long that she had a clear idea of the things she needed to work on. She had a longer list of weaknesses than strengths. Listening to her, it was not always easy to see what Becky-Sue got out of spending so much time and money on dance. Yet it organized her life and was central to her identity. First, she believed that dancing was good for her:

> I'm a true believer that dancing really truly keeps you young. I don't think I've ever met a ballroom dancer that is not sharp, their body's physically fit, and they're happy. They've done studies and found out that that's true. They've determined that not only is it good for you, but it's mentally good. It prevents Alzheimer's because you're constantly having to think about music and timing and choreography and steps, all kinds of stuff.

Whether ballroom dancing prevents Alzheimer's is not the point. What is important to remember is that Becky-Sue believed it to be so.

In addition, Becky-Sue loved to dance:

> It's something people ask me when we're dancing. They go, "I love watching you, 'cause you're always smiling." It's 'cause I'm having a good time. . . . I figure you're doing it for yourself. . . . There's a saying I read about dancing: "It's an expression of the inner soul. It's an expression of who you are on the inside." What I am on the inside is I'm fun. I'm a happy person. I have a lot of energy. It's a release for me in so many ways, emotionally, physically. It allows me to be who I feel I really am.

As someone who has watched Becky-Sue dance many times, I can attest to the obvious pleasure she takes in performing. She told me that she often wished she had gone into show business instead of following her father's advice for a safe career.

Another benefit of dancing was the friendships Becky-Sue had made on the dance floor. Her teacher took a number of students to competitions:

> To me we're a competitive team. If I'm dancing, they cheer for me, and I cheer for them, especially for new dancers. [My teacher] dances a lot. He goes to bed early. The good thing about it is I've become friends with so many people. I go to dinner and people go, . . . "Come over and sit with us." It's like a family. When I go to a competition, everyone's kissing and hugging each other, because we all know each other. It's wonderful to go, because we cheer for each other. When we're competing against each other —even if we win or lose—we say, "Hey, great job."

This emotional support among dancers was something reported by many women competitors. They wanted to please men, and they made friends with women.

Although Becky-Sue complained about her teacher, she saw him as caring:

> I see teachers out there that don't really put the effort into dancing with their students. That really bothers me, because it's almost like they don't think that they're capable of it. I think that if you don't think a student's capable of it, they never rise to the occasion. I think that's the reason [my

teacher] is tough on me. He expects so much out of me. . . . He says, "I know you think I'm hard on you, but I know, deep down, you have the potential to do so much more. That's why I keep pushing you. I'm trying to get it out."

A final reason why Becky-Sue loved to dance was because it kept her husband on his toes. She liked to tease and flirt with men, and she thought that dancing with another man made him jealous and cognizant of her value. Becky-Sue believed that marriages benefited from a little outside competition:

> When I first started. [my husband] didn't like it. Number one, I think most men don't like their wives or girlfriends dancing with another man. Number two, the financial aspect of it. We did have quite a few arguments when I first started; the problem being is I'm a very stubborn person. We just kept butting heads, but eventually he realized how important dancing is to me. . . . He is a wonderful man, and he realizes that it is the thing that will make me happy. . . . He realized that there's no threat. I'm not running off with some Latin lover. Don't ask me why they think that happens. They think they're all Latin. . . . My teacher's married with two kids, so he's okay with it now.

The encouragement of jealousy is typical of women who use flirting as a way of obtaining power in a relationship.[20]

Becky-Sue believed that her husband "talked out of both sides of his mouth" about her dancing. He complained about the expense to his friends, but he also boasted about how good she was and how she knew everyone in the ballroom world. When a professional on *Dancing with the Stars* gave her tickets to see it live, Becky-Sue's husband told everyone.

Pro/Am Women: Spending Their Own Money

Wendy was a successful career woman making her own choices about money. She had been dancing almost as long as Becky-Sue had and was about the same age. They had often competed against each other, but there the comparison ends. Although Wendy was married, she had her own income and did not rely on her husband, or his permission, to enroll in dancing. She ran a profitable small business in a male-dominated field and viewed herself as a woman who had made it in a man's world.

Unlike Becky-Sue, Wendy had not always loved to dance. As a child, she had enrolled in ballet lessons for a short while but gave it up when it proved difficult and painful. She had never played competitive sports, describing herself as the "kind of kid who would come home and say, 'I think I'm going to get all As, but there's a chance I might flunk gym.'" She started dancing as a result of work:

> [My husband] and I had been to a number of social events, and he was the worst white man dancing on two legs. Prior to our son going away to college, I had been on the board of an organization where there was a guy who was ten years older than I was, and his big shtick was to say, "Who wants to go dancing?" at the events of the board meeting. . . . We were in New Orleans, and . . . we got down on the dance floor—my father had taught me how to dance a regular waltz and foxtrot when I was nine years old. The music was playing; we couldn't have been dancing more than seven and a half seconds, and he dropped his arms and he stepped back about four feet, and he said, "I don't make the rules. I lead. You follow. Do you want to do it?" I said, "Yeah," sort of changed gears, and it worked. . . . [Our son] went off to college, and [my husband] and I looked at one another and said, "So what are we going to do together?" Like an idiot, I said, "Let's go learn to take dance lessons?"

The experience was terrible at first because Wendy learned quickly but her husband "couldn't hear the music." She felt stuck, because she did not want to hurt his feelings. Just as she was about to ask the studio if she and her husband could have separate lessons, they said, "We have to split you up. You're dancing at very different levels." Deciding there was "a God in Heaven" after all, Wendy never looked back. When I interviewed her, she had gone from once weekly with her husband to four double lessons per week by herself.

When she first had lessons with the teacher they assigned her to, she described the interchange as follows:

> He looks at me with those dark eyes, and he goes, "I've been looking forward to this." And I thought, "Oh, you pile of shit. That may work on women who don't have good-looking guys ever talk to them." Then he

said—and this is the part that I love, the part that got to me—"I like my women to dance strong; there's a really fine line between lead and follow." I thought, "I have no idea what the man said, but this could be a lot more entertaining than I thought."

Wendy was in a different social location than Becky-Sue was, but she responded as enthusiastically to the flirting, although she interpreted it differently.

Wendy is the kind of successful woman that writers often refer to as a queen bee—a woman who has succeeded in a world dominated by men and who thinks of herself as getting along better with men than with women.[21] When Wendy started competing, her attitude was quite different from that of Becky-Sue. She did not like her teacher to compete with a professional partner at the same competition, because doing so made him "very absorbed in his own stuff." Furthermore, she reported that if he did not place well, "he was self-indulgent and immature and out of control and a pain in the ass." Neither did she like it when he took other students, because "he would take them through their paces, and they didn't compete as much as I did, so they were more nervous than I was, and I would get short shrift in the whole thing."

Unlike Becky-Sue, Wendy did not make friends with other women who competed:

> I'm much better on my own. . . . I don't like group experiences, because other people do not have the same standards I do. . . . I'm intolerant of their personal anxieties. . . . There are also tensions between me and the other students in the dancing thing. It's kind of weird. Some of it has to do with women, and I don't hang out with women very much. Women have strange things about body image, jealousies of things that I'm not engaged in. . . . I don't understand the style of communication. Most of my friends are men.

Eventually, Wendy decided that her teacher, with whom she had competed many times, was paying her too little attention. He was taking other students as well, and he had a new, talented student competing at a level Wendy could not hope to achieve, so she dumped him for a different teacher. This new teacher, she believed, was better than the old one; he knew more and was top in his field. "What he knows about dance," she said, "is unbelievable." Wendy wanted to believe she had the best, unlike Becky-Sue, who thought that there might be a better teacher somewhere. Wendy described her current teacher's decisions as evidence of his excellence. For example, in answer to a question about coaching (many top students have coaching), she replied, "Now that I am with [the new teacher] I almost never have coaching, because he coaches everybody else in the world. He is not very likely to accept much in the way of coaching [from anyone else] 'cause he *is* the coach." This appears to have been something of an exaggeration; no professional ever mentioned having used her teacher as a coach, but Wendy wanted to believe that she had the best.

Although Wendy did not make friends with other women, she defined herself in terms of the male gaze, like Becky-Sue did.[22] She wanted men to admire her, she wanted to believe she danced with the most talented men, and she wanted to be special in their eyes. She was particularly inclined to see herself this way, but, as can be seen in comparing the women's stories with the men's, she was not alone in this.

One aspect of the queen bee syndrome is the desire to draw attention to oneself. Wendy used dancing to do this in her work, an occupation far removed from dancing. She did it with a self-deprecating wit:

> I once showed a client of mine years ago. I'd been doing it so much, I didn't get what a disconnect it was from who I am and how I'm perceived in my professional life. . . . He looks at the picture, and he just walks off. . . . The next day he called me on business, and I said to him, "That was a weird reaction to looking at those photos. It's not like you don't know who I am. You've heard me say, 'Fuck!' nine million times." He said, "No, you don't understand. I couldn't even get my head around that."

Once again, Wendy described herself through the male gaze.

Nevertheless, Wendy lost no opportunity to describe herself as tough. She explained that her current teacher understood that she was "a pretty volatile personality" and that he was too. She described their relationship as involving "an enormous amount of yelling and banter," which she loved. Dancing, she enthused, is "competitive, there's fashion, you get to hear good music, and I get to dance with gorgeous guys." Here, Wendy's commitment to heterosexuality and womanhood is clear, but she saw herself as a woman among men. In this sense, dancing with great male partners suited her perfectly. Like Becky-Sue, the relationship with the teacher was important, but the interpretation of its meaning differed.

Part of Wendy's self-identity came from her success in a man's world; she had never done anything by halves. Learning to dance had been hard for her because, she said,

> I had to come up against the fact that it didn't matter how smart I was; this was a different transaction. I'm at the top of my field. I'm the best in the country at what I do—acknowledged as the best. . . . I knew I was competitive, although I don't compete [at work], but I found out I really was competitive. . . . [Another student] one day said to me—I'd probably been dancing for like two years—she said, "What is your goal in competing?" I thought this was a dumb question. I said, "It's to be the best in the country at what I do."

Becky-Sue also wanted to be a winner, but whereas Wendy thought wanting to win made her unusual as a woman, Becky-Sue justified this desire by adding, "We all want to win." Whereas Wendy thought winning meant being number one, Becky-Sue qualified it this way: "if you walk off the floor and you feel that you did the best that you could do and that's all there was—they didn't like it—I don't feel bad." Hers was not the "winning is everything" attitude of men's competitive sports.[23] In this example, we see two different ways of performing femininity. Wendy, with her elaborate makeup, thick head of hair, and voluptuous figure, liked to play the bad girl with a foul mouth who had no time for women but could vamp men. Becky-Sue was the attractive older wife of a successful man; she loved to dance and was friends with everyone. Both of them used flirting as a form of power, but whereas Becky-Sue wanted to be viewed as adorable, Wendy used it to disarm men.

Younger women are frequently highly competitive. Natalka Cap, seen in figure 2.1 dancing rhythm with Jose DeCamps, won her heats at both the United States Dance Competition and the Ohio Star Ball. Another equally competitive student, Christine Stanko Burkholder, seen in figure 7.2 practicing with Jean Paulovich, has won these events as well as the Latin events dancing with other partners. Although she was taking a maternity break during this picture, she retains her performance skills. The intense focus of teacher and student in this picture shows how important pro/am is to them.

Fig. 7.2. Focus. Christine Stanko Burkholder, in a coaching session with Jean Paulovich, shows the focus that enabled her to win national titles in pro/am Latin and rhythm. © 2010 Jonathan S. Marion.

Challenges to Romance: Dancing with Gay Men

One thing Becky-Sue and Wendy had in common was the illusion of ro-mance they enjoyed on the dance floor. Here are their answers when I asked them how they would feel dancing with a gay partner. Becky-Sue:

> I have danced with gay men. Don't get me wrong. I don't know how I would feel dancing with a gay man knowing their sexuality preference. You don't know whether the chemistry would be the same between you. . . . I don't mean that I hate gay men. . . . I feel very comfortable. In fact they're wonderful. They're like girlfriends to me, . . . like all the same things you do and love to talk. Frankly, they're much more personable than straight men as far as conversing and company and things like that. I don't know if I could feel the same connection knowing that that man doesn't like women that way.[24]

Wendy:

> I would not do it if they were gay. . . . For me, there's a man-woman thing that goes on. I don't screw them, I'm not involved with them, but definitely the essence of what dancing is all about is sex. It's a legitimized form of sexual interacting with people who you otherwise are not having physical relations with. Although I will tell you that one of my two most fabulous dance moments, . . . an older guy, gay, but built—he works out . . .—asked me to do the foxtrot. We got on the floor. This was like Fred and Ginger. He led, I followed. It was stuff—like it was unbelievable. The dance ended. . . . He went, "Wow! I need a cigarette. How about you?" I said, "That was fucking amazing." . . . [Being gay] didn't matter. It was just terrific dancing. But on a regular basis if you were to ask me, I would go, "Yeah, it matters."

These comments underscore the point that the intimacy typically pur-chased in dance lessons is heterosexual.[25] Even though neither woman ex-pected, or wanted, a romance with her teacher, each liked the safe sexual fantasy that ballroom provided. Imagination could only go so far. They could not fantasize about heterosexual romance with an openly gay part-ner. Yet, as Wendy describes, in the heat of the moment, she did have an erotic dancing experience with a gay teacher. Perhaps the dance itself can transcend conversation in practice, if not in theory. No doubt there are other students—I consider myself to be an example—who find lessons with a gay teacher to be just as exciting as those with one who is straight.[26]

Social Dance

Many students who competed were not as serious as Becky-Sue and Wendy. Most had not been dancing as long, nor had they been to as many competitions. Most of these students were career women, either married to men who did not dance or not currently married. Many of the serious competitors I interviewed did not spend as much as Becky-Sue or Wendy did. They were more like Phoebe, whom we met in chapter 1, scrimping and sacrificing other aspects of their lives in order to compete. In addition, many women I interviewed were social dancers, and it is to these that I now turn.

Hazel started learning to dance in her midfifties. Her husband was home on disability, suffering from congenital heart failure. He had been a competitive athlete in his youth but now could not easily leave the house. She needed an outlet, other than the long hours she put in at work. She had always loved to dance:

> When I was a little girl, I always used to dance by myself around the house. . . . When I got to be about ten years old, my girlfriend was fourteen, and she started learning all these dances from going to big dances. At ten years old, I learned to do all these dances, and I was actually very good. Then I saw *West Side Story*, and I just died over it, so I was constantly doing jazz along with the ballet. I used to do ballet by myself because my mother would never send me to dance school. . . . I went to at least two dances a week growing up. . . . I started going at twelve. . . . There were thousands of kids in that ballroom. . . . We would just dance and dance. When I got older—I was about twenty-seven—and I was looking through the phonebook, and I saw a ballet school. All of a sudden, I said, "Well, why don't I try it?" . . . It was all pink and Tchaikovsky. It was wonderful. She was a stickler. Everything had to be perfect.

Like many women, Hazel thought of herself as creative and sensitive. She had been an art major and was "very much into what is beautiful."

Hazel had to stop ballet after an injury, but she still loved to dance. One day, she persuaded a German co-worker to teach the Viennese waltz to a group of her friends, "all crowded into a room at work." He then taught them cha-cha, rumba, and swing. Then a group of them started going to local social dances. Hazel liked it but did not think "it was great" because, she said, she wanted to know exactly what she was doing wrong. At that point, she joined the group classes of a local social dance teacher and had not looked back.

Hazel loved her teacher but found the lessons frustrating. She blamed this on the men:

> I've been shown a step, and they've been shown a step, and they cancel out my step. I'm trying to execute it the way she showed, and—this happens a lot—they see it in a different way than she showed it, because people do not always do what you tell them to. They walk across you, and they block you. . . . I know where I'm supposed to be, but I'm supposed to follow. . . . The other thing is that if you don't lead at all, because they're thinking with their feet so much, they're completely limp. They have no frame, zero frame. I just dance the step myself then. . . . They're grateful. . . . People often feel like their teacher's looking at them and thinking, "Oh, good, she didn't see me mess up." They do worry about what the teacher thinks. Men look for approval more than women, I think.

Once again, we see the common theme that men are different from women. Whereas Becky-Sue complained that men always wanted to take charge, Hazel complained when they were unable to. All the women in this chapter, in spite of their different gender performances, believed in a gender divide.

Hazel also saw herself as bolder than the men. She described herself as the only one she knows "that gives hot and heavy looks," adding, "You look at them, and then you snap your head back to look at them again."[27] She said that "it just unglues the men" with whom she danced. Furthermore, they did not know how to read her intent and sometimes started flirting with her. Hazel enjoyed their confusion. It made her feel powerful. She described herself as thinking, "Just go ahead. I will surprise you, honey."

Hazel claimed to be indifferent to the social aspects of dancing, reporting that she could not care less if she was "dancing with a broomstick if that broomstick could dance." However, her dream was to dance with a professional dancer who had coached group classes at her studio and was tall, like her. She sounded wistful when she said that she would think she had died and gone to heaven if she could "just be able to do a whole dance with him." She brought his name up several times during the interview and appeared to have the kind of harmless crush on him that is common in the

Fig. 7.3. Hands-on. Teacher Cristina Rodrighes-Mueller is comfortable putting her hands on Emma Farber's head to demonstrate the head roll in the cha-cha. DanceSport Academy, Ardmore, PA, July 2010. © 2010 Jonathan S. Marion.

dance world. After the interview, she cross-examined me about how much he might charge for lessons. When I told her, she thought she would not be able to afford it. However, I saw her at a social dance party sometime after the interview, and she was now having lessons from this teacher and had even been to a local competition with him. Like Phoebe, she had somehow found the resources.

Although the concept of doing gender is an imperfect one, it is quite useful for understanding the development of a dancing identity. No matter the type of gender performance—"tough broad," "party girl," "sweet young thing," "the opposite sex," to name but a few—dancing was always compatible. It told the viewer that this was a real woman. Learning to dance is compatible with the way women learn to perform gender in American society, because in the end there are strict gender roles enforced in dancing, namely, that men lead and women follow. Although men's performances seem unconventional at first, and in some ways they truly are, they do not really challenge the concept of "doing gender," and their performance embodies a strict and powerful masculinity.

However, teaching dance is difficult for women. First, it is difficult to make a living. As discussed in previous chapters, women are more frequent purchasers of the intimacy of partner dancing and the illusion of romance that this brings with it.[28] There are opportunities for women to teach social dancing, but this is difficult for women who compete.[29] One way that women are able to make a living teaching dance is by teaching children, an activity which has increased as a result of children watching *So You Think You Can Dance* and even *Dancing with the Stars*. Women have more permission to touch children than do men, as can be seen in figure 7.3, in which Cristina Rodrighes-Mueller instructs Emma Farber and her partner, Isaac Bredbenner, how to do a head roll in the cha-cha. It is hard to imagine a man feeling comfortable doing this or parents allowing their child to be handled in this way by a man.

Becoming a dancer, as we have seen, is a somewhat different process for men and for women. But what happens when dancers age? As we will see in the next chapter, this also varies by gender. As in the rest of the society, aging has different meanings for men than for women.

8

The Music Hasn't Stopped

The Aging Dancer

A *NEW YORK TIMES* article entitled "Seeing Old Age as a Never-Ending Adventure" described a surge in extreme activities among the elderly, who increasingly view their later years as a time to explore new endeavors once viewed as exclusive to the young.[1] The story included a woman who went hiking in the South African wilderness at age ninety, and an eighty-nine-year-old man who strapped his feet to the top of a single-engine biplane and crossed the English Channel at 160 miles per hour. In reading the article, I recalled a dancer who was still competing at eighty-nine. Although she was older than most, there are many competition dancers in their sixties and seventies. Many of them are like me—they danced a little when they were young but took it up seriously in their later years. While dancing is not as extreme as "wing walking," it still requires courage and an appetite for the unknown to learn something physically and mentally challenging in one's later years. And one has to be willing to subject oneself to visual appraisal, something that is not always easy for an aging body to withstand.

While many amateurs discover the joys of partner dancing in their later years, professional dancers face a relentless emphasis on youth. Professionals, particularly the men, tease one another about aging—some take years off when discussing their age in public—and most expect their competitive careers to be over by their fortieth birthday. When dancers continue to compete after that, their age is constantly mentioned. For example, an interview in *Dance Beat* with retiring professional rhythm dancer Michael Neil focused on how long he had competed—twenty years—how old he was at retirement, and how he had managed to "dance for such a long time":

> There has been a lot of speculation about how old Michael Neil is, would he tell us now? "Michael Neil is 46 years old and fortunately through good genes, keeping my hair and my teeth, I've been able to dance for such a

long time. Dancing keeps you youthful, and through being involved in dancing and being an active person I've been able to keep a youthful look for a very long period of time. So at 46, I've been able to keep up with the younger, faster, smaller people."[2]

The story was replete with pictures of a youthful-looking Michael with his family, including teenage daughters, testifying to dancing's ability to keep one young. His ageless appearance was especially important when Michael danced with his final partner, Danielle Wilson, who was much younger than he. It is hard to imagine a forty-six-year-old woman still competing professionally.

Intimacy and Age

Most portrayals of intimacy are only deemed appropriate for young people. Think of the movies: the great romances are for the young, sometimes the middle-aged, but rarely the old. This is especially true for women. In popular culture, love and sex are the province of the young and the beautiful; indeed, beauty itself belongs to the young.[3] When older people are described as beautiful, their youthfulness is always mentioned. In a study asking people of different ages to rate the beauty of images, raters of all ages classified adolescent faces as more beautiful than those of either children or adults.[4] It should be no surprise that dancers in their twenties—old enough to have experienced love and loss but young enough to look perfect—can more believably portray a love and intimacy that audiences recognize.

Even among pro/am teachers who no longer compete professionally, youth is the order of the day. While some are in their fifties or older, most are younger. The same is true in competition dance studios, where teachers are typically younger than age fifty. Given the rigors of hours of private lessons or of competing with several students in one day, it is not surprising that pro/am dancing is largely a young person's occupation. This creates problems for students, many of whom are older women.

We are culturally uncomfortable when older women dance with young men. On *Dancing with the Stars*, eighty-two-year-old Cloris Leachman was considered too old to dance with any of the show's young regulars. Instead, she partnered forty-eight-year-old Corky Ballas. The age difference was still sufficiently problematic that the couple hammed it up throughout each performance with pseudodramatic looks, pratfalls, and unlikely moves such as using Cloris as a wheelbarrow in the jive.[5] In contrast, eighty-year-old Buzz Aldrin was comfortable dancing with twenty-eight-year-old Ashley DelGrosso.

Injury and Age

Dancers' attitudes toward aging are reminiscent of those professed by young athletes who use a "decline narrative" when asked to imagine what would happen to their bodies as they age.[6] Drawing on images of parents and grandparents, these athletes describe aging as a process of getting weaker and feebler, which they regard with horror. The sports-science curriculum these young athletes were enrolled in emphasizes aging "in biological terms rather than a more social and relational context."[7] Students worried about declining bodies, rather than about developing emotional skills and connections to sustain them as they get older. In addition to the physical rigors of dance, teachers, unlike athletes, must maintain their instant-intimacy skills as they age. Yet dance teachers also ignore the socioemotional aspects of aging. Furthermore, their lifestyles leave them vulnerable in this respect.

Competition, even pro/am competition, is so physically taxing that many professionals get injured. This is one of the main reasons they stop competing. Of the dancers I interviewed, even those who remained injury free gave superstitious answers to my questions about injuries, such as "So far, no," as they looked around for a piece of wood to knock on. Some dancers became injured because of poor technique; others hurt themselves during intense exercise regimes. Colin hurt his knee practicing yoga:

> I was actually stretching, doing a lot of yoga at the time. It's just one of the moves when you're rolling like a ball, and you get up without using your hands. I must have had an injury to my knee, and I just got up very quickly, without the hands. I pushed down, and as I pushed down, it just popped.

Colin was sufficiently debilitated that he was unable to compete for several months.

In a study of ballet dancers, Bryan Turner and Steven Wainwright describe dancers' injuries as social constructions.[8] Ballet dancers have constant injuries and pain. They live in a community of dancers who accept injuries as part of the experience, while simultaneously fearing an injury serious enough to interfere with a planned performance or even to put a stop to their career. Turner and Wainwright note that the decision to stop dancing because of injury is often arbitrarily determined.

This attitude toward injury and pain was shared by the dancers in my study. As Pamela, a top professional ballroom competitor, put it, "If you work hard, play hard, then things get sore." Many professional dancers echoed this matter-of-fact sentiment. Even serious problems were met with stoicism. For example, when Sofiya had surgery for varicose veins, she said, the "fourth day after the operation, I still had bandages on, and I was doing routines." She added, "I cannot take 'no' from my body for an answer." This emphasis on making one's body respond as ordered adds to dancers' fears of aging, because they envision a day when they are unable to do this.

When Competing Ends

In addition to physical anxieties, aging brings financial and emotional problems for professionals. Unless they own studios, many dancers save little retirement money, having moved around during their teaching careers. As a result, most continue searching for work in the dancing business, because they do not have the skills and experience to succeed elsewhere. As many dancers told me, when you have grown up dancing, there are few opportunities to make a comfortable living outside the ballroom.

Some successful former competitors become judges who also provide coaching to competitors. Some judges travel to competitions almost every week—a tiring and alienating way to make a living as one gets older, because judges must travel constantly and stand at the edge of the dance floor, hour after hour, judging heat after heat. It also requires intense emotional labor, because judges are always "on" in public competition spaces, as can be seen in figure 6.2.

Judges all know one another and exhibit a joking intimacy and camaraderie while passing the time between heats. They know most of the top dancers and teachers and often joke with them. However, they do not always know each other well, because they only meet at competitions. When they are judging, they work the floor for several hours at a time, from early morning until late evening, so they may spend only a few hours, at most, with friends. Since judges work different hours from most Americans and travel constantly, they may know few people outside the dance world. The fortunate ones travel as couples, and there are several well-known longtime partnerships. However, many judges are single, with former spouses and partners inhabiting the same world they do. The lasting partnerships are noted because they are uncommon. As people get older, they typically become more isolated as friends move away or die, but this is particularly true for dance professionals because they have so few friends in their home neighborhoods.

Douglas had danced professionally since he was a young adult, having first learned social dancing when it was popular among young people in Britain during and after World War II. Over his long career, he had won many competitions. Though he had ventured out from the ballroom world from time to time to work as a choreographer in other fields of dance, he never strayed far. He now spent his days coaching young couples and judging competitions. His greatest coaching strength, he said, was in helping couples sort out their conflicts:

> One encounters the full spectrum in a dancing school. When I was a young man, it used to scare me a little bit; now I embrace the problems. I can't wait for someone to have a problem because the greatest thing you can do is resolve breakdowns. Out of resolving breakdowns, you can make breakthroughs. . . . To me it's a challenge, being able to sit down and listen to this person's problems and for me to be their sounding board.

Douglas had come by these skills the hard way. He described the most difficult aspect of learning to dance as his "own immaturity in the dance relationship with a girl." Conflicts came, he said, from "two people seeing things only from their own position and not being able to have a common ground and ultimately needing a third party to resolve it." Coaches could do this, especially those who had experience. Couples now go to him not so much for technique as for "counseling in relationships."

Douglas said, "I just think I am the luckiest person in the world to have been . . . able to make my living doing what I love." When asked how hard it was to make a living as a dancer, he answered,

> There are more opportunities nowadays to make a good living for the dancer than ever before. Probably the whole aspect of ballroom dancing has been raised in the public consciousness to a point where it's about to become a megatrend. Dancing schools are doing better than they've ever done before. Given that a teacher knows their work and is a good teacher

—I'm not just saying a good dancer—they can make a very good living.
. . . You don't have to be a millionaire.

Douglas was financially stable but had paid a price for his unsettled life. He was no longer married to his former partner—they remained friends, but their careers had moved in different directions, and they lived in different parts of the country. Douglas lived alone, and when he developed a travel-related illness, he struggled to obtain help. He had many friends in the dance world, and "to see friends" was his reason for continuing to judge competitions. Dance was his world, and he had given it his all. Although he knew how to perform intimacy and to help couples resolve intimacy problems on the dance floor, he experienced little day-to-day intimacy in his personal life.

Many older professional dancers were less fortunate than Douglas, because they had not had the same level of competitive success. Most dance teachers had competed only occasionally. Hans had grown up in Germany at a time when most young people learned to dance. He had begun teaching there as a teenager but soon moved to America, where he became an Arthur Murray teacher just as the international style was becoming popular here. He always loved everything about the "English style," explaining, "I loved the precision of it. I loved the look of it. I loved the naturalness of it, the nature of it."

Though his parents were horrified at his career choice, Hans became a professional teacher. Throughout his adult life, he had worked as a journeyman dance teacher, holding several jobs simultaneously and even teaching at both Arthur Murray and Fred Astaire at one point: "Of course, that was a big taboo. I made sure one did not know about the other." He had taught a ballroom course for several years in a university's dance department. Eventually he opened his own studio in a large city and taught there for "many years," but the building was in disrepair, and he had to close. When I interviewed him, he was teaching one class a week for a local social dance studio. He also taught individuals and couples in his home, having turned his dining room into a small dance studio. Since the room was "not really big enough to do international," he said, "I do American style and social dancing. I teach weddings and Latin, and if I need to have a larger premises, there's a church right down the street here has a ballroom."

Hans enjoyed teaching but had trouble obtaining enough students to make a living. Having taught for forty-three years, he was at retirement age with no retirement in sight. He had been much busier at one time, "especially during the hustle era," he said. "I needed extra teachers, because it was so popular." Even at the best of times, none of his teachers had been on salary, nor could they afford health insurance. They worked as independent contractors (mostly teaching group classes) paid by the class and often teaching for several studios. He used to teach "eight hours a day," he said. "That kind of strength you have only when you are young. Now, I do four or five hours; that's enough." Now that Hans was older, he experienced worsening eye problems and was no longer able to drive. He also told me that he had lost much of his flexibility: "With age it disappears." And he added, "It takes longer to warm up, and my steps might get a little shorter."

Hans had many dance acquaintances but few close dance friends. Like Douglas, he had struggled with the intimacy dancing required. He, too, blamed this on immaturity. Problems between Hans and his partner "didn't always get resolved, because when you are young, you're arrogant." These problems, he explained, "don't go away." Instead, "they continue to threaten." Hans's solution to this was to look for a partner who "was able to put up with arrogance," because, he said, "I was in charge." He was now married to his second wife, whom he had met when she came for lessons.

Patrick, a chain school dancer, also found it difficult to sustain a decent standard of living as he got older and found himself with little in the way of savings. He was long married to Doreen, the Catholic schoolgirl whom he had met when she worked at the same studio. Patrick had switched from Arthur Murray to Fred Astaire and, at one point, had owned several franchises. By the 1980s, declining enrollments forced him to close, with little to show for all their work. He and his wife still worked as independent teachers, each teaching group lessons in different parts of town. They had a small dance floor in their basement where individual lessons could be taught, and they ran a bimonthly dance party using a rented space. Patrick was fastidious about his appearance, with carefully combed hair and neat clothes, habits instilled in him in the early days. When he worked for the chains, he had had to wear a suit or jacket and slacks and always a tie. When I asked him what he thought of the changes in the dress code, he answered, "I wasn't aware it had changed," adding, "I'm from the old school."

As might be expected, most of Patrick's friends were dancers. Even now, past retirement age, Patrick and Doreen worked almost every night of the week, with one night off to eat dinner together with their daughter and her husband, after which the parents taught the children to dance. Doreen commented, "It's not a money business. It is hand to mouth. If I stop working, my lifestyle is drastically cut." In addition, she was used to a busy evening life. She worried, "If and when I retire, that's drastic too, so I don't look forward to that part of it."

Of course, younger dancers do not envisage this as their fate. They may worry about the future occasionally, particularly if competitions are not going as well as they hoped, but most look ahead to the next competition or the next partner who might fix their performance problems and take them to the top. As we have seen, they also focus on creating bodies as youthful and glamorous as possible. Youthful dancers who no longer compete, or never did, imagine the day when they will open their own business and achieve financial security. Like others their age, young dancers do not worry about the absence of intimacy in their later years.

The major difference between these dancers and other young people is that the latter spend much of their time living and socializing with peers of their own age. In contrast, most American dancers teach those older than themselves. The young teachers are in positions of authority, but the older students are paying the bill. Though much of American society is age segregated, the ballroom world is not. Young and fit teachers must not only hold and caress the old and the wrinkled but are constantly reminded of the pains of aging as they deal with the problems of their students' bodies.

The Aging Woman

In recent years, those who write about the lifestyles of the elderly have emphasized the importance of staying active. Using the term "the new aging," this literature asserts that consumption, continued into old age, can help an individual retain the vigor of youth.[9] However, the elderly also face assumptions about their frailty and vulnerability and discover that others view their aging bodies as problematic.[10] This was certainly true for many of the women dancers I interviewed, who loved the idea of breaking what they saw as age rules but feared being thought of as foolish if they did. They worried, especially, about sustaining intimate relations with men much younger than themselves.

Older women face a choice between being "resolutely natural" or "relentlessly improved." For example, a study on resistance and aging compared Jane Fonda and Barbara Bush, showing that while Fonda celebrated the hard work of defying aging, Bush put equal effort into sustaining an image of aging gracefully and naturally.[11] Although the world of dance is one of elaborate artifice, some older dancers choose to show their age, albeit elegantly. Others go to great lengths to display youthful, even ageless bodies.

This contrast can be seen in color plate 8. The two student dancers, Beverly Moore and Joan Goddard, both compete in Ladies C Scholarship, which is for women fifty-one and older. At the 2009 Ohio Star Ball, Beverly narrowly beat Joan to win the Latin for the first time.[12] The photographs tell contrasting stories about aging. Both women are attractive, but the comparison ends there. Joan has the tanned and toned body and face of a much younger woman. Her sexy orange and pink Latin dress reveals her muscular bare legs, arms, and chest to the viewer. The dance pose also reveals her flexibility. In contrast, Beverly's long-sleeved black, filmy Latin dress is longer and goes straight from the neck to the knees. Her platinum-blond hair is neatly coiled into a bun, and her face does not appear to have seen plastic surgery. Only her back is bare. She presents herself like the elegant grandmother that she is.[13]

Each of these women looks comfortable dancing with a younger partner, and in their age category, this is the norm. However, dancers and students also live in the larger American culture, where partner age differences are the exception. This can intrude on a dancer's comfort. Furthermore, children and old people are expected to avoid some types of meaningful social interaction,[14] particularly displays of romantic passion—the young because they are excluded from sexual scripting in our culture[15] and the old because erotic love is considered inappropriate for them. When teachers are younger than the students with whom they dance pro/am, the older students have a particular problem. They are not only breaking the age rules about portraying intimacy and love; they are defying cultural norms about appropriate partners. Interestingly enough, while viewers of *Dancing with the Stars* are uncomfortable when older women dance with young men, at social dances and practices parties this happens all the time, as can be seen in figure 8.1. No one at the dance studios that I visited found this at all unusual.

Isabel, a showcase dancer, looked younger than her seventy-something years. She was in great shape and exercised regularly. She had started dancing after her husband died, in part because she was lonely. She had been a beginning-level teacher at Arthur Murray for a few years in her early twenties but had given that up when she married, although she regretted it afterward. At one point, she had persuaded her husband to take dance lessons with her, but he could never get the hang of it, and they had dropped it.

Fig. 8.1. Age differences matter less in dance studios. Here Jackie Murphy parties with Alex Jacobs. DanceSport Academy, Ardmore, PA, July 2010. © 2010 Jonathan S. Marion.

Isabel yearned for the physical and emotional contact she got from dancing, but she was nervous about being misunderstood and looking foolish:

> I'm uncomfortable. I don't want to seem like I'm making a move towards
> them. Yet they'll say, "You have to move in. The hips have to be here."
> Once I know this, I can do this. Once I get permission, I'm fine. . . . Some
> of the things that we do, and which I feel I can still do, I would like to do
> it just there at the studio or something. For somebody to see me, I would
> feel like they'll think, "What the heck is she doing? Her age, she's gonna
> do this?" If it calls for emotion, and it's supposed to be a sexy dance, and
> you're supposed to be looking at your partner, I think, "Is this for real or
> what?" I feel silly, I feel like, "Oh, this is ridiculous. I'm supposed to look at
> him?" I would love to be able to do it in the way it's supposed to be done,
> but once people see you, they're gonna think, "No!"

These sentiments were common among older women students. In our
culture, emotional rules are different for men than for women.[16] Whereas
older men are allowed to enjoy dancing with beautiful young women, older
women's romantic feelings about young men are considered laughable,
even shocking. Isabel wanted to abandon herself to the thrill of close and
intimate dancing, but the emotional boundaries interfered.

Isabel also worried that her teachers did not push her hard enough because they believed that her body would not cooperate:

> Some of the things they try with me—naturally the first time you ever did
> this, it's not going to be so good. But if they had done it a few more times,
> I think I could have done it. Right now, in the bolero—I wouldn't say it's a
> split, but your leg is up. He takes your leg. You wrap it around his, and then
> the other leg is back here, and he's pulling you along. It's sort of like a split.
> That was fine. I had no problem with that. We tried this once, a leg goes
> back in between his—I'd love to try some of these things, but I don't think
> they think I will do it well.

Isabel was still flexible, but her balance had worsened. To improve it for
the more difficult dance moves, she worked with weights and balls, and she
walked several miles every morning; at the gym, she said, "I have no problem." Balance problems occurred when "they're spinning you or turning
you." This would have made her teachers hesitant to do the kind of moves
Isabel described.

In addition to balance problems, Isabel thought that her teachers let her off easily, believing she could not remember complex routines because she was old. She imagined them saying, "Oh, well, she's not gonna remember this. Oh, you'd better do an easier [routine]." This made her think, "Darn. They're being easier with me, and I don't like that." She added, "I want to be able to do what I feel I could still do. I want them to think that I can still do this." Yet, when Isabel competed, she felt unsure of herself. Although she did not like it when her teachers made it easier or assumed she would not remember steps, she reported, "I don't think I look good when I am doing it. I'm always afraid I won't remember what I'm doing." Furthermore, she said, "I wished I had known more" because "the steps I was doing, they were all repetitions, repetitions, repetitions, and I wish I could do something better."

When competing, Isabel had won most of her entries but dismissed this success as reflective of the abilities of the other women in her age group: "Anybody would have walked in off the floor and been better than them." While at the competition, Isabel found it difficult to interact with her young teacher. She did not know what to say when they ate together and worried that he would rather be elsewhere. Although Isabel loved to dance, considering it a "type of therapy," her fears that she was not taken seriously by her teachers led her to stop having lessons. These student fears are difficult for teachers to assuage. Isabel was so certain that her teacher did not want to spend time with her that his assurances to the contrary did not convince her. Ours is a culture where it is hard to imagine handsome young men enjoying the company of older women. The media has made much of the rise of the "cougar," but the term refers to a beautiful woman in her forties enjoying a sexual liaison with a man ten to fifteen years younger.[17] Isabel was in her midseventies; one of her teachers was in his twenties, and the other in his thirties. Even though she did not want or expect romance, she could not even imagine the kind of instant intimacy that ballroom requires.

Isabel's was not the only type of story about age and the purchase of intimacy. Some older women reveled in the intimacy that dancing brought and in the permission dancing gave them to transgress age rules. Wendy, who was, as she put it, "fifty-seven, sadly" at the time of our interview, reported, "The age thing never bothered me." She was amused by what she termed "dance teacher bullshit," which she explained this way: "They invade your personal space about three inches more than is appropriate in a business setting." She added, "Their hands are all over you, and you're doing all these kinds of [intimate physical] things."

Although Wendy enjoyed the portrayal of intense intimate emotion with a younger man, she did not like her aging body. She had always been "really thin," but when she looked at her last showcase photographs, she said, "I looked pregnant, and I decided that weight was an issue." This was "extremely annoying" to her. She had been on the "evil South Beach diet" and lost weight, but when she went for her annual physical examination, she had gained nine pounds in a year. Although Wendy claimed that concern over weight had nothing to do with dancing, she told a revealing story:

> When I looked at the pictures after Showcase, I literally had to say to myself, "There's something wrong with these pictures from the angles they are taken. You do not have a body dysmorphia problem. You don't look pregnant. You actually look quite thin." You can't look at it like it's a real thing. Because I had a brief moment when I looked at the pictures, and I said, "Who the fuck are you kidding? You're just another fat old lady getting out there, working out some kind of a fantasy of one form or another." Once I got myself past the fact that I'm not actually fat, then I got myself past the fact that mostly how old I am is irrelevant—most people don't know how old I am. They don't think I'm that old, and it's mostly irrelevant.

Surrounded by beautiful, hard, young bodies such as those in the dance world, it is hard not to be judgmental about one's aging self. Wendy was critical of "fat old ladies" who had fantasies about dancing with young men, even though she was spending a lot of money on this herself. She had to perform considerable emotional labor to convince herself that she was not part of this group, that, instead, she was young looking and not fat.[18]

Claudia was another student in her midfifties who enjoyed the touching and flirting aspects of dance. In fact, the only time she found it difficult to dance with a partner was when, she said, "my partner won't connect with me." In that case, she said, "I've got to try to get them there." Like Wendy, however, Claudia had issues with her aging body. Indeed, she sometimes felt uncomfortable performing because of size and age issues. She found Latin dances particularly difficult—she did not think she looked sexy, so she had trouble feeling sexy. She compared herself to another student her teacher had performed with at her studio's annual showcase:

> She did a swing, and she was wearing the little red polka-dot dress, and she's real young and cute as a bug in a rug. They look fabulous together; they look like Daisy Mae and Li'l Abner or something. I really feel silly

doing it, so I think it's hard to overcome that. My biggest inspiration is [another student] because she is bigger than I. She does the jive, she does Latin like nobody's business, and her size does not get in the way at all. She's older than I am, so I shouldn't be intimidated. I find it very hard to do those steps, to look elegant and sexy and do them well. I am much less intimidated by smooth.

Older women's appearance concerns were sometimes exacerbated by the clothing demands of competitive dancing. There is a long literature on clothing and the aging body, some of which argues that although there is an increased freedom for older women to transgress rules about aging and clothing, these rules still dictate that they should dress conservatively and wear loose, longer clothes in subdued colors.[19] These rules form "moral prescriptions," which cause people to police the presentation of their bodies.[20] Older dancers often did this, even as they enjoyed violating color rules. Isabel, for example, had become concerned about her weight after taking lessons, because, she said, "you're there in front of the mirrors all the time." Unfortunately, she added, "I have a tendency to gain around [my middle]. When I look in the mirror, I think, 'Oh, goodness, look at that stomach— God!'" Isabel dieted constantly because, she said, "The only way that goes away is if I lose weight. I never wanted to be heavy."

In addition to concerns about weight, Isabel did not like her chest. Her neck and small breasts had become scrawnier as she aged. Before she went to her first and only competition, she bought a Latin dress with the help of her teacher. They had several dresses from Chrisanne delivered after seeing them on the Web:

> When they sent the dresses up, there were two I loved: the one I have and the other one. . . . It was a red one. I loved the skirt of it. I'm so skinny and boney up top. Even [my teacher] said, "I think the first one." He says, "Oh, they both look great, but I think the blue one is the best. . . ." The red one came down kind of low, but I loved the skirt of it, and the blue one came down and covered my boney bones.

This story is one of both complicity and transgression in aging. Although red has long been a color considered unsuitable for older women,[21] Isabel did not worry about this, and, indeed, the blue dress she bought was bright and sparkly with a short skirt. Although she often felt awkward in her teacher's company, Isabel appreciated his emotional support—he was careful to tell her that he loved both dresses on her. However, she still agonized over the "salt cellars" in her neckline, and she liked the blue dress because it concealed them, as well as her flat chest. Women of all ages feel obligated to cover what they view as the most disfiguring aspects of their bodies, but older women typically believe that they have more problem areas.[22] Like Isabel, they fear that others will judge harshly if they dress in a manner that looks too young. Negative comments about appearance in the dance world rarely focus on age; however, older women bring the assumptions of the larger culture with them when they perform.

Even so, outsiders quickly notice the amount of age transgression at competitions, both in performance and in dress. This is an aspect of pro/am that Juliet McMains takes issue with:

> Directly in the center of the floor is a woman of well over three hundred pounds whose round and rolling flesh is adorned in traffic-officer orange, trimmed with rhinestones the size of quarters. Her partner, who is dwarfed by her, attempts to match the magnitude of her girth with expressive presentation of his arms and slender body. Beside them dances a woman well into her sixties, her fuchsia fringe dress whipping the chest of her twenty-year-old partner as she distorts her face into exaggerated caricatures of sensual delight. Another couple flanks them, deadly serious in their execution of an advanced sequence of turns and checks. He pauses to steady her as she wobbles ever so slightly in her three-inch heels, her knobby knees and spindly legs struggling to support her. Her disorientation is palpable, but he strikes the floor with determination as intense as her canary yellow dress, carrying her resistant body with apparent ease.[23]

Although McMains claims no desire to insult these women by describing them as "grotesque," it is hard to imagine the women agreeing.[24] She includes stereotypes about aging bodies struggling to perform, clothed in unsuitable colors, and showing far more skin than is appropriate. McMains's language is surprising coming from an avowed feminist, and it illustrates the extent of prejudice about the aging and overweight female body that exists in this culture.

From a different perspective than that of McMains, the competition floor is a place where women can take pleasure in flouting societal conventions telling them to fade into the background now that they are old and romance is over for them. Furthermore, while many older women competitors look their age, as a group they are remarkable for their fitness and stamina, as can be seen in figure 7.1, which shows a typical lineup of young professional men with Ladies C students, that is, women over age fifty. Like Joan Goddard, seen in color plate 8, some have bodies that can compete with younger ones anywhere. Others are not so toned but still quite fit, and they revel in the permission that dance gives them to transgress clothing rules. In addition, while older women often find it difficult to buy everyday clothes that fit properly, this is less of a problem with dance dresses, which are made of stretch fabric and are kind to a variety of figures. Dance dress-makers are always willing to alter a dress to fit better or reveal less.

The current generation of elderly people grew up during the development of a youth culture and is loathe to forgo the pleasures of consumption.[25] As a result, they are less inclined to view clothing as constrained by cultural norms. Although appropriateness still loomed large, most of the older women I interviewed enjoyed dressing in clothing which might be considered more appropriate for the young. Isabel, for example, loved wearing the blue Latin gown in part because she felt she was breaking age rules, which she yearned to discard. Women make their own decisions about dress—often with advice from professional partners—and some are more transgressive than others.

Hazel, a social dancer, was fifty-eight and did not worry about her appearance. She did, however, explain that when you are older, "it's harder to remember patterns." Ballroom had actually improved her memory, but she still found this "the hardest thing to do." She also hated seeing herself in dance photographs, because the pictures never lived up to the image she had of herself performing. Her posture was particularly challenging, because, even when she thought she was standing straight, she saw that she was not. A tall woman, she had a lifetime's habit of slouching to overcome. However, she said that she enjoyed her ability to "express things" with her body. She claimed not to worry about trivia such as age differences.

Hazel also loved watching professional dance on television, and when a competition was held in her town, she went to watch. When I asked what she had liked, she answered, "Color, color, color." She explained, "Tchai-kovsky to me is pink, but ballroom to me is like bright colors: bright yellow, bright green, bright turquoise, pink, and of course everything glows, which is rhinestones. I love that." Clearly Hazel did not believe that color is only appropriate for the young.

Lulu, the Chinese dancer we met in chapter 3, had a different attitude toward age and dancing than did most of the students I interviewed who grew up in America. She had one goal when she danced: to win. She was disappointed when she did not do as well as she had hoped, and she explained that this was because she had started too late to become as good as she might have been. She had tried taking dance lessons while still married, but her husband had forbidden it because he was suspicious of her intentions.[26] Lulu started dancing in her early forties, but it took her ten years to find a good teacher who could help her compete at the level she wished. She noted that she was "physically not able to do" all the things she wanted to, because her "body doesn't listen" to the instruction, as would a young woman's body. After about four years, having reached the silver scholarship level, she developed a hip injury which made it difficult for her to continue competing. Now she confined herself to social dancing but regretted the dance career that she might have had. Lulu found competing difficult, because she was so competitive that she became discouraged when she competed against a student who danced better than she did. This made Lulu feel like she was "not good enough."

As discussed before, the Asian dancers I interviewed often had difficulty expressing emotion—particularly older women who came here as adults. Lulu saw her teachers as people she learned from and danced with, not as people she was intimate with, and she reported that she and her teachers did not become friends. The lack of interest in the emotional side of dancing made it difficult to succeed on the ballroom floor, where judges look for an emotional connection. Younger Asian American dancers did not feel his way; they were acculturated into the American ideals of emotional intimacy and personal revelation. Françoise, the young Chinese American student, answered the question as to whether she was comfortable with the hot and heavy looks required in Latin dancing with a giggle, explaining, "That's what I'm so good at. That's what I love. Yeah, I think that's what makes it fun." Françoise explained, "[My teacher] is very good looking. He's fun to get along with, and the fact that we dance together, it's very exciting but more so, like, funny, I think." Françoise had coaching from her teacher's professional partner, with whom he was romantically involved. Unlike Lulu, she thought of her teachers as friends. She viewed the mild flirtation as one of life's pleasures but not something to take seriously, and she was disdainful of those who "try to make something more of the student-teacher relationship," describing it as "very uncomfortable" for the teacher. Françoise's comments show her Westernized understanding of the emotional rules when performing instant intimacy.[27]

The Aging Man

The issues for older male students are different than those for women. As discussed previously, men must learn to take charge of the dance, yet they typically learn this from a woman much younger and more skilled than they are. This leads to potential ego problems for men who view the ability to take charge of the situation as central to masculinity.[28] In dance, they are called on to take charge, yet they feel vulnerable when they ask women to dance, many of whom dance better than they do.

Some of the older men I interviewed had developed physical problems that they had to overcome in order to dance. In social dancing, physical problems interfered with the men's dancing more than the women's, because the women tended to lean on the men. Gordon had such issues. A gymnast as a young man, he had once been in fine physical shape. Now, among other injuries, he had no cartilage in one knee, and it swelled sometimes when he danced. He was no longer as flexible as he once was, which he regretted, because dancing requires flexibility. He had gained about twenty-five pounds after giving up exercise. However, he had danced through everything, even dancing one armed with his wife after shoulder surgery. His viewed his main weakness as a dancer to be the result of his physical problems, because, he said, "depending on the woman I am dancing with—if I'm moving a sofa around the floor—I get terribly, terribly fatigued." However, he was fine "if the woman is light on her feet and dances holding her own frame as opposed to dropping, to sagging, to leaning, or not picking up leads."

The difficulties of teaching "sofas" is one reason older professionals find teaching hard, but Gordon's story differed from that of the professional dancers. He was retired on a generous teaching pension and had a loving wife and many friends. He could not do everything he wanted to do in dancing, because of both mental and physical limitations. However, he regarded dancing as one of the main joys in his life, something which enhanced the already strong relationship he had with his wife. When I asked him about his best dancing fantasy, he answered,

> I'm living it. I'm dancing. I'm enjoying it. It's social. For example, last year in Sorrento, we went to a beautiful outdoor place. . . . There was another couple that danced. It was great. They were from England, and they put a Viennese waltz on, and, in international, you never break. [Our dance teacher] has taught us all kinds of crazy swirls or whatever. It was kind of

funny, because that couple actually stopped and watched for a little while, and we came back to the table with them. . . . It's kind of nice when you dance, and other people look at that and say, "My God." We've made a lot of friends all over Europe by dancing. When you go out dancing, people come over, and they want to talk to you. It's my biggest fantasy just to be able to continue to do it.

Gordon had made many friends in his dance studio. His own teacher, and others who worked there, had been to his house for dinner, and he regarded their friendship as important.

Aging is viewed differently for men than for women. It is more acceptable for older men to become involved with younger women, but such behavior may still be viewed as foolish and even nasty. Gerald, the sixty-nine-year-old competitive pro/am dancer, had felt awkward dancing with very young teachers. When he got a teacher who was a little older and married, it became easier. His friends teased him about his getting his "jollies over it," but he argued that it was the last thing he thought about when on the floor, because learning to dance—particularly learning to lead a champion dancer such as his teacher—was so difficult. He had had several physical problems which interfered with his dancing (including bunion surgery and a fairly serious heart attack), but each time he came back to the floor ready to go again. Gerald had a charming, relaxed persona, and he was friendly with everyone. Like Gordon, he was connected to family and friends both inside and outside the dance world, so being older was only a problem insofar as he felt his physical and mental limits. His wife competed with the husband of Gerald's partner, which made pro/am competition seem respectable to him. Gordon and his wife had become friendly with their teachers, and his teacher told me that Gordon was one of the first people she turned to for advice.

As professional dancers age, they frequently suffer from a lack of long-term intimacy and remain stuck in a world where emoting is a commodity to be turned on and off at will. The buyers, however, get the benefits of fun and glamour to enhance their already full lives. This, of course, has social class implications of a profound kind. I return to this issue in the next chapter.

9

Connection Is Key

I AM WATCHING the pro/am dancing at the Manhattan DanceSport Competition, a famously tough event. In addition to the high quality of the performances, participants are younger and more ethnically diverse than is typical at pro/am competitions. Ballroom is a passion typically indulged in by older students, especially in the south, although it is experiencing a growing interest among the young. The crowd at Manhattan is mostly white, but many have accents that mark them as Russian speakers. In addition, there are a number of Latino and Filipino professionals and several from Haiti.[1] The students are also more mixed than usual, with African Americans, Latinos, and Asians, including Indians. This makes for an interesting variety on the floor.

Manhattan is an intense competition where winning is emphasized over fun. Like most big competitions, the organizers provide an extra floor for practice. While most couples use this to prepare for the next day, a surprising number are going through their paces immediately before they compete. The atmosphere is tense. The teachers push the students hard and are brutal in their assessments. One teacher makes a student go through a cha-cha routine by herself to ensure that she knows all the steps and directions. This technique, though common during lessons, can be terrifying if one is about to perform. In rapid succession, another teacher tells his student the following:

> Your steps are too large. How can you get back to me if you travel so far?

> You need to give me something. Your arms are like noodles. I need to have a connection between your body and mine, so I can lead you where you need to go.

> Take the step *before* you do the underarm turn. Walk, *then* turn. It looks better.

> Your problem is you don't know where you are going. You don't know what you're doing.

By this time, the student looks lost. I realize that the teacher is nervous too. He wants his student to do well, but his own anxieties make it hard for him to calm hers. When he realizes that she is upset, he switches into nurturing mode as he tries to reassure her that she will be fine. I later ask a professional friend how to interpret what I saw. She tells me that students frequently make the mistake of thinking that pro/am is not really a partnership, because they are the only ones being judged.[2] However, she notes, "It *is* a partnership, and there are partnership issues in dancing pro/am just like in any other dance partnership. Partners," she adds, "often get tense with one another right before they perform." Her advice is to "ignore the talk and focus on your performance."

Although the Manhattan competition is an extreme case, everyone in the ballroom world has partnership issues. The pressures of competition exacerbate these issues, because one's performance is always judged in comparison to others'. Dancers learn to look as if they are having a wonderful time holding the most marvelous person in the world, no matter how they feel. Yet long-term relationship maintenance involves more than the portrayal of a connection. It requires working out conflicts and difficulties and sharing real, possibly painful feelings. A typical dance career provides little practice for learning these skills. In pro/am, economics further complicate the relationships. Teachers need to keep students wanting to dance with them, and students often find it easier to change teachers than to explain how they feel. In the example from the Manhattan competition, it is hard to imagine the student and the teacher talking frankly about partner insecurities. This is why I use the term "instant intimacy" to describe the quality of many dance relationships. Closeness between partners develops quickly but may not go deep. A dance relationship can become more than this, but even then, a quick and superficial intimacy remains a tool to be called on at any moment as necessary. For professionals who spend much of their day in these relationships, this fallback position may have a marked impact on identity. Couples in long-term relationships become aware of how the other feels without being told. In the dance world, partners often move on before this stage is reached. Competitive couples with a personal relationship sometimes report that this relationship is hard to maintain after competing is over, because so much of their togetherness is focused on performance and so little on private life. Without private ties, dancers must rely on their relationships with students and those with other professionals.

There is a sparse literature on relationships such as these. Much relationship literature deals with married couples engrossed in family life. It is an accepted truism that "the family is a vital institution in American society and often serves as the major source of support for individuals."[3] Less is known about more transitory relationships, even though these are rising in frequency as marriage and family decline in importance. The fastest growing type of household is persons living alone, and this is becoming an accepted way of life.[4] Between 1970 and 2007, one-person households increased from 17 to 27 percent of all U.S. households.[5] Factors such as a later age at marriage, an increase in divorce, and a decreased likelihood of remarrying help to explain this trend. Economists call this a decline in the opportunity cost of being single. They cite a number of factors, including the free availability of sex outside marriage, women's increased ability to support themselves, and fewer potential stay-at-home wives to provide a full array of services. Furthermore, since individuals only improve their economic standing by marrying someone who makes at least as much as they do, rising income inequality has made marriage a poorer economic choice.[6] Writers of advice books sometimes view friendships as more permanent than marriage.[7] Yet friendship has not diminished the desire for romance. Furthermore, while those living alone may need a social network to a greater degree than those who are enmeshed in nuclear families,[8] such persons frequently find that they enjoy living by themselves and that they do not want a permanent relationship.[9] The attempt to create meaningful social contacts in a world which is changing so rapidly involves what Anthony Giddens calls "everyday social experiments" in interpersonal intimacies.[10]

Friendships with the other sex can take on particular importance for singles. Men and women view such relationships as different from same-sex friendships.[11] A number of studies have shown that many individuals, of all ages, consider the sexual component of flirting or teasing as well as the potential for actual sexual involvement to be benefits of such friendships.[12] In fact, heterosexuals do not typically distinguish between cross-sex friendships and potential sexual partners.[13] One of the advantages of dancing with a teacher is that it involves a safe cross-sex friendship, even as it suggests the potential for more. As we have seen in earlier chapters, most dancers know this potential is not real, even though a few—Daniel and Brenda, for example—had fantasies.

Although some students and teachers of dance are married, most are single. Many of these singles are in their late twenties and thirties. Whereas earlier generations were tied down with the economic and temporal burdens of family, young people today have the freedom and money to indulge in ballroom. This makes it attractive to those who are happy to live alone but want romance and glamour in their lives, and it explains the increase in interest among the young.

In chapter 1, I outlined four research questions, the answers to which can be found throughout the book and are discussed further in this chapter, although not necessarily in the same order. Intimacy has been understood by sociologists to have implicit economic ties,[14] but if adults increasingly live alone, it becomes an explicit commodity, something purchasers, such as Phoebe, understand. Dance allows individuals to create both the appearance and the reality of an emotional connection which arises quickly and which satisfies the need for romance. Women are the major purchasers of dance intimacy and men the major purveyors. Outside the dance word, when men purchase connection, they frequently purchase sex from a sex worker, even if they want it as a "girlfriend experience," that is, a relationship with no strings attached but which provides a transitory feeling of love and intimacy.[15] Men who take dance lessons sometimes confuse the meaning of the intimacy offered.

The historical understanding of romance as something that women want and will buy makes the dance world difficult for men. Professional male dancers must integrate elements of culturally acceptable masculinity, including relationship control and athleticism, into their "male dancer" performance. They add elements of masculinity exclusive to the dance world, learning to dance in the masculine way admired by other male dancers while taking care of students' emotional desires. This pattern is not always established in the same way. Colin, for example, was dancing as a young boy before he became a man. His dancing success and his class mobility strengthened his sense of masculinity. Matt was gay, and he valued his dancing identity, although heterosexuals sometimes assumed he could not create a believable emotional connection to female partners. Eastern European dancers do not face the same struggles. In those countries, dance is an honorable career, assuming a man can support himself doing it. Ballroom success may facilitate economic mobility with immigration to America. Even so, eastern European male dancers take pains to perform masculinity on the dance floor, as can be seen in images throughout this book. They are especially concerned with how they appear to other male dancers.

Women dance professionals also challenge and reinforce gender stereotypes. Women teachers control the relationship and take care that students not misunderstand the intimacy they offer. Even though the dance performance is one of men leading and women following, many professional women live independent lives without expectations of domesticity.

For American dancers, teaching pro/am creates upward mobility. Most come from working-class or lower-middle-class homes, but they learn to spend their days socializing with affluent students: dressing well, feeling comfortable in luxurious hotels, and putting students at their ease, both physically and emotionally. Women become career oriented and often put family aside in doing so. For immigrants, particularly those from eastern Europe, the story is different. Most grew up in educated homes and graduated from college. However, with the collapse of the former Soviet Union, many fell on hard times. A move to America led to lateral social mobility but vertical economic mobility. As dancers age, they continue to work in the dance industry, teaching, judging, or working in one of the ancillary activities such as dressmaking, because they spent much of what they have earned on their competitive careers, and they do not have skills outside the world of ballroom.

Male students also challenge the rule that men do not dance. Some are comfortable dancing, having achieved masculinity through long-term heterosexual relationships, occupational success, and their ability to support a family. They dance to please their wives and are amused when other husbands feel threatened. Other men dance for the same reasons as single women: a desire for a social life and for emotional intimacy without commitment. These are men who prefer a brief romance to the purchase of sex.

Women students delight in the joie de vivre created for them by their male teachers. Women control the purse strings, but what they buy is a safe expedition into a romance novel. For many successful career women, particularly those who are no longer young, this fits their lifestyle better than looking after a husband does. Those women students who are married find in dancing a relief from the demands of domestic life or at least a way to keep husbands on their toes.

The commodification of intimacy involves work, especially on the part of the provider. Regardless of age, attractiveness, or sexual identity, the portrayal of an emotional connection always implies a heterosexual love relationship. While students understand that this portrayal is not real, they want teachers to care about them and to enjoy their company. Furthermore, audiences want to see a believable performance. Teachers learn to quickly charm students with the appearance of closeness, affection, and a belief in the student's dance potential. Regardless of gender, teachers engage in emotional labor typically thought of as women's work.

In performing intimacy, some dancers, such as Mark, believe in authenticity. In producing an emotionally intense performance, they try to let audiences in on genuine feelings. Others are not convinced, although many think that practice produces the appearance of feeling. Still others are more cynical and argue that the portrayal of intimacy has little to do with actual feeling. American students understand intimacy as a performance, but from what I have seen and from what they and their teachers have told me, East Asian students find this difficult. They do not like to emote on the dance floor and fear that others will assume the feelings are genuine. They are more interested in performing well than in creating an intimate bond with a teacher whose time they have purchased. These dancers do not understand the concept of instant intimacy, as it is not a feeling or experience that is part of their culture.

When children and youth learn to dance, their lack of connection is palpable.[16] This can be seen at the 2008 National Youth Final of USA Dance, where the top Latin dancers ages seventeen to nineteen competed to represent the United States at the IDSF final in Moscow.[17] In the video of the event, the dancers show a remarkable athleticism and energy. However, partners rarely look at one another, except to glance and look away. Couples wear typical Latin attire; the women show lots of skin, and the men's shirts are unbuttoned to the waist, but they appear to be uncomfortable with touching and emoting, preferring instead to strike sexy poses aimed at no one. This removes the special character of each different dance; only the speed differs. Another illustration of this lack of connection is shown in figure 9.1, of Anthony Kinevsky and Ilana Zorin dancing in the Youth Latin at Desert Classic in 2010. Both dancers are intent on their performance, but they are not emotionally connected.

As we saw in chapter 6, the ability to portray emotion varies from couple to couple. In the 2010 Winter Olympics, Tessa Virtue and Scott Moir won the gold medal for ice dancing. On the YouTube page showing video of their performance,[18] commenters said that Virtue and Moir reminded them of all-time emoters Jane Torvill and Christopher Dean, a couple who revolutionized ice dancing with their ability to dance as if in love—but not just in love: they exuded a real enthusiasm and sense of fun, an authenticity of emotion that seemed shared and almost to be encouraged by each other. The 2010 silver medalists, Meryl Davis and Charlie White, though charming, did not stir viewers to the same degree.[19] It is hard to explain why, but viewers recognize intimacy when they see it, even if the performance is artificial. Torvill and Dean, who remain the highest scoring skating pair of all time, having scored perfect 6.0s for artistic expression from every judge, were never romantically involved.[20] Actors portray feelings all the time, but

Fig. 9.1. Young dancers may have great technique, but they do not have the life experience to draw on in producing emotional intensity. Anthony Kinevsky and Ilana Zorin at the 2010 Desert Classic DanceSport Championships, Palm Desert, CA. © 2010 Jonathan S. Marion.

to do it without speaking gives romance extra meaning. We see this displayed in a number of the pictures in this book.

In dance, the right appearance helps in portraying intimacy. Viewers are more willing to believe that love exists when young and beautiful couples have perfect bodies, glamorous clothing, and the right hair and makeup. This look takes continuous and intense labor to produce. Although both men and women perform aesthetic labor, appearance is more central for women, many of whom remember dresses rather than performances from their early years. Clothing creates contradictions for older women; although often self-conscious, they frequently enjoy the outrage of wearing "unsuitable" clothes. Even social dancers work to produce the right look on the dance floor, and social dance teachers often coach students in the importance of doing so. In pro/am competition, teachers become involved in students' appearances, helping them buy dresses and jewelry and sending them for professional hair and makeup. Appearance work provides its own pleasures even as it enhances the experience of the dance.

The production of an intimate connection finds its ultimate expression in performance. Facial expressions and emotions must look real; their creation is part of the emotional labor of dance. Most audiences at competitions know what to look for, and while they want the performers to look authentic, they understand that acting is involved. In contrast, viewers of shows such as Dancing with the Stars know little about ballroom. These audiences often convince themselves of the authenticity of the love portrayed by the professionals and their celebrity students.

At competitions, teachers work hard to create a sense of partnership with their amateur students. Students who do well enhance a teacher's reputation within the dance world, so teachers constantly assure students of their success while pressuring them to do better. These contradictory pressures do not always work as intended, even though teachers try to help their students to feel like insiders.

My analysis of the economics of ballroom underscores the profitability of providing intimacy for pay. Studios are a curious combination of intimate revelation and frontstage artifice. Students must believe in the value of what they receive. One way of demonstrating the value of dance occurs when students compete. Competitions are organized to maximize student involvement, and professional competition helps by enhancing the glamour of the experience. Since many students cannot afford this expensive hobby, social dance teachers make dance affordable by selling a briefer version of the same instant intimacy.

In a world that worships youth and beauty, aging is often traumatic. Professional dancers frequently lie about their age, and as they get older, they find that their lifestyle is not conducive to the achievement of deep emotional commitment or even intense friendship. Thus, older dancers who excel at portraying intimacy and making students feel a connection are often quite alone. Older students struggle with the cultural norms about age difference but enjoy the continuing pleasures of dancing with young professionals who assure them of their desirability. The dance world is a place where those who are considered too old to flirt may still indulge.

Although our culture valorizes love at first sight, most people believe that time and effort are essential to maintain romantic relationships. Yet, in this society, time is money, and the successful pay others to provide their pleasures. Many industries support the pleasures of those who have little time to spare: restaurants, clubs, bars, gyms, and social networking. These help people to feel connected and cared about, without involving the work of entertaining at home or sustaining a relationship with a cohabiting partner. Instead of dancing with an equally skilled partner, a professional dance teacher can open the world of professional dancing and of competition with minimal effort on the part of the student. Like other venues, a big part of dance studios' business is in the provision and facilitation of instant intimacy to those who seek a quick emotional bond.

Dancing, however, provides a special kind of intimacy. It involves the pleasures of touch. We value personal space; in urban areas, we are unpleasantly jostled by crowds, and a stranger's touch can seem threatening rather than the safe erotic pleasure that dancers report it to be. The physicality of partner dancing is sometimes difficult for students to come to terms with —Asian students find it particularly hard. However, many of the dancers I interviewed reported that the physicality was one of their main pleasures from dance. They enjoyed the safe, mildly erotic physicality of the close connection on the ballroom floor. When I last saw Phoebe in the summer of 2010, she was still dancing with the same teacher and wearing a new dress. She asked me how the book was going, and when I told her that hers was the first story, she repeated for me the physical and emotional pleasures she got from dance.

To summarize, dancers learn to integrate a capacity for instant intimacy into their identities. Although there are differences, both men and women incorporate aspects of conventional gender performance into their dancing identities while simultaneously challenging traditional scripts. Professional dancers become part of the American middle class through dance and through the association with affluent students. This dynamic plays out differently for immigrants. Students experience the intimacy of the dance world differently than teachers do; they are the clients with the resources to facilitate a professional career in return for romance and glamour. The performance of intimacy in dance becomes believable when encased in perfect bodies, perfectly adorned. The commodification of intimacy has implications for professionals and their ability to develop long-term relationships and an intimacy that lasts off the dance floor as well as on it.

It is not surprising that partner dancing is experiencing a comeback. Nor is the increased attention unexpected. As I finish writing this chapter, the *New York Times* features a full-page article listing the many places to dance Latin in New York City, carefully distinguishing places for beginners from those too intimidating for the inexperienced. The message is that "the number of places featuring Latin dance seems to be growing" and that anyone who wishes to dance can find the right place almost any night of the week. This implicit recognition of the pleasures of "dancing happily with each other" acknowledges that even for major newspapers, marketing the joys of instant intimacy is an important business.[21]

Glossary

American smooth is a category of American-style dances in ballroom competitions. It includes waltz, tango, foxtrot, and Viennese waltz. This category loosely corresponds to the ballroom (or standard) category of international style. However, unlike ballroom, it allows dancers to open and separate while dancing.

American style is a style of ballroom dancing developed in the United States that contrasts with international (or English) style. It consists of two categories: American smooth and American rhythm.

American rhythm is a category of American-style dances in ballroom competitions. It includes cha-cha, rumba, swing, bolero, and mambo. This category loosely corresponds to the Latin category of international style ballroom, although the dances differ somewhat.

Ballroom (sometimes called standard) is a category of international style dances in ballroom competitions. It includes waltz, tango, foxtrot, quickstep, and Viennese waltz. This category loosely corresponds to the smooth category of American style, although in ballroom, dancers are always in closed position.

Bolero is one of the five competition dances in American rhythm. The first step is typically taken on the first beat and held during the second beat, with two more steps falling on beats three and four. This dance is quite different from the other American rhythm dances in that it requires not only Cuban motion but also rises and falls and contra body movement more typically found in dances such as the waltz.

Cha-cha (sometimes called cha-cha-cha) is one of the five dances in both American rhythm and Latin competitions. It is danced to the music of the same name introduced by Cuban composer and violinist Enrique Jorrín in 1953. This rhythm was developed from syncopation of the fourth beat.

Closed position occurs when partners face each other with their bodies approximately parallel. In ballroom and smooth, the bodies are also offset about half a body width such that each person has his or her partner on the right side, with the left side somewhat unobstructed.

Core (sometimes called center) refers to the group of muscles in the center of the body, encompassing the abdomen, lower and upper back, hips, buttocks, and inner thighs. In all dance movements the core must be engaged. Beginning dancers often have a hard time finding the core in their bodies and engaging it.

East Coast swing. See **Swing**.

Follow is typically the role of the woman in mixed-gender couples. She follows the lead of the man.

Foxtrot is one of two competition dances invented in the United States. It is danced to 4/4 time with a slow-quick-quick or slow-slow-quick-quick rhythm. It is danced in both American smooth and ballroom, although the tempo is slower in ballroom. It is typically danced to swing-band music.

Frame involves the upper-body positions of the dancers. A strong frame provides connection between partners and conveys intended movement. The dancers' arms and upper bodies are held firmly in place, neither relying on a partner to maintain his or her frame nor applying force that would move the partner or the partner's frame.

Hold refers to the way the couple holds each other during the dance. The classic dance hold involves the man's left hand in the woman's right held at about the woman's eye level. The man's right hand is on her back, and her left hand is on his bicep.

International style describes the style of ballroom dance competed the world over. It consists of two categories, ballroom and Latin. The term is used in the United States to distinguish it from American style.

Jive is one of the five Latin dances. In competition, it is danced at a speed of forty-four bars per minute, which makes it faster than its American rhythm counterpart, the swing. The basic step is a six-beat pattern, comprising eight weight changes because some steps are triple steps.

Latin dance is one of the two sets of competition dances in international ballroom. It consists of cha-cha, samba, rumba, paso doble, and jive.

Latin motion is a characteristic type of hip motion found in the technique of performing a step in Latin and rhythm dances. Although it is most visible in the hips, much of the effect is created through the action of the feet and knees.

Lead, typically male in a mixed-gender couple, refers to who is responsible for choosing appropriate steps to suit the music if the dance is improvised and leading the follow by hand and body signals to complete the chosen steps smoothly and safely. If the dance is a choreographed routine, the lead is still responsible for initiating each move, which ensures smooth coordination between the two dancers.

Lift is when a dancer's feet (typically the woman's) are both off the floor at the same time. Lifts are not permitted in ballroom competition except for cabaret and showdance events.

Lindy hop is a dance based on the popular Charleston and named for Charles Lindbergh's Atlantic crossing in 1927. It evolved in Harlem in the 1920s and '30s and originally evolved with the jazz music of that time. Lindy was a fusion of many dances that preceded it or were popular during its development. It is a member of the swing-dance family, but unlike swing it has an eight-count basic step.

Line of dance is conceptually a path along and generally parallel to the edge of the dance floor in the counterclockwise direction. To help avoid collisions, it is agreed that in traveling dances, dancers should proceed along the line of dance.

Mambo is a dance of Cuban origin that corresponds to mambo music. It is one of the five dances of the rhythm competition. Mambo music was invented in Havana in the 1930s by Cachao and his contemporaries and made popular around the world. The music was heavily influenced by the jazz musicians brought to entertain American customers in Cuban casinos. It is similar to salsa, except that in mambo the dance pauses on the first step (pause, 2, 3, 4, pause, 6, 7, 8), whereas in salsa the pause is typically on the last step (1, 2, 3, pause, 5, 6, 7, pause).

Quickstep is an international style ballroom dance that follows a 4/4 time beat, at about fifty bars per minute. From its early beginning as a faster foxtrot, the quickstep has become distinctive for its speed across the floor. It is danced to the fastest tempo of the ballroom dances, which necessitates that partners stay in closed position throughout the dance.

Paso doble, like samba, is a progressive international Latin dance. It is the Latin dance most resembling the ballroom style, in that forward steps are taken with the heel lead, the frame is wider and more strictly kept up, and there is significantly different and less hip movement. It actually originated in southern France but is modeled after the sound, drama, and movement of the Spanish bullfight.

Rhythm. See **American rhythm**.

Rumba is danced in both Latin and rhythm competition, and it originated in Cuba based on rhythms brought over by slaves. The Latin version is slower. The dance is considered the most romantic of the Latin dances and involves hip action over the standing leg.

Samba is a progressive Latin dance of Brazilian origin in 2/4 time. However, there are three steps to every bar (slow-quick-quick). There are two major streams of samba that differ considerably: the modern ballroom samba and the traditional samba of Brazil. Traditional Brazilian samba includes a partner dance but is danced solo at carnivals.

Smooth. See **American smooth**.

Spotting is a technique used during turns. The dancer chooses a reference point, often the partner or a distant point along the line of travel, and focuses on it as long as possible. Then the dancer flips his or her head as fast as possible to "spot" the reference point again.

Swing (sometimes called East Coast swing) is one of the five rhythm dances. It has a six-count basic step. This is in contrast to the meter of most swing music, which has a four-count basic rhythm. In practice, however, the six-count moves of the East Coast swing are often combined with eight-count moves from other swing dances such as the Lindy hop and the Charleston.

Tango is a ballroom dance that branched away from its original Argentine roots by allowing European, American, Hollywood, and competitive influences into the style and execution of the dance. Dance partners hold the classic dance position, with top line held away and legs and hips held close, unlike Argentine tango, in which heads and bodies may be close and legs held away.

Viennese waltz is the original form of the waltz. It was the first ballroom dance performed in the closed hold or "waltz" position. It is danced at about 180 beats (58–60 measures) a minute, much faster than the waltz.

Waltz is danced at approximately ninety beats per minute with three beats to the bar (the international standard of thirty measures per minute). Dancers follow line of dance and incorporate rise and fall into their steps.

West Coast swing is derived from Lindy hop. It is characterized by a distinctive elastic look that results from its basic extension-compression technique of partner connection, and it is danced primarily in a slotted area on the dance floor. The dance allows for both partners to improvise steps while dancing together. Typically the follower walks into new patterns, traveling forward on counts 1 and 2 of each basic pattern, rather than rocking back, as in East Coast swing.

Notes

Notes to the Introduction to Photographing Emotion

1. I was attending and photographing the 2004 Yankee as fieldwork for my doctoral dissertation (completed in 2006) on the cultures of competitive ballroom and salsa dancing, with the permission of competition coorganizer Judi Hatton.

2. See Jonathan S. Marion, *Ballroom: Culture and Costume in Competitive Dance* (Oxford: Berg, 2008), 10–11; and Jonathan S. Marion, "Photography as Ethnographic Passport," *Visual Anthropology Review* 26, no. 1 (2010): 24–30.

3. Chris Jenks, "The Centrality of the Eye in Western Culture: An Introduction," in *Visual Culture*, ed. Chris Jenks, 1–25 (London: Routledge, 1995).

4. Quoted in Gregory Bateson, *Steps to an Ecology of Mind* (New York: Ballantine Books, 1972), 134, 137.

5. Sara Pink makes a related point in her book *Doing Visual Ethnography* (2d ed.; London: Sage, 2007): "images . . . are inextricably interwoven with our personal identities, narratives, lifestyles, cultures and societies, as well as with definitions of history, space and truth" (21).

6. Richard Freeman, "Photography and Ethnography," in *Viewpoints: Visual Anthropologists at Work*, ed. Mary Strong and Laena Wilder (Austin: University of Texas Press, 2009), 61.

7. For an early formulation of this point, see Robert Gardner, "Anthropology and Film," *Daedalus* 86 (1957): 348.

8. Pink, *Doing Visual Ethnography*, 151.

9. See, for example, Dirk Nijland, "Ritual Performance and Visual Representations," in *Reflecting Visual Ethnography: Using the Camera in Anthropological Research*, ed. Metje Postma and Peter I. Crawford, 26–49 (Leiden: CNWS, 2006).

10. John Collier Jr. and Malcolm Collier, *Visual Anthropology: Photography as Research Method* (Albuquerque: University of New Mexico Press, 1986), 158.

11. For more on this idea, see Pink, *Doing Visual Ethnography*, chapter 2.

12. I try to focus on the couple as a unit, especially when partners physically move apart from one another (as they do in all styles other than Standard); however, the "couple" can sometimes be hard see. Likewise, and as Ericksen points out in her introduction to this book, newcomers to ballroom competitions sometimes struggle and have to learn how to focus on one couple at a time amid the

spectacle of multiple couples, costumes, colors, and choreography performing simultaneously.

13. Karl Heider, *Ethnographic Film* (Austin: University of Texas Press, 2006), 78–82.

14. Figure 4.1, of J. T. Damalas and Thomas Mielnicki, is a postproduction example of such cropping. The original image is full length, but in publication the facial expressions might have been lost.

15. Freeman, "Photography and Ethnography," 59.

16. When this is not possible, such as when I take close-up images, I always try to juxtapose this with a wider-angle, contrasting image taken at the same time —providing context I can subsequently reference, draw from, or show.

17. For more on line and shape in DanceSport, see Marion, *Ballroom*, 42–43.

18. As per Pink (*Doing Visual Ethnography*, 28), "visual methods can be especially pertinent in investigating embodied experiences." A closely related point —based on ideas posited by David MacDougal (see *The Corporeal Image: Film, Ethnography, and the Senses* [Princeton: Princeton University Press, 2006], 1–4) —is made by Metje Postma and Peter I. Crawford, when they note that "image speaks directly to the senses and emphasizes the human body and objectifications of culture and social aesthetics and social interaction, instead of ideas, meanings, and concepts." "Introduction: Visual Ethnography and Anthropology," in Postma and Crawford, *Reflecting Visual Ethnography*, 2.

19. Laena Wilder, "Documentary Photography in the Field," in Strong and Wilder, *Viewpoints*, 49, original emphasis.

20. For a recent overview of the current state of ethics in visual anthropology and allied disciplines, see Sara Perry and Jonathan S. Marion, "State of the Ethics in Visual Anthropology," *Visual Anthropology Review* 26, no. 2 (2010).

21. Malcolm Collier, "Photographic Exploration of Social and Cultural Experience," in Strong and Wilder, *Viewpoints*, 18.

22. For a concise overview of the method in anthropology and sociology, see Douglas Harper, "Talking about Pictures: A Case for Photo Elicitation," *Visual Studies* 17, no. 1 (2002): 13–26.

23. Pink, *Doing Visual Ethnography*, 23.

Notes to the Introduction

1. In competition, all Latin dances are performed in this order.

2. As Jonathan Marion notes, because the steps of ballroom are standardized, dancers from different countries can dance together immediately. This enables professional couples to develop a partnership in a short time, although it takes about eighteen months to become perfect together. See Marion, "Beyond Ballroom: Activity as Performance, Embodiment, and Identity," *Human Mosaic* 36, no. 2 (2004): 7–16.

3. Ruud Vermey, *Latin: Thinking, Sensing, and Doing in Latin American Dancing* (Munich: Kastell Verlag, 1994), 19. Although Vermeij uses the Dutch spelling of his name, his published book translates this into "Vermey." Thus, I use "Vermeij" in the text and "Vermey" in book citations.

4. This devotion to the dancers is spreading. Describing "balletomanes" as people who think "dancers matter more than choreography," *New York Times* dance critic Alastair Macaulay bemoaned the decision of the American Ballet Theatre to announce dancers' names months before a scheduled performance. See Macaulay, "Joy of Being Groupies in Lofty Halls of Ballet," *New York Times*, May 13, 2010.

5. This has changed recently. Many dancers have immigrated to the United States from the former Soviet-bloc countries to dance for America in international competition. Since this event, Riccardo and Yulia have won the World Championship.

6. This competition was held in St. Petersburg, Florida, each June. In 2011, it moved to Tampa. The term "DanceSport" is often used to denote the combination of dance and competition.

7. This was the Lithuanian couple's first professional competition together. Both have had previous partners, and she has danced with several well-known men. Rankings for international style dancers who have competed in recognized competitions can be found on dancesportinfo.net.

8. "Closed" means that only those who dance for the United States were allowed to compete.

9. Keith Todd, "Bigger! Better! Bolder! USDC 2008," *Dance Beat* 0908 (2008).

10. In this book, I use the term "ballroom," a usage that is becoming popular in the United States.

11. Unlike regular competition, in which dancers are on the floor together and lifts are not allowed, in showdance and in cabaret, dancers perform to their choice of music with the whole floor to themselves, and lifts are expected. Showdance involves a carefully choreographed narrative version of the recognized dances, whereas cabaret has many more daring lifts.

12. See www.ndca.org.

13. See www.wdcdance.com.

14. See http://usadance.org/about-usa-dance/our-organization.

15. See www.idsf.net.

16. Students dance at bronze, silver, or gold levels and in categories within each level: beginner, intermediate, full, and scholarship. The levels vary slightly from competition to competition.

17. This is not the first time I have put my academic skills toward understanding my personal experience. When I had three young children, I wrote my dissertation on women's struggle to manage career and home: "Women and Work" (Ph.D. diss., University of Pennsylvania, 1976). And when I developed breast cancer, I

interviewed other women about their experiences: *Taking Charge of Breast Cancer* (Berkeley: University of California Press, 2008).

18. Viviana Zelizer, *The Purchase of Intimacy* (Princeton: Princeton University Press, 2005).

19. Barbara Cohen-Stratyner, "Social Dance: Contexts and Definitions." *Dance Research Journal* 33, no. 2 (2001): 121–124.

20. Argentine tango has spawned an extensive literature. Books about falling in love with Argentine tango include Camille Cusamo, *Tango: An Argentine Love Story* (Berkeley, CA: Seal, 2008); Marina Palmer, *Kiss and Tango* (New York: Harper, 2006); and Irene D. Thomas and Larry M. Sawyer, *The Temptation to Tango: Journeys of Intimacy and Desire* (Victoria, BC: Trafford, 2005). Books with a history of tango, an account of its pleasures, and sometimes academic analysis include Christine Denniston, *The Meaning of Tango: The Story of the Argentinean Dance* (London: Portico, 2007); Virginia Gift, *Tango: A History of Obsession* (www .booksurge.com, 2008); Julie Taylor, *Paper Tangos* (Durham: Duke University Press, 1998); and Robert Harris Thompson, *Tango: The Art History of Love* (New York: Pantheon, 2005); An academic study of tango and its relationship to race and colonialism is Marta E. Savigliano, *Tango and the Political Economy of Passion* (Boulder, CO: Westview, 1995).

21. See Bill Keveney, "Nielsen Ratings: 'Dancing with the Stars,' 'Idol' in Virtual Tie," *USA Today*, March 31, 2010, www.usatoday.com/life/television/news/ 2010-03-31-nielchatter31_ST_N.htm.

22. I used a mixed approach to recruiting dancers. I started with a small snowball sample, asking dancers I knew either to give me names or to introduce me to dancers—either in person or by email—I wanted to interview. When I traveled to interview professionals around the country, I asked them to put up a notice in their studio asking folks to contact me if interested in an interview. I specifically targeted some top dancers and owners of social dance studios, contacting them via their websites. I asked respondents a variety of open-ended questions, starting with general ones about how they started dancing and letting them shape what they told me. I asked everyone questions about the connection, both physical and emotional, and the work involved in developing and maintaining it. Topics differed somewhat for professionals and students. I had a list of areas to explore and asked these in an open-ended way, with more specific questions if necessary. Not every dancer emphasized the same thing. Interviews lasted between one and a half and two hours, occasionally longer. Most interviews with students took place in the respondent's home or occasionally in a coffee shop or in his or her place of work. Professionals always conducted interviews in their studios. This sometimes structured the amount of time I had. Lessons typically last forty-five minutes, and I understood that the professionals were not earning money during an interview. I told them that interviews would last one and a half hours, so they could be fit in

between lessons. Often with couples one would do the interview while the other was teaching, and then they would switch. Sometimes I had to skip topics that I would have normally asked about because the dancer told me so much about other topics that the ninety minutes were up.

Notes to Chapter 1

1. Viviana A. Zelizer, *The Purchase of Intimacy* (Princeton: Princeton University Press, 2005); Viviana A. Zelizer, *The Social Meaning of Money: Pin Money, Paychecks, Poor Relief, and Other Currencies* (New York: Basic Books, 1994). These books are important in framing this chapter.

2. In June 2010, Jose Manuel Carrero, dancing the lead in *Sleeping Beauty*, at American Ballet Theatre, partnered Gillian Murphy and guest artist Alina Cojocaru five days apart. Carrero was comfortable switching from one dancer to another, and Cojocaru was able to bring the same choreography with her from London.

3. Therapeutic massage is another example, but it lacks the mutuality of ballroom.

4. In *The Social Meaning of Money*, Zelizer argues that professional theater contains a subset of markets, such as Broadway musicals or repertory theater, which survive by appealing to groups of wealthy patrons who keep the enterprise afloat. Money spent on theatergoing has a different meaning to these people and is kept separate from money for everyday activities.

5. Independent teachers are self-employed and rent space lesson by lesson.

6. Students may purchase a package consisting of hotel stay, tickets, and meals.

7. Judith Lynne Hanna, *Dance, Sex, and Gender: Signs of Identity, Dominance, Defiance, and Desire* (Chicago: University of Chicago Press, 1988), xv.

8. Michael S. Kimmel, "Masculinity as Homophobia: Fear, Shame, and Silence in the Construction of Gender Identity," in *Privilege: A Reader*, ed. Abby L. Ferber and Michael S. Kimmel, 51–74 (Boulder, CO: Westview, 2003); C. J. Pasco, *Dude, You're a Fag: Masculinity and Sexuality in High School* (Berkeley: University of California Press, 2007).

9. Personal life in the modern world is more democratic than formerly. This has allowed women to take the lead in forging intimate connections and to establish the boundaries needed to manage relationships successfully. See Anthony Giddens, *The Transformation of Intimacy: Love, Sexuality, and Eroticism in Modern Societies* (Malden, MA: Polity, 1992).

10. Arlie Russell Hochschild, *The Managed Heart: Commercialization of Human Feeling* (Berkeley: University of California Press, 1983).

11. Eva Illouz, *Consuming the Romantic Utopia: Love and the Cultural Contradictions of Capitalism* (Berkeley: University of California Press, 1997).

12. Herbert Marcuse, *Eros and Civilization: A Philosophical Inquiry into Freud* (Boston: Beacon, 1955).

13. Illouz, *Consuming the Romantic Utopia*, 7; Erich Fromm, *The Art of Loving* (New York: Harper and Row, 1956); Steven Seidman, *The Social Construction of Sexuality* (New York: Norton, 2003).

14. Heike Wieschiolek has found that dancers enjoy salsa clubs for this reason. See "'Ladies, Just Follow His Lead!' Salsa, Gender and Identity," in *Sport, Dance and Embodied Identities*, ed. Noel Dyck and Eduardo P. Archetti, 115–137 (Oxford: Berg, 2003).

15. Illouz, *Consuming the Romantic Utopia*.

16. See Phillies Phantasy Camp, "2008 Team Pictures," www.philliescamps .com/PhantasyCamp/team2008pictures.htm.

17. See Mike Krzyzewski's website, www.coachk.com/camps-and-clinics/ k-academy/.

18. Elizabeth Bernstein, *Temporarily Yours: Intimacy, Authenticity, and the Commerce of Sex* (Chicago: University of Chicago Press, 2007).

19. Kathleen Bogle, *Hooking Up: Sex, Dating, and Relationships on Campus* (New York: NYU Press, 2008).

20. Francesca M. Cancian, *Love in America: Gender and Self-Development* (New York: Cambridge University Press, 1987), 5.

21. The men's shirt read, "How to please 20 women in one night: On the dance floor."

22. Arlie Russell Hochschild, "The Commercial Spirit of Intimate Life and the Abduction of Feminism: Signs from Women's Advice Books," *Theory, Culture, and Society* 112, no. 3 (1995): 1–24.

23. Bogle, *Hooking Up*.

24. James Mahood and Kristine Wenberg, *The Mosher Survey* (New York: Arno, 1980); Clelia Dues Mosher, *Health and the Woman Movement* (New York: Woman's Press, 1918).

25. Kathy Peiss, *Hope in a Jar: The Making of America's Beauty Culture* (New York: Owl Books, 1998).

26. Some Protestants still believe that dancing paves the way to Hell. A student at Heritage Christian School in Findlay, Ohio, faced suspension if he attended his girlfriend's prom at the local public school. See Mary Kate Malone, "Don't Go to Prom, School Tells Teen," *TheCourier.com*, May 8, 2009, www.thecourier .com/Issues/2009/May/08/ar_news_050809_story3.asp?d=050809_story3 ,2009,May,08&c=n.

27. This brief history of dancing relies on the following: Peter Buckman, *Let's Dance: Social, Ballroom, and Folk Dancing* (New York: Penguin Books, 1978); Julie Malnig, "Two Stepping to Glory: Social Dance and the Rhetoric of Social Mobility," in *Moving History/Dancing Cultures: A Dance History Reader*, ed. Ann Dils

and Ann Cooper Albright, 271–287 (Middletown, CT: Wesleyan University Press, 2001); Richard M. Stephenson and Joseph Iaccarino, *The Complete Book of Ballroom Dancing* (New York: Doubleday, 1980); Christine Zona and Chris George, *Gotta Ballroom: Waltz, Tango, Foxtrot, and Viennese Waltz* (Champaign, IL: Human Kinetics, 2008); Lyndon Wainwright, *The Story of British Popular Dance* (Brighton, UK: International Dance Publications, 1996).

28. In *Pride and Prejudice*, Mr. Darcy first meets Lizzie at a dance.

29. Mary Clarke and Clement Crisp, *The History of Dance* (London: Orbis, 1981).

30. Julie Malnig, "Athena Meets Venus: Visions of Women in Social Dance in the Teens and Early 1920s," *Dance Research Journal* 31, no. 2 (1999): 34–62.

31. Julie Malnig, *Dancing Till Dawn: A Century of Exhibition Ballroom Dance* (New York: NYU Press, 1992).

32. Stephen G. Jones, *Workers at Play: A Social and Economic History of Leisure, 1918–1939* (London: Routledge and Kegan Paul, 1986); John Stevenson, *British Society, 1914–45* (New York: Penguin Books, 1990).

33. The 1930s song "Ten Cents a Dance" (Richard Rogers, music; Lorenz Hart, lyrics) is a taxi dancer's lament. This is also the title of a 1931 film starring Barbara Stanwyck (Columbia Pictures).

34. Paul G. Cressey, *The Taxi-Dance Hall* (Chicago: University of Chicago Press, 1932). Taxi-dance halls declined after the Second World War. See Clyde B. Vedder, "The Decline of the Taxi-Dance Hall," *Sociology and Social Research* (1954): 387–391. They persist in some cities. See Mary V. Meckel, "Continuity and Change Within a Social Institution: The Role of the Taxi-Dancer" (Ph.D. diss., University of Nebraska–Lincoln, 1988).

35. Kathy Peiss, *Cheap Amusements: Working Women and Leisure in Turn-of-the-Century New York* (Philadelphia: Temple University Press, 1986).

36. Dorothy Richardson, *The Long Day: The Story of a New York Working Girl*, in *Women at Work*, ed. William O'Neill, 3–303 (Chicago: Quadrangle Books, 1972).

37. Ibid., 94–95.

38. Thomas A. Faulkner, *From the Ballroom to Hell* (Chicago: Church Press, 1894), reprinted in *I See America Dancing: Selected Readings, 1685–2000*, ed. Maureen Needham (Urbana: University of Illinois Press, 2002), 112.

39. Some of this debate appears in Elizabeth Aldrich, *From the Ballroom to Hell: Grace and Folly in Nineteenth-Century Dance* (Evanston, IL: Northwestern University Press, 1991).

40. Belle Lindner Israels, "The Way of the Girl," *Survey* 22 (July 3, 1909), reprinted in Needham, *I See America Dancing*, 121.

41. Ibid.

42. Illouz, *Consuming the Romantic Utopia*. Concerned with rising divorce rates, experts emphasized the importance of sex in saving marriage. See Julia A.

Ericksen, *Kiss and Tell: Surveying Sex in the Twentieth Century* (Cambridge: Harvard University Press, 1999).

43. See www.arthurmurray.com; www.fredastaire.com.

44. Juliet McMains and Danielle Robinson, "Swingin' Out: Southern California's Lindy Revival," in Needham, *I See American Dancing*, 84–91; Randal Doane, "The Habitus of Dancing: Notes on the Swing Dance Revival in New York City," *Journal of Contemporary Ethnography* 35 (2006): 84–116.

45. The Oxford University team—the most successful British student team —started in 1968 and grew from 91 to 428 members in twenty years. See http:// oudancesport.co.uk/Home.

46. Leslie Kaufman, "Ballroom Dance Resurgence Reaches Classrooms," *New York Times*, April 21, 2005; Carin Rubinstein, "Mad Hot Classrooms Are Abundant This Summer," *New York Times*, July 31, 2005.

47. Stephanie Cox, "1, 2, Cha-Cha-Cha: More Getting in Step with Ballroom Dancing," *Connecticut Post*, March 19, 2004; Aaron Bailey, "This Isn't Your Grandma's Ballroom Dancing," Associated Press, August 8, 2005; Robert Lipsyte, "High Hopes for Ballroom Dancing," *USA Today*, October 11, 2005.

48. In the 1980s, as the Soviet Union collapsed, Russians, particularly Russian Jews, were admitted to the United States. The *New York Times* first noted the effect of immigration on ballroom dancing in 2000 and has reported on it periodically since. Lynn Ames, "The View from Dobbs Ferry: Ballroom Dance Pizazz from Russian Émigrés," *New York Times*, March 26, 2000; Patricia Vowinkel, "Ballroom Dancing with a Russian Flair," *New York Times*, December 30, 2001; Shayna Samuels, "And One and Two and the Dancers Are On," *New York Times*, April 21, 2002; Joseph Berger, "The Russians Are Coming, Stepping Lightly," *New York Times*, June 11, 2003. See also Kathleen Megan, "American Ballroom Dance Gets Big Lift from Soviet Émigrés," *Hartford Courant*, March 13, 2004.

49. Marjorie Werz, "Dance Fever," *Pittsburgh Tribune-Review*, August 8, 2005. Ballroom dancing has a complex and contentious governance system. Not all amateur dancers are members of the USABDA, now called USA Dance.

50. Juliet McMains, *Glamour Addiction: Inside the American Ballroom Dance Industry* (Middletown, CT: Wesleyan University Press, 2006).

51. J. Thomas Cottle, "Social Class and Social Dancing," *Sociological Quarterly* 7, no. 2 (1966): 179–196.

52. Irene Castle, *Castles in the Air* (New York: Da Capo, 1980).

53. Carlos G. Groppa, *The Tango in the United States* (Jefferson, NC: McFarland, 2004).

54. Philip J. S. Richardson, *A History of English Ballroom Dancing* (London: Herbert Jenkins, 1946), 43.

55. Ibid., 23.

56. Clarke and Crisp, *The History of Dance*, 111.

57. Richardson, *A History of English Ballroom Dancing*, 93.

58. Ibid., 114.

59. Alex Moore, *Ballroom Dancing* (London: Sir Alex Pittman and Sons, 1933); the tenth edition was published in 2002. See also Alex Moore, *The Revised Technique of Ballroom Dancing* (Kingston-on-Thames, UK: Alex Moore, Zeeta Dance Studios, 1948).

60. See www.istd.org.

61. Ruud Vermey, *Latin: Thinking, Sensing and Doing in Latin American Dancing* (Munich: Kastell Verlag, 1994).

62. Barbara Browning, *Samba: Resistance in Motion* (Bloomington: Indiana University Press, 1995).

63. Debate about samba can seen in the comments about two YouTube videos showing the contrasting styles: sambatribe, "How to Dance Samba, Basic Samba Step, www.learnsamba.com," July 17, 2007, www.youtube.com/watch?v=JkfiXd8BIRQ&NR=1; and xxMTBxx, "Slavik and Karina Samba Video," January 14, 2007, www.youtube.com/watch?v=wsyc_VVrO-A.

64. In *Glamour Addiction*, McMains posits a racial dynamic as the basis for many of the decisions made about the curriculum and marketing of ballroom, especially Latin dancing.

65. According to Caroline Joan S. Picart, the term "DanceSport" had been used in Europe for some years before it was adopted in 1989 by the IDSF in its bid to make ballroom an Olympic sport. See Picart, *From Ballroom to DanceSport: Aesthetics, Athletics, and Body Culture* (Albany: SUNY Press, 2006), 70.

66. McMains, *Glamour Addiction*.

67. Erving Goffman. *The Presentation of Self in Everyday Life* (New York: Doubleday Anchor, 1959).

68. The Ohio Star Ball hosts a joint party for teachers and students. A student there complained to me that her teacher was hanging out with his friends and not including her.

69. Judith Butler, *Gender Trouble: Feminism and the Subversion of Identity* (New York: Routledge, 1990).

70. In *Glamour Addiction*, McMains argues that teachers are always frontstage when dancing with students. This has not been my experience. Furthermore, several teachers told me that they felt relaxed around students they knew and trusted.

71. For a discussion of the racial implications of Latin dance performance, see McMains, *Glamour Addiction*.

72. Helen Thomas and Nicola Miller, "Ballroom Blitz," in *Dance in the City*, ed. Helen Thomas, 89–110 (London: MacMillan, 1997).

73. Mark Padilla, *Caribbean Pleasure Industry: Tourism, Sexuality, and AIDS in the Dominican Republic* (Chicago: University of Chicago Press, 2007).

74. Bernstein, *Temporarily Yours*.

75. The truth of these rumors is unclear. When I questioned how a speaker

244 Notes to Chapter 1

knew that a particular man must be gay, the answer was that he "danced gay"; that is, the male dancer did not have a macho presentation of self.

76. Peter Brinson, "Scholastic Tasks of a Sociology of Dance," *Dance Research: The Journal of the Society for Dance Research* 1, no. 1 (1983): 100–107.

77. Helen Thomas, *Dance, Modernity, and Culture* (New York: Routledge, 1995).

78. Donald S. Blumenfield-Jones, Dance as a Mode of Research Representation," *Qualitative Inquiry* 1, no. 4 (1995): 391–401.

79. Two exceptions are Cottle, "Social Class and Social Dancing"; and Helena Znaniecki Zopata and Joseph R. Noel, "The Dance Studio—Style without Sex," *Transaction* 4, no. 3 (1967): 10–17.

80. Examples include Gediminas Karoblis, "Question Concerning Dance Technique," *Phenomenology* (2005): 363–398; Jonathan S. Marion, *Ballroom: Culture and Costume in Competitive Dance* (Oxford: Berg, 2008); McMains, *Glamour Addiction*; Sally Peters, "The Elegant Passion," *Journal of Popular Culture* 25 (Spring 1992): 163–171; Sally Peters, "From Eroticism to Transcendence: Ballroom Dance and the Female Body," in *The Female Body: Figures, Styles, Speculations*, ed. Laurence Goldstein, 145–158 (Ann Arbor: University of Michigan Press, 1991); Picart, *From Ballroom to DanceSport*.

81. Examples include Eve Babitz, *Two by Two: Tango, Two-Step, and the L.A. Night* (New York: Simon and Schuster, 1999); Janet Carlson, *Quick, Before the Music Stops: How Ballroom Dancing Saved My Life* (New York: Broadway Books, 2008); Gregory Causey with Natasha Yushmanov, *Dancing with Natasha* (Springboro, OH: Romance Divine, 2007); Lydia Raurell, *A Year of Dancing Dangerously* (Woodstock, NY: Overlook-Duckworth, 2008).

82. Examples include Bill Irvine and Bobbie Irvine, *The Dancing Years* (London: W. H. Allen, 1970); Kathryn Murray with Betty Hannah Hoffman, *My Husband, Arthur Murray* (New York: Simon and Schuster, 1960); Doris Eaton Travis, *The Days We Danced: The Story of My Theatrical Family from Florenz Ziegfeld to Arthur Murray* (Seattle: Marquand Books, 2003).

83. Examples include Beth Kephart, *House of Dance* (New York: HarperTeen, 2008); Dorothy Truex, *The Twenty Million Dollar Give-Away: An Exposé of Competitive Ballroom Dancing* (Bloomington, IN: Xlibris, 2000).

84. Jonathan Marion has conducted extensive interviews with ballroom dancers, which informed his book *Ballroom*. However, as of 2010, he had written about these sparingly.

85. McMains, *Glamour Addiction*; Truex, *The Twenty Million Dollar Give-Away*.

86. Hochschild, *The Managed Heart*.

87. In the online version of *Dance Beat* (December 17, 2008), Park West Photography advertised two calendars, showing male and female dancers, respectively, and emphasizing the dancers' unattainable looks. See www.dancebeat.com/store/products.asp.

Notes to Chapter 2

1. Bill Irvine and Bobbie Irvine, *The Dancing Years* (London: W. H. Allen, 1970).

2. Peter Eggleton and Brenda Winslade won Blackpool after the Irvines stepped down. However, the Irvines are said to have changed ballroom dancing competition forever.

3. Irvine and Irvine, *The Dancing Years*, 80.

4. In most competitions, there are five ballroom dances, but at Blackpool the Viennese waltz is not performed.

5. Irvine reports that Albach, a former dancer who was now a photographer, timed the event with a stopwatch.

6. Irvine and Irvine, *The Dancing Years*, 82–83.

7. Ibid., 88.

8. Julie Malnig, *Dancing Till Dawn: A Century of Exhibition Ballroom Dance* (New York: NYU Press, 1992); Juliet McMains, *Glamour Addiction: Inside the American Ballroom Industry* (Middletown, CT: Wesleyan University Press, 2006).

9. Although *The Dancing Years* purports to be written by both Bill and Bobbie Irvine, the voice is always first-person Bill.

10. This is common in the competition world, although it is slowly changing, especially for certain charismatic "girls" such as Katusha Demidova, Yulia Zagoruychenko, or Joanna Leunis.

11. The competition is held in the Winter Gardens Ballroom. The Tower Ballroom is still open for social dancing.

12. John H. Gagnon, "Scripts and the Coordination of Sexual Conduct," in *An Interpretation of Desire: Essays in the Study of Sexuality* (Chicago: University of Chicago Press, 2004), 59–87.

13. Two dancers born in America have won the Latin competition at Blackpool, but not for the United States. Corky Ballas and his British wife, Shirley, won for England in 1995 and 1996, and in 1993 Nadia Eftedal and Johan Eftedal won for his native Norway.

14. Two couples from each participating country compete at the world competition, which moves from country to country each year.

15. The Irvines' closest competition for "best ever" are Marcus and Karen Hilton, who won nine times in the 1990s.

16. "Modestly" because, for three years prior to the interview, they had placed higher than that.

17. They have since retired from professional competition.

18. Maximiliaan Winkelhuis, *Dance to Your Maximum: The Competitive Ballroom Dancer's Workbook* (www.DancePlaza.com, 2001), 280.

19. Ibid, 18.

20. In *Ballroom: Culture and Costume in Competitive Dance* (Oxford: Berg, 2008), Jonathan Marion discusses the tension between sport and art.

21. See www.idsf.net.

22. This is only one conflict among several involving these and other dance organizations, including national organizations.

23. See www.wdcdance.com/download/mj2DWmgAikNE6YETDuHMQwO xa/WDC Competition Rules current June 2010.pdf.

24. Ruud Vermey, *Latin: Thinking, Sensing and Doing in Latin American Dancing* (Munich: Kastell Verlag, 1994), 22.

25. The performance can be seen on YouTube: chemdance, "Gekhman Silver Robot Ballroom Dance," March 1, 2007, www.youtube.com/watch?v=SE-nH0G 6toY.

26. Meredith and his former wife, Melanie LePatin, won the U.S. National Professional Latin Championship in 1995. He was the color commentator on *America's Ballroom Challenge* for several years.

27. dapenda, "Ben Ermis & Shalene Archer-Ermis Smooth Viennese Waltz," YouTube, July 22, 2007, www.youtube.com/watch?v=3VNMWAHDI-I.

28. Winkelhuis, *Dance to Your Maximum*, 47.

29. The performance can be seen on YouTube: Shpealer, "2007 IDSF World Latin—Eugene & Maria—Jive," June 9, 2008, www.youtube.com/watch?v=b0gk A1wQosk.

30. The performance can be seen on YouTube: jaziac, "International Ballroom Jive—Bryan Watson & Carmen Vincelj," October 8, 2006, www.youtube.com/ watch?v=QdtgCYGKVb4.

31. Alastair Macaulay, "Ballroom: More Sexily, Less Strictly," *New York Times*, August 13, 2009.

32. Macaulay has fond memories of the golden age of dancing in Hollywood movies, which he contrasts unfavorably with contemporary ballroom dancing. Alastair Macaulay, "They Seem to Find the Happiness They Seek," *New York Times*, August 14, 2009.

33. This also happens on Broadway sometimes. For example, the Twyla Tharp musical *Come Fly Away* depicts the erotic connections between four pairs of dancers in a nightclub. Macaulay found this musical to be tawdry. See Alastair Macaulay, "Sinatra, Focused on Sex and Sizzle," *New York Times*, March 27, 2010.

34. Most Russian dancers do not turn professional unless they are able to leave the country. It is difficult to make a living there as a professional dancer.

35. Arlie Hochschild, *The Managed Heart: Commercialization of Human Feeling* (Berkeley: University of California Press, 1983).

36. This story is reminiscent of Eleanor Langer's account of telephone operators handling customer complaints for the New York Telephone Company. Company policy was that customers could not ask for a particular representative with whom they had previously discussed a problem. Customers, who had to keep ex-

plaining the same problem, became frustrated. Women were hired as operators because of their natural feminine charm but did not always respond well to being shouted at by angry callers. The company organized training sessions with specific responses to be learned for each situation. Not surprisingly, the workers became alienated. See Eleanor Langer, "Inside the New York Telephone Company," in *Women at Work*, ed. William O'Neill, 307–360 (Chicago: Quadrangle Books, 1972).

37. At that time, dancers were expected to retire from competition after winning Blackpool three times. Bill and Bobby Irvine bent the rules when after winning the ballroom competition they stayed out for a year, after which they won Latin and ballroom. Currently, winners may continue competing for as long as they are able.

38. Len Scrivener, *Just One Idea: Ballroom Dancing Analysed by Len Scrivener*, ed. Bryan Allen (privately published by Bryan Allen, 1983), 37. These lectures and articles are from the 1950s.

39. Ibid., 28.

40. Marion, *Ballroom*. Radler's article, "How a Ballroom Dance Competition Is Judged," may be found at www.ballroomdance.net/How_a_Competition_is_Judged_.html.

41. Vermey, *Latin*.

42. Waiting in the wings at a student showcase, I remember thinking how embarrassed I would be to mess up in front of family and friends.

43. These include Mary Murphy, Toni Redpath, and Jason Gilkinson.

44. Dancers who have done this include Jonathan Roberts, who won the American smooth competition after he joined the show; Anna Trebunskya, who was a finalist in several important competitions; and Tony Dovaloni, who won the American rhythm championship while on the show. Other dancers who joined the show after successful competitive careers include Karina Smirnoff and Louis Van Amstel.

45. This couple did not win at Blackpool, but they made the finals in jive and rumba in 2007.

46. This has changed in recent years. Many immigrants from eastern Europe compete as Americans.

47. The dancing at Blackpool is so popular that most of the seats are long spoken for and rarely turn over. Former dancers who own seats but cannot attend in a particular year will sell or give seats to friends, rather than give them up.

48. Michael Chapman runs the Millennium competition in St. Petersburg, Florida. He brings in top European competitors to do floor shows.

Notes to Chapter 3

1. Eva Illouz, *Consuming the Romantic Utopia: Love and the Cultural Contradictions of Capitalism* (Berkeley: University of California Press, 1997).

2. Viviana A. Zelizer, *The Purchase of Intimacy* (Princeton: Princeton University Press, 2005).

3. Sometimes top students compete in the evening.

4. The rules for this can be found on the DanceSport Series website, at www.dancesportseries.com/rules.html.

5. A video of this event can be seen on the DanceSport Series website, at www.dancesportseries.com.

6. For more information, see Starlite Ballroom and Dance Studio, "Biographical Data for Rauno and Kristiina Ilo," www.starlitedanceindy.com/html/ilobio.html.

7. Prize amounts listed in an advertisement for the American Ballroom Company, which runs USDC, in *Dance Beat* 0909 (2009).

8. Their current ranking, along with those of other pro/am students, can be seen on the DanceSport Series website, at www.dancesportseries.com. They can be seen dancing on YouTube: NationalDanceCouncil, "World Pro Am C Standard Alain and Beverley," June 30, 2009, www.youtube.com/watch?v=a5TW6O9RDQ8. Doucet is a former ten-dance champion.

9. Didio Barrera, "Like a Good Wine: Interview with Beverly Moore and Alain Doucet," *Dance Beat World* 1209-3 (2009).

10. Single dances typically cost thirty-five dollars per entry, but scholarship dances, which are fewer and involve a set of dances, are about eighty to one hundred dollars per entry. This is how I arrived at the figure of forty dollars.

11. This is approximate. Some heats with several dances, such as open competition, have higher entry fees. Also, there are other sources of revenue like a share of students' hotel packages.

12. The NDCA keeps a list of the dates and websites of all its approved dance events. See www.ndca.org/events.cfm?showsection=events&cfid=6296899&cftoken=37609285. In 2010, there were seventy-three approved competitions.

13. Illouz, *Consuming the Romantic Utopia*.

14. See, for example, the Outback Golf tournament (www.outbackproam.com), where pairs of players compete to play with professionals. At the ATT Pebble Beach Pro/Am competition, celebrities are paired with professional golfers (www.attpbgolf.com).

15. See U.S. Bureau of Labor Statistics, "Occupational Employment and Wages, May 2008: 27-2031 Dancers," www.bls.gov/oes/2008/may/oes272031.htm#(4).

16. Coaches, particularly those with an international reputation, may charge much more than this.

17. Arlie Russell Hochschild, *The Managed Heart: Commercialization of Human Feeling* (Berkeley: University of California Press, 1983).

18. An example would be George's comment in chapter 1 that he needed down time with his friends when he went to competitions.

19. Every summer, top international couples are invited to Tokyo to perform in the Superstars Dance Festival, which are televised and sold all over the world. Typically only five or six couples in each of the two styles are invited. Each couple dances about five dances of their choosing.

20. This list is not comprehensive but covers most places.

21. Teaching wedding couples their first dance is a big business for dance studios, and studio websites always feature it prominently. At big weddings, this can extend to dances for other members of the wedding party, such as the bride and her father.

22. "Modern Living: A Lifetime of Arthur Murray" (*Time*, November 24, 1948) describes the case of a widow in Albany, New York, who at age seventy-nine was persuaded to spend $11,800—half her life savings—for a lifetime membership, which meant unlimited lessons forever. Dorothy Cohen describes a case before the FTC in which the chains were accused of unfair practices and sales techniques. As a result, the FTC placed a limitation of $1,500 on lesson contracts and forbade the practice of advertising free lessons to lure consumers into signing dance contracts. Dorothy Cohen, "Remedies for Consumer Protection: Prevention, Resolution, or Punishment," *Journal of Marketing* 28 (1975): 24–31.

23. Russel B. Nye, "Saturday Night at the Paradise Ballroom; or, Dance Halls in the Twenties," *Journal of Popular Culture* 7, no. 1 (1973): 14–22.

24. Arthur Murray uses the medal system from Britain for students and teachers. Dancers are tested to move up to the next level. In the Murray system, balls are held after testing sessions, and students are awarded their medals at these balls.

25. There are more Arthur Murray studios than Fred Astaire's nationally, 158 versus 130. Counted from their websites in October 2009.

26. In Philadelphia and suburbs, there are at least sixty independent schools (including schools using temporary rentals) where students can learn to dance. Most are in the suburbs.

27. Brigitt Mayer-Karakis, *Ballroom Icons* (self-published, 2009), 116.

28. Dance Forums is a ballroom-dancing discussion board. It can be accessed at www.dance-forums.com.

29. Erving Goffman, *The Presentation of Self in Everyday Life* (New York: Doubleday Anchor, 1959).

30. When my husband's dance teacher was pregnant, we gave a baby shower for her and her husband to which almost all of the teachers and many of the students came. At our studio, this was not a unique event.

31. For example, Bob Powers and Julia Gorchakova, twelve times undefeated American rhythm champions, are on the board and coach at studios around the country.

32. Bill Irvine and Bobbie Irvine, *The Dancing Years* (London: W. H. Allen, 1970), 149–150.

33. Ann Swidler, "Love and Adulthood in American Culture," in *Themes of Work and Love in Adulthood*, ed. Neil J. Smelser and Erik H. Erikson, 120–150 (Cambridge: Harvard University Press, 1980), 128.

34. At a social dance near Philadelphia, the organizers have "mixers," where and men women line up. The first man in line has to dance the first woman around the floor to the end of the line and take the first woman lined up. While dancing a mixer, I asked my partner what he liked about it. He answered, "It's like having a one-minute affair. You pick a woman up, dance around the floor with her, and then leave with no hard feelings."

35. My husband told a Russian teacher that he was not going to continue dancing with her because he was not enjoying his lessons, only to be told that he was not good enough to have fun.

36. Donald Greenless, "Hong Kong Banker Wins Back Millions for Dance Lessons," *New York Times*, September 6, 2006.

37. Kate Linebaugh, "Banker Now Regards $15.4 Million Lessons as a Serious Mistake," *Wall Street Journal*, August 3, 2006.

38. Greenless, "Hong Kong Banker."

Notes to Chapter 4

1. Dancing with the Stars website, "The Erin Andrews and Maskim [*sic*] Chmerkovskiy Thread," abc.go.com/shows/dancing-with-the-stars/discuss?cat=23170&tid=809524&tsn=1.

2. The World Congress held every year alongside the Blackpool Dance Festival consists of lectures and demonstrations by champions and former champions and is attended by competitors.

3. Ruud Vermey, *Latin: Thinking, Sensing and Doing in Latin American Dancing* (Munich: Kastell Verlag, 1994), 90–91. Peter Townsend is Vermeij's longtime romantic partner.

4. Judith Butler, *Gender Trouble* (New York: Routledge, 1990).

5. Vermey, *Latin*.

6. Although same-sex dancing is not allowed in any of the world amateur or professional competitions, a number of same-sex competitions are held in Europe and the United States. Since 2007, the European Same-Sex Dance Association has been working to promote this. See www.essda.eu.

7. Jennie Livingston, director, *Paris Is Burning*, Miramax Films, 1990.

8. Butler, *Gender Trouble*, 187–188. For a reading of the drag performances in *Paris Is Burning*, see Judith Butler, *Bodies That Matter: On the Discursive Limits of "Sex"* (New York: Routledge, 1993).

9. "Top" means that he ranked highly at important international competitions.

10. Arlie Russell Hochschild, "The Economy of Gratitude," in *The Sociology of*

Emotions: Original Essays and Research Papers, ed. David Franks and Doyle McCarthy, 95–113 (Greenwich, CT: JAI, 1989).

11. Traveling to a competition, I sat next to a former American rhythm champion who told me that when he was the U.S. champion year after year, he and his partner disliked each other and could barely stand to practice together. Sometimes coaches would put them in opposite corners of the dance floor.

12. Arlie Hochschild, *The Managed Heart: Commercialization of Human Feeling* (Berkeley: University of California Press, 1983).

13. The sociology of emotions, on which this chapter draws, is a relatively new field. For early overviews of the main ideas, see Peggy Thoits, "The Sociology of Emotions," in *Annual Review of Sociology* 15 (1989): 17–42; and Theodore Kemper, ed., *Research Agendas in the Sociology of Emotions* (Albany: SUNY Press, 1990).

14. Arlie Russell Hochschild, "Emotion Work, Feeling Rules, and Social Structure," *American Journal of Sociology* 85, no. 3 (1979): 551–565.

15. Jane P. Tompkins, ed., *Reader-Response Criticism: From Formalism to Post-Structuralism* (Baltimore: Johns Hopkins University Press, 1980); David Bordwell, *Making Meaning: Inference and Rhetoric in the Interpretation of Cinema* (Cambridge: Harvard University Press, 1989). Although ballet audiences do not expect to see authentic feelings portrayed on the stage, a former member of the Pennsylvania Ballet Company described watching *Romeo and Juliet* just after the dancer playing Romeo proposed to the dancer playing Juliet. The dancers watching backstage thought their performances had an increased emotional intensity: "We could tell they were in love."

16. The speed of relationship changes in the dance world makes viewers unsure about the meaning of what they are seeing. There is constant gossip and speculation about this.

17. Hochschild, *The Managed Heart*.

18. This is interesting given that Tornsberg was successful with all three of his recorded partners, Vibeke Toft, Carmen Vincelj, and Serena Lecca. He made the finals at Blackpool with each of them, and each partnership lasted at least several years.

19. Feeling rules dictate how one is supposed to feel in a particular situation. Emotional labor is performed to bring feelings into line with these rules. Hochschild, *The Managed Heart*, 118.

20. For a look at the Japanese interest in ballroom, see Masayuki Suo's *Shall We Dansu?*, a film produced by Yasuyoshi Tokuma (Japan: Toho, 1996).

21. Hans Galke, a prominent Latin dancer and coach, won the amateur Latin at Blackpool in 1990 and made the finals in professional Latin about seven times.

22. Many jobs have a sexual component to them. For example, Hooters' waitresses understand that their job is not limited to serving food. See Meika Loe,

"Working for Men: At the Intersection of Power, Gender, and Sexuality," *Sociological Inquiry* 66 (1996): 399–422.

23. Arlie Hochschild, *The Commercialization of Intimate Life* (Berkeley: University of California Press, 2003), 84.

24. Kathleen A. Bogle, *Hooking Up: Sex, Dating, and Relationships on Campus* (New York: NYU Press, 2008).

25. Correct technique in ballroom is for there to be "no daylight" between partners when dancing in closed position. Latin allows for more space. Even though Latin looks sexier, it is ballroom that gives beginning students the most discomfort. See Richard M. Stephenson and Joseph Iaccarino, *The Complete Book of Ballroom Dancing* (New York: Doubleday, 1980).

26. Arlie Russell Hochschild, "The Sociology of Emotions as a Way of Feeling," in *Emotions in Social Life: Critical Theories and Contemporary Issues*, ed. Gillian Bendelow and Simon J. Williams, 3–15 (New York: Routledge, 1998).

27. Viviana Zelizer, *The Purchase of Intimacy* (Princeton: Princeton University Press, 2005).

28. Bogle, *Hooking Up.*

29. Eva Illouz, *Consuming the Romantic Utopia: Love and the Cultural Contradictions of Capitalism* (Berkeley: University of California Press, 1997).

Notes to Chapter 5

1. *New York Times* theater critic Charles Isherwood described *Burn the Floor*, a Broadway ballroom dancing show, as "every bit as flashy and tacky as you would expect." He described the costumes as "clingy, sequin-spattered and fringe trimmed dresses for the women and tight black slacks (and the occasional shirt) for the men," which, he stated, "sometimes look cheap." Charles Isherwood, "Shaking, Rattling and Shimmying, under a Broadway Disco Ball," *New York Times*, August 3, 2009.

2. Maximiliaan Winkelhuis, *Dance to Your Maximum: The Competitive Ballroom Dancer's Workbook* (www.DancePlaza.com, 2001).

3. Gyrotonics is an exercise system developed by former dancer Julio Horvath after he experienced injuries from dancing. Like Pilates, it is intended to enable users to simultaneously stretch and strengthen muscles and tendons while also articulating and mobilizing the joints. Practitioners often describe it as "three-dimensional Pilates." While the exercises are being performed, practitioners breathe in prescribed ways in order to increase coordination, endurance, and aerobic activity. It is popular among dancers because of its impact on bodily health and appearance but is used by others also. Because of the expense and difficulty of teacher training, it is concentrated in New York and on the West Coast. More information is available at www.gyrotonic.com.

4. "U.K." refers to the United Kingdom Open Competition held annually in

Bournemouth. Along with the Blackpool Dance Festival and the International at London's Royal Albert Hall, it is one of the three most important competitions on the international circuit.

5. Depending on a ballroom's decor, some colors look better than others on a particular floor.

6. Bryan S. Turner, *The Body and Society*, 2nd ed. (New York: Sage, 1996), 5.

7. Susan Bordo, *Unbearable Weight: Feminism, Western Culture, and the Body* (Berkeley: University of California Press, 1993).

8. Sophie Flack, a former dancer with New York City Ballet, reported that she was not cast in some roles because she has visible breasts. Flack appeared slender in the picture that accompanied the article. Gia Kouris, "Sophie Flack: A Nine-Year Veteran Discusses Her Recent Lay-Off," *Time-Out New York*, July 2–8, 2009.

9. Mike Featherstone, "The Body in Consumer Culture," in *The Body: Social Process and Cultural Theory*, ed. Mike Featherstone, Mike Hepworth, and Bryan S. Turner, 170–197 (London: Sage, 1991).

10. Chris Warhurst, Dennis Nickson, Anne Witz, and Anne Marie Cullen, "Aesthetic Labor in Interactive Service Work: Some Case Study Evidence for the 'New' Glasgow," *Service Industries Journal* 20 (2000): 103–120.

11. Chris Warhurst, Diane van den Broek, Richard Hall, and Dennis Nickson, "Lookism: The New Frontier of Employment Discrimination?" *Journal of Industrial Relations* 51 (2009): 131–136.

12. Elizabeth Wissinger, "Modeling Consumption: Fashion Modeling Work in Contemporary Society," *Journal of Consumer Culture* 9 (2009): 273–296.

13. Jonathan S. Marion, *Ballroom: Culture and Costume in Competitive Dance* (Oxford: Berg, 2008).

14. Julia Twigg, "Clothing, Age and the Body: A Critical Review," *Ageing and Society* 27 (2007): 285–305.

15. Joan B. Eicher, "Dress: Gender and the Public Display of Skin," in *Body Dressing*, ed. Joanne Entwistle and Elizabeth Wilson, 233–252 (Oxford: Berg, 2001).

16. Elizabeth Wilson, "A Note on Glamour," *Fashion Theory* 11, no. 1 (March 2007): 95–107.

17. It was the longest-running television show in BBC history—1949 to 1988.

18. Conversation with ball-gown designer Deirdre Baker, August 3, 2009.

19. Ibid.

20. This was not the first long dress. Marion Welsh, before she married her partner, Kenny Welsh, had worn a long dress for about two years. But she was not yet a star, and the dress was not noticed.

21. As a result, Deirdre was left with "an awful lot of net," she told me.

22. Latin dresses had already become less bulky and more clingy, and men had stopped wearing the traditional dinner jacket to dance Latin some time earlier.

23. bmwsitgez, "World Champions Ballroom '60—Bill & Bobbie Irvine," YouTube, March 22, 2008, www.youtube.com/watch?v=8yNq2Me6ArY.

24. kcballroom, "2008 WSS Mirko Gozzoli & Alessia Betti Foxtrot," YouTube, November 7, 2008, www.youtube.com/watch?v=kCyejC4u1pU&feature=related.

25. Ballroom dances, including the foxtrot, are danced with knees slightly bent. Nowadays women's knees are covered by their long flowing dresses, which produces an elegant line.

26. theslumsofsoftfocus, "Fred Astaire and Ginger Rogers—Smoke Gets in Your Eyes," YouTube, June 24, 2007, www.youtube.com/watch?v=OMOBdQyk KQY.

27. Bill Irvine and Bobbie Irvine, *The Dancing Years* (London: W. H. Allen, 1970).

28. Marion, *Ballroom*, 59.

29. Roland Barthes, *Mythologies* (Paris: Granada/Editions di Seuil, 1957), 15.

30. Juliet McMains, *Glamour Addiction: Inside the American Ballroom Dance Industry* (Middletown, CT: Wesleyan University Press, 2006), 1.

31. Ibid., xi.

32. McMains uses terminology developed by Linda Mizejewska in her book *Ziegfeld Girl: Image and Icon in Culture and Cinema* (Durham: Duke University Press, 1997).

33. McMains, *Glamour Addiction*, 3.

34. Turner, *The Body and Society*.

35. Alastair Macaulay, "Ballroom: More Sexily, Less Strictly," *New York Times*, August 17, 2009.

36. Charles Isherwood and Alastair Macaulay, "One Loves It. One Loathes It. 'That's Life,' " *New York Times*, April 1, 2010; Alastair Macaulay, "Dancing Their Way to a Tony Nomination," *New York Times*, June 4, 2010.

37. Bordo, *Unbearable Weight*.

38. Kathy Peiss, *Hope in a Jar: The Making of America's Beauty Culture* (New York: Owl Books, 1998), 269.

39. Susan Bordo, *The Male Body: A New Look at Men in Public and in Private* (New York: Farrar, Straus and Giroux, 1999).

40. In dance today, this traditional obligation is lessening. Many men display themselves as much as they display their women partners.

41. Friendships between gay men and straight women have been popularized in shows such as *Will and Grace* and *Sex in the City*.

42. Chrisanne clothes are made in England and cost around twenty-two hundred to five thousand dollars depending on the amount of stoning and whether the dress is for Latin or ballroom. See www.chrisanne.us/index.html.

43. A competition held in the Los Angeles Hilton Airport Hotel each May.

44. Wire shoe brushes are used to rough up the suede sole of dance shoes and keep them from getting too slippery.

45. Vivian Beiswenger, "Dance Etiquette According to Beiswenger," *Delaware Valley Dance Spotlight*, November–December 2007, 3.

46. Eva Illouz, *Consuming the Romantic Utopia: Love and the Cultural Contradictions of Capitalism* (Berkeley: University of California Press, 1997).

47. Francesca M. Cancian, *Love in America: Gender and Self-Development* (New York: Cambridge University Press, 1987).

48. Julia A. Ericksen, *Taking Charge of Breast Cancer* (Berkeley: University of California Press, 2008).

Notes to Chapter 6

1. Mike Donaldson argues that working-class men's bodies are their economic assets. Mike Donaldson, *Time of Our Lives: Labor and Love in the Working Class* (Sydney, Australia: Allen and Unwin, 1991). With the decline of opportunities to make good salaries from manual labor, dance provides a different type of economic opportunity.

2. Helen Thomas, "Dancing the Difference," *Women's Studies International Forum* 19, no. 5 (1996): 505–511.

3. John Bryce Jordan, "Pricked Dances: The Spectator, Dance, and Masculinity in Early 18th-Century England," in *When Men Dance: Choreographing Masculinities across Borders*, ed. Jennifer Fisher and Anthony Shay, 181–206 (New York: Oxford University Press, 2009).

4. Candace West and Don H. Zimmerman, "Doing Gender," *Gender and Society* 9 (February 1987): 8–37. The concept of "doing gender" has been criticized as reifying gender as a category with its own set of rules. If this were true, masculinity would involve only one set of appropriate behaviors. Male dancers challenge this. For example, the ability to swivel one's hips is admired among male dancers, if not among males everywhere. Yet despite acceptance on the dance floor, heterosexual male dancers in a country such as the United States must integrate their dancer identity and their masculine identity, because the two do not appear to be compatible. They do this by negotiating an appropriate gender performance in ways that both reflect and challenge culture. See Dorothy Smith, "Categories Are Not Enough," *Gender and Society* 23 (2009): 76–81.

5. Barrie Thorne, *Gender Play: Boys and Girls in School* (New Brunswick: Rutgers University Press, 1993).

6. Doug Risner, "What Do We Know about Men Who Dance?" in Fisher and Shay, *When Men Dance*, 57–77.

7. R. W. Connell, *Masculinities* (Berkeley: University of California Press, 1995).

8. C. J. Pascoe, *Dude, You're a Fag: Masculinity and Sexuality in High School* (Berkeley: University of California Press, 2007), 69. Pascoe notes that African American boys admired boys who could swivel their hips.

9. Judith Butler, *Gender Trouble: Feminism and the Subversion of Identity* (New York: Routledge, 1990).

10. Francesca M. Cancian, *Love in America: Gender and Self-Development* (New

York: Cambridge University Press, 1987); Francesca M. Cancian and Stacey J. Oliker, *Caring and Gender* (Thousand Oaks, CA: Pine Forge, 2000).

11. Barbara J. Risman, "From Doing to Undoing Gender as We Know it," *Gender and Society* 23 (February 2009): 81–85.

12. Susan Bordo, *The Male Body: A New Look at Men in Public and in Private* (New York: Farrar, Straus and Giroux, 1999), 161. Bordo attributes this insight to movie critic Pauline Kael.

13. Gaylin Studlar, "Valentino, 'Optic Intoxication' and Dance Madness," in *Screening the Male: Exploring Masculinities in Hollywood Cinema*, ed. Steven Cohan and Ina Rae Hark, 23–45 (New York: Routledge, 1993).

14. Michael Gard, *Men Who Dance* (New York: Peter Lang, 2006), 2.

15. Connell, *Masculinities*.

16. Michael A. Messner, *Out of Play: Critical Essays on Gender and Sport* (Albany: SUNY Press, 2007).

17. Ted Shawn, *One Thousand and One Night Stands* (New York: Doubleday, 1960); Mary Clarke and Clement Crisp, *Dancer: Men in Dance* (London: British Broadcasting Association, 1984); Maura Keefe, "Is Dance a Man's Sport Too? The Performance of Athletic-Coded Masculinity on the Concert Dance Stage," in Fisher and Shay, *When Men Dance*, 91–106.

18. Timothy Jon Curry, "Fraternal Bonding in the Locker Room: A Profeminist Analysis of Talk about Competition and Women," *Sociology of Sport Journal* 8 (1991): 119–135.

19. Internationally, dancers may remain as amateurs for long periods of time and are often better than many professionals.

20. These are top professional dancers, mostly from the United Kingdom, Australia, and Canada. Some dance international ballroom, not American smooth, and others are Latin dancers. It is common for American smooth dancers to receive coaching in ballroom and Latin because smooth contains elements of each style.

21. Very top professionals are able to support themselves by coaching, by doing shows, and with sponsors.

22. Christine Zona and Chris George, *Gotta Ballroom: Waltz, Tango, Foxtrot, and Viennese Waltz* (Champaign, IL: Human Kinetics, 2008), 60.

23. Richard M. Stephenson and Joseph Iaccarino, *The Complete Book of Ballroom Dancing* (New York: Doubleday, 1980), 61.

24. Caroline Joan S. Picart and Kenneth Gergen, "Dharma Dancing: Ballroom Dancing and Relational Order," *Qualitative Inquiry* 10, no. 6 (2004): 864.

25. Ruud Vermeij, in his book on Latin dancing, is critical of the exaggerated portrayal of male/female roles. He argues that gender portrayals "are already there in the structure of the dance and need to be understood rather than exaggerated." Ruud Vermey, *Latin: Thinking, Sensing and Doing in Latin American Dancing* (Munich: Kastell Verlag, 1994), 97.

26. In closed position, the couple maintains a dance hold the whole time they

are dancing. James's students could also dance open position with him if they maintained a hold. They could not dance separately since this entails learning choreographed steps.

27. What Colin means by "bumped in" is that dancers' legs are intertwined such that the woman's legs are on both sides of his right thigh holding tight, while his legs are on both sides of her left thigh.

28. Juliet McMains states, "Although few standard male dancers identify themselves as homosexual, nearly half the professional male Latin competitors in the United States are openly gay." Juliet McMains, *Glamour Addiction: Inside the American Ballroom Dance Industry* (Middletown, CT: Wesleyan University Press, 2006), 143. Using a slightly different tack, Jonathan S. Marion states, "When I first started my fieldwork, half the men then in the World and Blackpool Professional Latin finals were homosexual." This involved fewer than ten men, and Marion knew the sexual identity of each. Marion adds, however, that this is not representative of "the general distribution of Latin dancers." Jonathan S. Marion, *Ballroom: Culture and Costume in Competitive Dance* (Oxford: Berg, 2008), 143.

29. Estimates of gay men in the professional dance world come from dancers. One frequently cited estimate of the preponderance of gay men is J. Michael Bailey and Michael Oberschneider, "Sexual Orientation and Professional Dance," *Archives of Sexual Behavior* 26, no. 4 (1997): 433–443. A more reliable estimate, but still not a scientifically defensible one, comes from a survey of several thousand dancers responding to a questionnaire in *Dance Magazine*. Half of the male respondents said they were gay. See Linda H. Hamilton, *Advice for Dancers: Emotional Counsel and Practical Strategies* (San Francisco: Jossey-Bass, 1998).

30. Marion, *Ballroom*, 143.

31. Eric Marx, "In the Ballroom, a Redefinition of 'Couple,'" *New York Times*, July 14, 2004.

32. Peter Lyman argues that men use sexist and racist jokes to creates a sense of insider bonding. Homophobic jokes serve this purpose also. Peter Lyman, "The Fraternal Bond as a Joking Relationship: A Study of the Roles of Sexist Jokes in Male Group Bonding," in *Men's Lives*, ed. Michael S. Kimmel and Michael A. Messner, 169–178 (Boston: Allyn and Bacon, 2004).

33. Steven Seidman, *The Social Construction of Sexuality* (New York: Norton, 2003), 52.

34. Helena Wulff, *Ballet across Borders: Career and Culture in the World of Dancers* (Oxford: Berg, 1998).

35. Jonathan Ned Katz, *The Invention of Heterosexuality* (New York: Dutton, 1995); Connell, *Masculinities*; Seidman, *The Social Construction of Sexuality*.

36. This example is from an actual conversation and refers to Ricardo Cocchi, who dances with Yulia Zagorochenko.

37. Ramin Setoodeh, "Straight Jacket," *Newsweek.com*, April 30, 2010, www.newsweek.com/2010/04/30/straight-jacket.html.

38. This is the typical way of teaching men how to dance the woman's steps. All male dancers become comfortable dancing with another man either taking the lead or following.

39. Peter Nardi argues that gay men's friends are usually gay because these friends have shared experiences of marginalization and form a substitute family. Almost four-fifths of the gay men he interviewed said their best friend was also gay. Peter M. Nardi, *Gay Men's Friendships: Invincible Communities* (Chicago: University of Chicago Press, 1999).

40. Successful dancers are often sponsored, particularly by clothing and shoe manufacturers. They may also have wealthy patrons.

41. McMains, *Glamour Addiction*.

42. For a summary of research showing that long-married couples who learn something new and challenging rekindle romance, see Tara Parker-Pope, "Reinventing Date Night for Long-Married Couples," *New York Times*, February 12, 2008.

43. Several writers have argued that Americans are increasingly socially isolated today and that this is bad for health. Dancing is one way of combating isolation for those who live alone. See John T. Cacioppo and William Patrick, *Loneliness: Human Nature and the Need for Connection* (New York: Norton, 2008); Thomas Dumm, *Loneliness as a Way of Life* (Cambridge: Harvard University Press, 2008); Jacqueline Olds and Richard S. Schwartz, *The Lonely American: Drifting Apart in the Twenty-First Century* (Boston: Beacon, 2009); and Robert Putnam, *Bowling Alone: The Collapse and Revival of American Community* (New York: Simon and Schuster, 2000).

44. A friend of my husband's and mine told our daughter that he had always thought my husband and I had a romantic relationship but that dance had enhanced it.

45. When my husband and I go to our dance-studio parties, I may only dance a couple of times with him all evening.

46. In Sally Peters's description of learning to follow, she describes the lead as "almost entirely physical." She adds that it is considered an "unforgivable sin" for the woman to anticipate the man's lead, something Gordon expected from his wife. Sally Peters, "From Eroticism to Transcendence: Ballroom Dance and the Female Body," in *The Female Body: Figures, Styles, Speculations*, ed. Laurence Goldstein, 145–158 (Ann Arbor: University of Michigan Press, 1991), 152.

47. Eva Illouz, *Consuming the Romantic Utopia: Love and the Cultural Contradictions of Capitalism* (Berkeley: University of California Press, 1997).

Notes to Chapter 7

1. Julie Bettie, *Women without Class: Girls, Race, and Identity* (Berkeley: University of California Press, 2003).

2. Mark Knowles, *The Wicked Waltz: Outrage at Couple Dancing in the 19th and Early 20th Centuries* (Jefferson, NC: McFarland, 2009).

3. Richard Dwyer, *Stars* (London: Routledge, 1998). For a discussion of America's love affair with fame, see Jake Halpern, *Fame Junkies: The Hidden Truths behind America's Favorite Addiction* (New York: Houghton Mifflin, 2007); and John Maltby, Liz Day, David Giles, Raphael Gillet, Marianne Quick, Honey Lancaster-James, and P. Alex Linley, "Implicit Theories of a Desire for Fame," *British Journal of Psychology* 99 (2008): 279–291.

4. Juliet McMains, *Glamour Addiction* (Middletown, CT: Wesleyan University Press, 2008), 1.

5. Sally Peters, "The Elegant Passion," *Journal of Popular Culture* 25, no. 4 (Spring 1992): 163–171.

6. John A. Clausen, *American Lives: Looking Back at the Children of the Great Depression* (New York: Free Press, 1993).

7. Candace West and Don H. Zimmerman, "Doing Gender," *Gender and Society* 9 (February 1987): 8–37.

8. Dorothy E. Smith, "Categories Are Not Enough," *Gender and Society* 23, no. 1 (2009): 76; Dorothy E. Smith, "Ideology, Science, and Social Relations: A Reinterpretation of Marx's Epistemology," *European Journal of Social Theory* 7, no. 4 (2004): 445–462.

9. Candace West and Sarah Fenstermaker, "Doing Difference," *Gender and Society* 9 (1995): 8–37. See also Candace West and Don H. Zimmerman, "Accounting for Doing Gender." *Gender and Society* 23, no. 1 (2009): 112–122.

10. Nikki Jones, "I Was Aggressive for the Streets, Pretty for the Pictures," *Gender and Society* 23, no. 1 (2009): 89–93.

11. Sally Peters, "From Eroticism to Transcendence: Ballroom Dance and the Female Body," in *The Female Body, Figures, Styles, Speculations*, ed. Laurence Goldstein, 145–158 (Ann Arbor: University of Michigan Press, 1991).

12. Jonathan S. Marion, "Beyond Ballroom: Activity as Performance, Embodiment, and Identity," *Human Mosaic* 36, no. 2 (2004): 10.

13. Kathleen Gerson finds that young men and women hope for relationships of gender equality. However, men are more likely to pursue a relationship which allows them to put career first while a partner provides child care. Kathleen Gerson, "Falling Back on Plan B: The Children of the Gender Revolution Face Uncharted Territory," in *Families as They Really Are*, ed. Barbara J. Risman, 378–392 (New York: Norton, 2009).

14. An example can be seen on YouTube: igorglinka, "Dancing Rock-and-Roll," May 26, 2007, www.youtube.com/watch?v=34FyB1DoHag.

15. For most of the world, couples start out as amateurs and do not turn professional until they are close to the top. It is more difficult to make a living as a professional because there is little pro/am outside the United States. With the

popularity of the British show *Strictly Come Dancing* and its offshoots such as the American *Dancing with the Stars*—shows based on pro/am, with the star playing the role of amateur—pro/am is spreading. In 2009, competitions were held in the Bahamas, Russia, South Africa, and Mexico, among other places.

16. Clive Jones, *Soviet Jewish Aliyah, 1989–1992* (London: Frank Cass, 1996); Larissa Remennick, *Russian Jews on Three Continents* (New Brunswick, NJ: Transaction, 2007). After 1988, as a result of pressure from Israel, the United States made it more difficult for Jewish émigrés from the former Soviet Union to come here. Several dancers I interviewed came to the United States after first going to Israel.

17. Immigrants from the former Soviet Union and its satellites, particularly Jews, have caused a resurgence in ballroom dancing in places such as New York. See Lynn Ames, "The View from Dobbs Ferry: Ballroom Dance Pizazz from Russian Emigres," *New York Times*, March 26, 2000; Patricia Vowinkel, "Ballroom Dancing with a Russian Flair," *New York Times*, December 30, 2001; Shayna Samuels, "And One and Two and the Dancers Are On," *New York Times*, April 21, 2002; Joseph Berger, "The Russians Are Coming, Stepping Lightly," *New York Times*, June 11, 2003. See also Kathleen Megan, "American Ballroom Dance Gets Big Lift from Soviet Emigres," *Hartford Courant*, March 13, 2004.

18. Clifford J. Levy, "Young Americans Embrace Rigors of the Bolshoi," *New York Times*, May 31, 2010.

19. Ann Harriman, *Women/Men Management* (New York: Praeger, 1985).

20. Elaine Hall, "Smiling, Deferring, and Flirting: Doing Gender by Giving 'Good Service.'" *Work and Occupations* 20 (1993): 452–471.

21. D. Elizabeth Pugel, "Points of Derailment: The Making of a Female Physicist," *Physics and Society* 26, no. 3 (1997), http://aps.org/units/fps/newsletters/1997/july/ajul97.html; Virginia W. Cooper, "Homophily or the Queen Bee Syndrome," *Small Group Research* 28, no. 4 (1997): 483–499.

22. E. Ann Kaplan, "Is the Gaze Male?" in *Women and Film: Both Sides of the Camera*, ed. E. Ann Kaplan, 35–46 (London: Methuen, 1983).

23. Michael A. Messner, *Out of Play: Critical Essays on Gender and Sport* (Albany: SUNY Press, 2007).

24. In this quotation, Becky-Sue conflates homosexuality with gender inversion, a longstanding practice in American society. See Steven Seidman, *The Social Construction of Sexuality* (New York: Norton, 2003).

25. Viviana A. Zelizer, *The Purchase of Intimacy* (Princeton: Princeton University Press, 2005); Viviana A. Zelizer, *The Social Meaning of Money: Pin Money, Paychecks, Poor Relief, and Other Currencies* (New York: Basic Books, 1994).

26. At a studio showcase, I danced a West Coast swing with an openly gay teacher, and we vamped it up to "My Aphrodisiac Is You," by Katy Melua.

27. This is a dance technique called "spotting."

28. Eva Illouz, *Consuming the Romantic Utopia: Love and the Cultural Contradictions of Capitalism* (Berkeley: University of California Press, 1997).

29. Sometimes social dance teachers compete in hustle, West Coast swing, or salsa, but these more informal competitions are outside this book's range.

Notes to Chapter 8

1. Kirk Johnson, "Seeing Old Age as a Never-Ending Adventure," *New York Times,* January 8, 2010.

2. Didio Barrera, "Being There! Interview with Michael Neil," *Dance Beat* 0210 (2010): 50.

3. Naomi Wolf, *The Beauty Myth: How Images of Beauty Are Used against Women* (New York: William Morrow, 1991).

4. John F. Cross and Jane Cross, "Age, Sex, Race, and the Perception of Facial Beauty," *Developmental Psychology* 5 (1971): 433–439.

5. An example of their dancing can be seen on YouTube: DanceDispatch, "Jive by Cloris and Corky—'Dancing with the Stars!'" October 6, 2008, www.youtube.com/watch?v=kHdMFS2uM7A&feature=related.

6. Cassandra Phoenix and Andrew Sparkes, "Young Athletic Bodies and Narrative Maps of Aging," *Journal of Aging Studies* 20 (2006): 107–121.

7. Ibid., 118.

8. Bryan S. Turner and Steven P. Wainwright, "Corps de Ballet: The Case of the Injured Ballet Dancer," *Sociology of Health and Illness* 25 (2003): 269–288.

9. Stephen Katz, "Fashioning Agehood: Lifestyle Imagery and the Commercial Spirit of Seniors Culture," in *Childhood and Old Age: Equals or Opposites?* ed. Jorgen Povlsen, Signe Mellemgaard, and Ning de Coninck-Smith, 75–92 (Odense, Denmark: Odense University Press, 1999)

10. Stephen Katz and Barbara Marshall, "New Sex for Old: Lifestyle, Consumerism, and the Ethics of Aging Well," *Journal of Aging Studies* 17 (2003): 3–16.

11. Myra Dinnerstein and Rose Weitz, "Jane Fonda, Barbara Bush and Other Aging Bodies: Femininity and the Limits of Resistance," *Feminist Issues* 14, no. 2 (1994): 3–4.

12. Didio Barrera, "The World of Pro/Am: The Ohio Star Ball," *Dance Beat World* 1209-3 (2009), www.dancebeatworld.com/cmsAdmin/uploads/1209-3-low .pdf.

13. Didio Barrera, "Like a Good Wine: Interview with Beverly Moore and Alain Ducette," *Dance Beat World* 1209-3 (2009), www.dancebeatworld.com/cmsAdmin/uploads/1209-3-low.pdf.

14. Sarah Irwin, "Later Life, Inequality, and Sociological Theory," *Ageing and Society* 19 (1999): 691–715.

15. John H. Gagnon and William Simon, *Sexual Conduct: The Social Sources of Human Sexuality* (Chicago: Aldine, 1973).

16. Arlie Russell Hochschild, "Emotion Work, Feeling Rules, and Social Structure," *American Journal of Sociology* 85, no. 3 (1979): 551–565.

17. In the TV reality show *The Cougar*, the star was forty, and the men competing for her affection were in their twenties. On screen, the age differences appeared minimal. See TV Land, "The Cougar," http://www.tvland.com/prime/fullepisodes/thecougar.

18. Arlie Hochschild, *The Managed Heart: Commercialization of Human Feeling* (Berkeley: University of California Press, 1983).

19. Julia Twigg, "Clothing, Age and the Body: A Critical Review," *Ageing and Society* 27 (2007): 286–305.

20. Ibid., 286.

21. Alison Lurie makes this point in *The Language of Clothes* (London: Bloomsbury, 1992), 197.

22. D. G. Smathers and P. E. Horridge, "The Effects of Physical Changes on Clothing Preferences of Elderly Women," *International Journal of Aging and Human Development* 9 (1978–1979): 273–278.

23. Juliet McMains, *Glamour Addiction: Inside the American Ballroom Dance Industry* (Middletown, CT: Wesleyan University Press, 2006), 39.

24. Ibid., 43.

25. Chris Gilleard and Paul Higgs, *Contexts of Ageing: Class, Cohort and Community* (Cambridge, UK: Polity, 2005).

26. This attitude is common among older Chinese men. One amateur dancer described earning money at Chinatown dances, where husbands did not want to dance, but their wives did. Husbands were jealous when their wives danced with other men, so they hired young men to dance with their wives while they supervised.

27. Hochschild, "Emotion Work."

28. Robert Brannon, "The Male Sex Role—and What It's Done for Us Lately," in *The Forty-Nine Percent Majority*, ed. Deborah S. David and Robert Brannon, 1–10 (Reading, MA: Addison-Wesley, 1976).

Notes to Chapter 9

1. I assume this when I see them speaking French with well-known Haitian rhythm dancer Emmanuel Pierre Antoine.

2. At the most competitive level, gold scholarship, the couple is judged.

3. Rose M. Kreider and Diana B. Elliott, "America's Families and Living Arrangements: 2007," U.S. Census Bureau, Current Population Reports, September 2009, www.census.gov/prod/2009pubs/p20-561.pdf.

4. Marc Molgat and Mireille Vézina, "Transitionless Biographies? Youth and Representations of Solo Living," *Youth: Nordic Journal of Youth Research* 16 (2008): 349–371.

5. Ibid.

6. Betsey Stevenson and Justin Wolfers, "Marriage and Divorce: Changes and Their Driving Force," *Journal of Economic Perspectives* 21 (Spring 2007): 27–52.

7. Lisa Gee, *Friends: Why Men and Women Are from the Same Planet* (New York: Bloomsbury, 2004).

8. Paul C. Glick, "Living Alone during Middle Adulthood," *Sociological Perspectives* 37 (1994): 445–457.

9. Molgat and Vézina, "Transitionless Biographies?"

10. Anthony Giddens, *The Transformation of Intimacy: Sexuality, Love, and Eroticism in Modern Societies* (Stanford: Stanford University Press, 1992), 8.

11. Michael Monsour, *Men and Women as Friends: Relationships across the Life Span in the 21st Century* (Mahwah, NJ: Erlbaum, 2002).

12. Ibid., 155; Lillian Rubin, *Just Friends: The Role of Friendship in Our Lives* (New York: Harper and Row, 1985), 156–158.

13. Linda A. Sapadin, "Friendship and Gender: Perspectives of Professional Men and Women," *Journal of Social and Personal Relationships* 5 (1988): 387–403.

14. Eva Illouz, *Consuming the Romantic Utopia: Love and the Cultural Contradictions of Capitalism* (Berkeley: University of California Press, 1997); Viviana Zelizer, *The Purchase of Intimacy* (Princeton: Princeton University Press, 2005).

15. Elizabeth Bernstein, *Temporarily Yours: Intimacy, Authenticity, and the Commerce of Sex* (Chicago: University of Chicago Press, 2007).

16. See wen88888, "2008 USA Dance National-Youth Latin Champ Final," YouTube, August 21, 2008, www.youtube.com/watch?v=0HlqzC6NE0A&feature=related.

17. For age categories, see USA Dance, "DanceSport: Forms & Resources," http://usadance.org/dancesport/forms-and-resources/rules-policies-and-bylaws.

18. bergengirl88, "Canadians Virtue & Moir's Flawless Freedance Wins Gold at 2010 Winter Olympics!" YouTube, February 23, 2010, http://www.youtube.com/watch?v=lE4TbwxMsCA.

19. See bergengirl88, "Americans Davis & White Win Olympic Silver Medal in Ice Dancing!" YouTube, February 23, 2010, http://www.youtube.com/watch?v=IK0UTdvSP78.

20. See Nicky Slater, "Torvill & Dean: What Really Went On When the Skates Came Off," *Daily Mail*, February 5, 2009, www.dailymail.co.uk/tvshowbiz/article-1136876/Torvill--Dean-What-really-went-skates-came-off.html.

21. Larry Rohter, "From Street to Club, Moving to a Latin Beat," *New York Times*, July 22, 2010.

Bibliography

Aldrich, Elizabeth. *From the Ballroom to Hell: Grace and Folly in Nineteenth-Century Dance*. Evanston, IL: Northwestern University Press, 1991.

Babitz, Eve. *Two by Two: Tango, Two-Step, and the L.A. Night*. New York: Simon and Schuster, 1999.

Bailey, J. Michael, and Michael Oberschneider. "Sexual Orientation and Professional Dance." *Archives of Sexual Behavior* 26, no. 4 (1997): 433–443.

Barthes, Robert. *Mythologies*. Paris: Granada/Editions di Seuil, 1957.

Bateson, Gregory. *Steps to an Ecology of Mind*. New York: Ballantine Books, 1972.

Bernstein, Elizabeth. *Temporarily Yours: Intimacy, Authenticity, and the Commerce of Sex*. Chicago: University of Chicago Press, 2007.

Bettie, Julie. *Women without Class: Girls, Race, and Identity*. Berkeley: University of California Press, 2003.

Blumenfield-Jones, Donald S. "Dance as a Mode of Research Representation." *Qualitative Inquiry* 1, no. 4 (1995): 391–401.

Bogle, Kathleen. *Hooking Up: Sex, Dating, and Relationships on Campus*. New York: NYU Press, 2008.

Bordo, Susan. *The Male Body: A New Look at Men in Public and in Private*. New York: Farrar, Straus and Giroux, 1999.

———. *Unbearable Weight: Feminism, Western Culture, and the Body*. Berkeley: University of California Press, 2004.

Bordwell, David. *Making Meaning: Inference and Rhetoric in the Interpretation of Cinema*. Cambridge: Harvard University Press, 1989.

Brannon, Robert. "The Male Sex Role—and What It's Done for Us Lately." In *The Forty-Nine Percent Majority*, edited by Deborah S. David and Robert Brannon, 1–10. Reading, MA: Addison-Wesley, 1976.

Brinson, Peter. "Scholastic Tasks of a Sociology of Dance." *Dance Research: The Journal of the Society for Dance Research* 1, no. 1 (1983): 100–107.

Browning, Barbara. *Samba: Resistance in Motion*. Bloomington: Indiana University Press, 1995.

Buckman, Peter. *Let's Dance: Social, Ballroom, and Folk Dancing*. New York: Penguin Books, 1978.

Butler, Judith. *Bodies That Matter: On the Discursive Limits of "Sex."* New York: Routledge, 1993.

Butler, Judith. *Gender Trouble: Feminism and the Subversion of Identity*. New York: Routledge, 1990.

Cacioppo, John T., and William Patrick. *Loneliness: Human Nature and the Need for Connection*. New York: Norton, 2008.

Cancian, Francesca M. *Love in America: Gender and Self-Development*. New York: Cambridge University Press, 1987.

Cancian, Francesca M., and Stacey J. Oliker. *Caring and Gender*. Thousand Oaks, CA: Pine Forge, 2000.

Carlson, Janet. *Quick, Before the Music Stops: How Ballroom Dancing Saved My Life*. New York: Broadway Books, 2008.

Castle, Irene. *Castles in the Air*. New York: Da Capo, 1980.

Causey, Gregory, with Natasha Yushmanov. *Dancing with Natasha*. Springboro, OH: Romance Divine, 2007.

Clarke, Mary, and Clement Crisp. *Dancer: Men in Dance*. London: British Broadcasting Association, 1981.

———. *The History of Dance*. London: Orbis, 1981.

Clausen, John A. *American Lives: Looking Back at the Children of the Great Depression*. New York: Free Press, 1993.

Cohen, Dorothy. "Remedies for Consumer Protection: Prevention, Resolution, or Punishment." *Journal of Marketing* 28 (1975): 24–31.

Cohen-Stratyner, Barbara. "Social Dance: Contexts and Definitions." *Dance Research Journal* 33, no. 2 (2001): 121–124.

Collier, John, Jr., and Malcolm Collier. *Visual Anthropology: Photography as Research Method*. Albuquerque: University of New Mexico Press, 1986.

Collier, Malcolm. "Photographic Exploration of Social and Cultural Experience." In *Viewpoints: Visual Anthropologists at Work*, edited by Mary Strong and Laena Wilder, 13–31. Austin: University of Texas Press, 2009.

Connell, R. W. *Masculinities*. Berkeley: University of California Press, 1995.

Cooper, Virginia W. "Homophily or the Queen Bee Syndrome." *Small Group Research* 28, no. 4 (1997): 483–499.

Cottle, J. Thomas. "Social Class and Social Dancing." *Sociological Quarterly* 7, no. 2 (1966): 179–196.

Cressey, Paul G. *The Taxi-Dance Hall*. Chicago: University of Chicago Press, 1932.

Cross, John F., and Jane Cross. "Age, Sex, Race, and the Perception of Facial Beauty." *Developmental Psychology* 5 (1971): 433–439.

Curry, Timothy Jon. "Fraternal Bonding in the Locker Room: A Profeminist Analysis of Talk about Competition and Women." *Sociology of Sport Journal* 8 (1991): 119–135.

Cusamo, Camille. *Tango: An Argentine Love Story*. Berkeley, CA: Seal, 2008.

Denniston, Christine. *The Meaning of Tango: The Story of the Argentinean Dance*. London: Portico, 2007.

Dinnerstein, Myra, and Rose Weitz. "Jane Fonda, Barbara Bush and Other Aging Bodies: Femininity and the Limits of Resistance." *Feminist Issues* 14, no. 2 (1994): 3–24.

Doane, Randal. "The Habitus of Dancing: Notes on the Swing Dance Revival in New York City." *Journal of Contemporary Ethnography* 35 (2006): 84–116.

Donaldson, Mike. *Time of Our Lives: Labor and Love in the Working Class.* Sydney, Australia: Allen and Unwin, 1991.

Dumm, Thomas. *Loneliness as a Way of Life.* Cambridge: Harvard University Press, 2008.

Dwyer, Richard. *Stars.* London: Routledge, 1998.

Eicher, Joan B. "Dress: Gender and the Public Display of Skin." In *Body Dressing*, edited by Joanne Entwistle and Elizabeth Wilson, 233–252. Oxford: Berg, 2001.

Ericksen, Julia A. *Kiss and Tell: Surveying Sex in the Twentieth Century.* Cambridge: Harvard University Press, 1999.

———. *Taking Charge of Breast Cancer.* Berkeley: University of California Press, 2008.

———."Women and Work." Ph.D. diss., University of Pennsylvania, 1976.

Faulkner, Thomas A. "From the Ballroom to Hell." Chicago: Church Press, 1894. Reprinted in *I See America Dancing: Selected Readings, 1685–2000*, edited by Maureen Needham, 112–118. Urbana: University of Illinois Press, 2002.

Featherstone, Mike. "The Body in Consumer Culture." In *The Body: Social Process and Cultural Theory*, edited by Mike Featherstone, Mike Hepworth, and Bryan S. Turner, 170–197. London: Sage, 1991.

Freeman, Richard. "Photography and Ethnography." In *Viewpoints: Visual Anthropologists at Work*, edited by Mary Strong and Laena Wilder, 53–75. Austin: University of Texas Press, 2009.

Fromm, Erich. *The Art of Loving.* New York: Harper and Row, 1956.

Gagnon, John H. "Scripts and the Coordination of Sexual Conduct." In *An Interpretation of Desire: Essays in the Study of Sexuality*, 59–87. Chicago: University of Chicago Press, 2004.

Gagnon, John H., and William Simon. *Sexual Conduct: The Social Sources of Human Sexuality.* Chicago: Aldine, 1973.

Gard, Michael. *Men Who Dance.* New York: Peter Lang, 2006.

Gardner, Robert. "Anthropology and Film." *Daedalus* 86 (1957): 344–352.

Gee, Lisa. *Friends: Why Men and Women Are from the Same Planet.* New York: Bloomsbury, 2004.

Gerson, Kathleen. "Falling Back on Plan B: The Children of the Gender Revolution Face Uncharted Territory." In *Families as They Really Are*, edited by Barbara J. Risman, 378–392. New York: Norton, 2009.

Giddens, Anthony. *The Transformation of Intimacy: Love, Sexuality, and Eroticism in Modern Societies.* Malden, MA: Polity, 1992.

Gift, Virginia. *Tango: A History of Obsession.* www.booksurge.com, 2008.

Gilleard, Chris, and Paul Higgs. *Contexts of Ageing: Class, Cohort and Community.* Cambridge, UK: Polity, 2005.

Glick, Paul C. "Living Alone during Middle Adulthood." *Sociological Perspectives* 37 (1994): 445–457.

Goffman, Erving. *The Presentation of Self in Everyday Life.* New York: Doubleday Anchor, 1959.

Groppa, Carlos G. *The Tango in the United States.* Jefferson, NC: McFarland, 2004.

Hall, Elaine. "Smiling, Deferring, and Flirting: Doing Gender by Giving 'Good Service.'" *Work and Occupations* 20 (1993): 452–471.

Halpern, Jake. *Fame Junkies: The Hidden Truths behind America's Favorite Addiction.* New York: Houghton Mifflin, 2007.

Hamilton, Linda H. *Advice for Dancers: Emotional Counsel and Practical Strategies.* San Francisco: Jossey-Bass, 1998.

Hanna, Judith Lynne. *Dance, Sex, and Gender: Signs of Identity, Dominance, Defiance, and Desire.* Chicago: University of Chicago Press, 1988.

Harper, Douglas. "Talking about Pictures: A Case for Photo Elicitation." *Visual Studies* 17, no. 1 (2002): 13–26.

Harriman, Ann. *Women/Men Management.* New York: Praeger, 1985.

Heider, Karl. *Ethnographic Film,* rev. ed. Austin: University of Texas Press, 2006.

Hochschild, Arlie Russell. *The Commercialization of Intimate Life.* Berkeley: University of California Press, 2003.

———. "The Commercial Spirit of Intimate Life and the Abduction of Feminism: Signs from Women's Advice Books." *Theory, Culture, and Society* 112, no. 3 (1995): 1–24.

———. "The Economy of Gratitude." In *The Sociology of Emotions: Original Essays and Research Papers,* edited by David Franks and Doyle McCarthy, 95–113. Greenwich, CT: JAI, 1989.

———. "Emotion Work, Feeling Rules, and Social Structure." *American Journal of Sociology* 85, no. 3 (1979): 551–565.

———. *The Managed Heart: Commercialization of Human Feeling.* Berkeley: University of California Press, 1983.

———. "The Sociology of Emotions as a Way of Feeling." In *Emotions in Social Life: Critical Theories and Contemporary Issues,* edited by Gillian Bendelow and Simon J. Williams, 3–15. New York: Routledge, 1998.

Illouz, Eva. *Consuming the Romantic Utopia: Love and the Cultural Contradictions of Capitalism.* Berkeley: University of California Press, 1997.

Irvine, Bill, and Bobbie Irvine. *The Dancing Years.* London: W. H. Allen, 1970.

Irwin, Sarah. "Later Life, Inequality, and Sociological Theory." *Ageing and Society* 19 (1999): 691–715.

Israels, Beth Lindner. "The Way of the Girl." *Survey* 22 (July 3, 1909). Reprinted in *I See America Dancing: Selected Readings, 1685–2000,* edited by Maureen Needham, 118–122. Urbana: University of Illinois Press, 2002.

Jenks, Chris. "The Centrality of the Eye in Western Culture: An Introduction." In *Visual Culture*, edited by Chris Jenks, 1–25. London: Routledge, 1995.

Jones, Clive. *Soviet Jewish Aliyah, 1989–1992*. London: Frank Cass, 1996.

Jones, Nikki. "I Was Aggressive for the Streets, Pretty for the Pictures." *Gender and Society* 23, no. 1 (2009): 89–93.

Jones, Stephen G. *Workers at Play: A Social and Economic History of Leisure, 1918–1939*. London: Routledge and Kegan Paul, 1986.

Jordan, John Bryce. "Pricked Dances: The Spectator, Dance, and Masculinity in Early 18th-Century England." In *When Men Dance: Choreographing Masculinities across Borders*, edited by Jennifer Fisher and Anthony Shay, 181–206. New York: Oxford University Press, 2009.

Kaplan, E. Ann. "Is the Gaze Male?" In *Women and Film: Both Sides of the Camera*, ed. E. Ann Kaplan, 35–46. London: Methuen, 1983.

Karoblis, Gediminas. "Questions Concerning Dance Technique." *Phenomenology* (2005): 363–398.

Katz, Jonathan Ned. *The Invention of Heterosexuality*. New York: Dutton, 1995.

Katz, Stephen. "Fashioning Agehood: Lifestyle Imagery and the Commercial Spirit of Seniors Culture." In *Childhood and Old Age: Equals or Opposites?* edited by Jorgen Povlsen, Signe Mellemgaard, and Ning de Coninck-Smith, 75–92. Odense, Denmark: Odense University Press, 1999.

Katz, Stephen, and Barbara Marshall. "New Sex for Old: Lifestyle, Consumerism, and the Ethics of Aging Well." *Journal of Aging Studies* 17 (2003): 3–16.

Keefe, Maura. "Is Dance a Man's Sport Too? The Performance of Athletic-Coded Masculinity on the Concert Dance Stage." In *When Men Dance*, edited by Jennifer Fisher and Anthony Shay, 91–106. New York: Oxford University Press, 2009.

Kemper, Theodore, ed. *Research Agendas in the Sociology of Emotions*. Albany: SUNY Press, 1990.

Kephart, Beth. *House of Dance*. New York: HarperTeen, 2008.

Kimmel, Michael S. "Masculinity as Homophobia: Fear, Shame, and Silence in the Construction of Gender Identity." In *Privilege: A Reader*, edited by Abby L. Ferber and Michael S. Kimmel, 51–74. Boulder, CO: Westview, 2003.

Knowles, Mark. *The Wicked Waltz: Outrage at Couple Dancing in the 19th and Early 20th Centuries*. Jefferson, NC: McFarland, 2009.

Kreider, Rose M., and Diana B. Elliott. "America's Families and Living Arrangements, 2007." U.S. Census Bureau, Current Population Reports. September 2009.

Langer, Eleanor. "Inside the New York Telephone Company." In *Women at Work*, edited by William O'Neill, 307–360. Chicago: Quadrangle Books, 1972.

Loe, Meika. "Working for Men: At the Intersection of Power, Gender, and Sexuality." *Sociological Inquiry* 66 (1996): 399–422.

Lurie, Alison. *The Language of Clothes*. London: Bloomsbury, 1992.

Lyman, Peter. "The Fraternal Bond as a Joking Relationship: A Study of the Roles of Sexist Jokes in Male Group Bonding." In *Men's Lives*, edited by Michael S. Kimmel and Michael A. Messner, 169–178. Boston: Allyn and Bacon, 2004.

MacDougal, David. *The Corporeal Image: Film, Ethnography, and the Senses*. Princeton: Princeton University Press, 2006.

Mahood, James, and Kristine Wenberg. *The Mosher Survey*. New York: Arno, 1980.

Malnig, Julie. "Athena Meets Venus: Visions of Women in Social Dance in the Teens and Early 1920s." *Dance Research Journal* 31, no. 2 (1999): 34–62.

———. *Dancing Till Dawn: A Century of Exhibition Ballroom Dance*. New York: NYU Press, 1992.

———. "'Two Stepping to Glory: Social Dance and the Rhetoric of Social Mobility." In *Moving History/Dancing Cultures: A Dance History Reader*, edited by Ann Dils and Ann Cooper Albright, 271–287. Middletown, CT: Wesleyan University Press, 2001.

Maltby, John, Liz Day, David Giles, Raphael Gillet, Marianne Quick, Honey Lancaster-James, and P. Alex Linley. "Implicit Theories of a Desire for Fame." *British Journal of Psychology* 99 (2008): 279–291.

Marcuse, Herbert. *Eros and Civilization: A Philosophical Inquiry into Freud*. Boston: Beacon, 1955.

Marion, Jonathan S. *Ballroom: Culture and Costume in Competitive Dance*. Oxford: Berg, 2008.

———. "Beyond Ballroom: Activity as Performance, Embodiment, and Identity." *Human Mosaic* 36, no. 2 (2004): 7–16.

———. "Photography as Ethnographic Passport." *Visual Anthropology Review* 26, no. 1 (2010): 24–30.

Mayer-Karakis, Brigitt. *Ballroom Icons*. Self-published, 2009.

McMains, Juliet. *Glamour Addiction: Inside the American Ballroom Dance Industry*. Middletown, CT: Wesleyan University Press, 2006.

McMains, Juliet, and Danielle Robinson. "Swingin' Out: Southern California's Lindy Revival." In *I See America Dancing: Selected Readings, 1685–2000*, edited by Maureen Needham, 84–91. Urbana: University of Illinois Press, 2000.

Meckel, Mary V. "Continuity and Change within a Social Institution: The Role of the Taxi-Dancer." Ph.D. diss., University of Nebraska–Lincoln, 1988.

Messner, Michael A. *Out of Play: Critical Essays on Gender and Sport*. Albany: SUNY Press, 2007.

Mizejewska, Linda. *Ziegfeld Girl: Image and Icon in Culture and Cinema*. Durham: Duke University Press, 1997.

Molgat, Marc, and Mireille Vézina. "Transitionless Biographies? Youth and Representations of Solo Living." *Youth: Nordic Journal of Youth Research* 16 (2008): 349–371.

Monsour, Michael. *Men and Women as Friends: Relationships across the Life Span in the 21st Century*. Mahwah, NJ: Erlbaum, 2002.

Moore, Alex. *Ballroom Dancing*. London: Sir Alex Pittman and Sons, 1933.

———. *The Revised Technique of Ballroom Dancing*. Kingston-on-Thames, UK: Alex Moore, Zeeta Dance Studios, 1948.

Mosher, Clelia Dues. *Health and the Woman Movement*. New York: Woman's Press, 1918.

Murray, Kathryn, with Betty Hannah Hoffman. *My Husband, Arthur Murray*. New York: Simon and Schuster, 1960.

Nardi, Peter M. *Gay Men's Friendships: Invincible Communities*. Chicago: University of Chicago Press, 1999.

Nijland, Dirk J. "Ritual Performance and Visual Representations." In *Reflecting Visual Ethnography: Using the Camera in Anthropological Research*, edited by Metje Postma and Peter I. Crawford, 26–49. Leiden: CNWS, 2006.

Nye, Russel B. "Saturday Night at the Paradise Ballroom; or, Dance Halls in the Twenties." *Journal of Popular Culture* 7, no. 1 (1973): 14–22.

Olds, Jacqueline, and Richard S. Schwartz. *The Lonely American: Drifting Apart in the Twenty-First Century*. Boston: Beacon, 2009.

Padilla, Mark. *Caribbean Pleasure Industry: Tourism, Sexuality, and AIDS in the Dominican Republic*. Chicago: University of Chicago Press, 2007.

Palmer, Marina. *Kiss and Tango*. New York: Harper, 2006.

Pascoe, C. J. *Dude, You're a Fag: Masculinity and Sexuality in High School*. Berkeley: University of California Press, 2007.

Peiss, Kathy. *Cheap Amusements: Working Women and Leisure in Turn-of-the-Century New York*. Philadelphia: Temple University Press, 1986.

———. *Hope in a Jar: The Making of America's Beauty Culture*. New York: Owl Books, 1998.

Perry, Sara, and Jonathan S. Marion. "State of the Ethics in Visual Anthropology." *Visual Anthropology Review* 26, no. 2 (2010).

Peters, Sally. "The Elegant Passion." *Journal of Popular Culture* 25, no. 4 (Spring 1992): 163–171.

———. "From Eroticism to Transcendence: Ballroom Dance and the Female Body." In *The Female Body: Figures, Styles, Speculations*, edited by Laurence Goldstein, 145–158. Ann Arbor: University of Michigan Press, 1991.

Phoenix, Cassandra, and Andrew Sparkes. "Young Athletic Bodies and Narrative Maps of Aging." *Journal of Aging Studies* 20 (2006): 107–121.

Picart, Caroline Joan S. *From Ballroom to DanceSport: Aesthetics, Athletics, and Body Culture*. Albany: SUNY Press, 2006.

Picart, Caroline Joan S., and Kenneth Gergen. "Dharma Dancing: Ballroom Dancing and Relational Order." *Qualitative Inquiry* 10, no. 6 (2004): 854–868.

Pink, Sarah. *Doing Visual Ethnography*, 2d ed. London: Sage, 2007.

Postma, Metje, and Peter I. Crawford. "Introduction: Visual Ethnography and Anthropology." In *Reflecting Visual Ethnography: Using the Camera in Anthropological Research*, edited by Metje Postma and Peter I. Crawford, 1–23. Leiden: CNWS, 2006.

Pugel, D. Elizabeth. "Points of Derailment: The Making of a Female Physicist." *Physics and Society* 26, no. 3 (1997). http://aps.org/units/fps/newsletters/1997/july/ajul97.html.

Putnam, Robert. *Bowling Alone: The Collapse and Revival of American Community.* New York: Simon and Schuster, 2000.

Raurell, Lydia. *A Year of Dancing Dangerously.* Woodstock, NY: Overlook-Duckworth, 2008.

Remennick, Larissa. *Russian Jews on Three Continents.* New Brunswick, NJ: Transaction, 2007.

Richardson, Dorothy. "The Long Day: The Story of a New York Working Girl." In *Women at Work*, edited by William O'Neill, 3–303. Chicago: Quadrangle Books, 1972.

Richardson, Phillip J. S. *A History of English Ballroom Dancing.* London: Herbert Jenkins, 1946.

Risman, Barbara J. "From Doing to Undoing Gender as We Know it." *Gender and Society* 23 (February 2009): 81–85.

Risner, Doug. "What Do We Know about Men Who Dance?" In *Men Who Dance: Choreographing Masculinities across Borders*, edited by Jennifer Fisher and Anthony Shay, 57–77. New York: Oxford University Press, 2009.

Rubin, Lillian. *Just Friends: The Role of Friendship in Our Lives.* New York: Harper and Row, 1985.

Sapadin, Linda A. "Friendship and Gender: Perspectives of Professional Men and Women." *Journal of Social and Personal Relationships* 5 (1988): 387–403.

Savigliano, Marta E. *Tango and the Political Economy of Passion.* Boulder, CO: Westview, 1995.

Scrivener, Len. *Just One Idea: Ballroom Dancing Analysed by Len Scrivener.* Edited by Bryan Allen. Privately published by Bryan Allen, 1983.

Seidman, Steven. *The Social Construction of Sexuality.* New York: Norton, 2003.

Shawn, Ted. *One Thousand and One Night Stands.* New York: Doubleday, 1960.

Smathers, D. G., and P. E. Horridge. "The Effects of Physical Changes on Clothing Preferences of Elderly Women." *International Journal of Aging and Human Development* 9 (1978–1979): 273–278.

Smith, Dorothy E. "Categories Are Not Enough." *Gender and Society* 23, no. 1 (2009): 76–81.

———. "Ideology, Science, and Social Relations: A Reinterpretation of Marx's Epistemology." *European Journal of Social Theory* 7, no. 4 (2004): 445–462.

Stephenson, Richard M., and Joseph Iaccarino. *The Complete Book of Ballroom Dancing.* New York: Doubleday, 1980.

Stevenson, Betsey, and Justin Wolfers. "Marriage and Divorce: Changes and Their Driving Force." *Journal of Economic Perspectives* 21 (Spring 2007): 27–52.

Stevenson, John. *British Society, 1914–45.* New York: Penguin Books, 1990.

Studlar, Gaylin. "Valentino, 'Optic Intoxication' and Dance Madness." In *Screening the Male: Exploring Masculinities in Hollywood Cinema*, edited by Steven Cohan and Ina Rae Hark, 23–45. New York: Routledge, 1993.

Swidler, Ann. "Love and Adulthood in American Culture." In *Themes of Work and Love in Adulthood*, edited by Neil J. Smelser and Erik H. Erikson, 120–150. Cambridge: Harvard University Press, 1980.

Taylor, Julie. *Paper Tangos*. Durham: Duke University Press, 1998.

Thoits, Peggy. "The Sociology of Emotions." *Annual Review of Sociology* 15 (1989): 17–42.

Thomas, Helen. *Dance, Modernity, and Culture*. New York: Routledge, 1995.

———. "Dancing the Difference." *Women's Studies International Forum* 19, no. 5 (1996): 505–511.

Thomas, Helen, and Nicola Miller. "Ballroom Blitz." In *Dance in the City*, edited by Helen Thomas, 89–110. London: Macmillan, 1997.

Thomas, Irene D., and Larry M. Sawyer. *The Temptation to Tango: Journeys of Intimacy and Desire*. Victoria, BC: Trafford, 2005.

Thompson, Robert Harris. *Tango: The Art History of Love*. New York: Pantheon, 2005.

Thorne, Barrie. *Gender Play: Boys and Girls in School*. New Brunswick: Rutgers University Press, 1993.

Tompkins, Jane P., ed. *Reader-Response Criticism: From Formalism to Post-Structuralism*. Baltimore: Johns Hopkins University Press, 1980.

Travis, Doris Eaton. *The Days We Danced: The Story of My Theatrical Family from Florenz Ziegfeld to Arthur Murray*. Seattle: Marquand Books, 2003.

Truex, Dorothy. *The Twenty Million Dollar Give-Away: An Exposé of Competitive Ballroom Dancing*. Bloomington, IN. Xlibris, 2000.

Turner, Bryan S. *The Body and Society*. 2nd ed. New York: Sage, 1996.

Turner, Bryan S., and Steven P. Wainwright. "Corps de Ballet: The Case of the Injured Ballet Dancer." *Sociology of Health and Illness* 25 (2003): 269–288.

Twigg, Julia. "Clothing, Age and the Body: A Critical Review." *Ageing and Society* 27 (2007): 285–305.

Vedder, Clyde B. "The Decline of the Taxi-Dance Hall." *Sociology and Social Research* (1954): 387–391.

Vermey, Ruud. *Latin: Thinking, Sensing and Doing in Latin American Dancing*. Munich: Kastell Verlag, 1994.

Wainwright, Lyndon. *The Story of British Popular Dance*. Brighton, UK: International Dance Publications, 1996.

Warhurst, Chris, Dennis Nickson, Anne Witz, and Anne Marie Cullen. "Aesthetic Labor in Interactive Service Work: Some Case Study Evidence for the 'New' Glasgow." *Service Industries Journal* 20 (2000): 103–120.

Warhurst, Chris, Diane van den Broek, Richard Hall, and Dennis Nickson. "Lookism: The New Frontier of Employment Discrimination?" *Journal of Industrial Relations* 51 (2009): 131–136.

West, Candace, and Sarah Fenstermaker. "Doing Difference." *Gender and Society* 9 (1995): 8–37.

West, Candace, and Don H. Zimmerman. "Accounting for Doing Gender." *Gender and Society* 23, no. 1 (2009): 112–122.

———. "Doing Gender." *Gender and Society* 9 (February 1987): 8–37.

Wieschiolek, Heike. " 'Ladies, Just Follow His Lead!' Salsa, Gender and Identity." In *Sport, Dance and Embodied Identities*, edited by Noel Dyck and Eduardo P. Archetti, 115–137. Oxford: Berg, 2003.

Wilder, Laena. "Documentary Photographs in the Field." In *Viewpoints: Visual Anthropologists at Work*, edited by Mary Strong and Laena Wilder, 33–51. Austin: University of Texas Press, 2009.

Wilson, Elizabeth. "A Note on Glamour." *Fashion Theory* 11, no. 1 (March 2007): 95–107.

Winkelhuis, Maximiliaan. *Dance to Your Maximum: The Competitive Ballroom Dancer's Workbook*. www.DancePlaza.com, 2001.

Wissinger, Elizabeth. "Modeling Consumption: Fashion Modeling Work in Contemporary Society." *Journal of Consumer Culture* 9 (2009): 273–296.

Wolf, Naomi. *The Beauty Myth: How Images of Beauty Are Used against Women.* New York: William Morrow 1991.

Wulff, Helena. *Ballet across Borders: Career and Culture in the World of Dancers.* Oxford: Berg, 1998.

Zelizer, Viviana A. *The Purchase of Intimacy.* Princeton: Princeton University Press, 2005.

———. *The Social Meaning of Money: Pin Money, Paychecks, Poor Relief, and Other Currencies.* New York: Basic Books, 1994.

Zona, Christine, and Chris George. *Gotta Ballroom: Waltz, Tango, Foxtrot, and Viennese Waltz.* Champaign, IL: Human Kinetics, 2008.

Zopata, Helena Znaniecki, and Joseph R. Noel. "The Dance Studio—Style without Sex." *Transaction* 4, no. 3 (1967): 10–17.

Index